Behind the
Palace Doors

Behind the Palace Doors

FIVE CENTURIES OF SEX, ADVENTURE, VICE,
TREACHERY, AND FOLLY FROM ROYAL BRITAIN

Michael Farquhar

RANDOM HOUSE TRADE PAPERBACKS

NEW YORK

A Random House Trade Paperback Original

Copyright © 2011 by Michael Farquhar

Published in the United States by Random House Trade Paperbacks,
an imprint of The Random House Publishing Group,
a division of Random House, Inc., New York.

RANDOM HOUSE TRADE PAPERBACKS and colophon are
trademarks of Random House, Inc.

Library of Congress Cataloging-in-Publication Data
Farquhar, Michael.
Behind the palace doors: five centuries of sex, adventure, vice, treachery,
and folly from royal Britain / Michael Farquhar.
p. cm.
Includes bibliographical references.
ISBN 978-0-8129-7904-6
eBook ISBN 978-0-679-60453-2
1. Great Britain—Kings and rulers—Biography—Miscellanea.
2. Queens—Great Britain—Biography—Miscellanea.   3. Royal houses—
Great Britain—History—Miscellanea.   4. Great Britain—History—
Miscellanea.   I. Title.
DA28.1.F37 2011
941.009'9—dc22   2010021116

Printed in the United States of America

www.atrandom.com

2 4 6 8 9 7 5 3 1

Book design by Caroline Cunningham

CONTENTS

PART III

House of Hanover

PART IV

House of Saxe-Coburg-Gotha to Windsor

PART I

House of Tudor

HENRY VII

(reigned 1485–1509)

HENRY VIII

(r. 1509–1547)

EDWARD VI

(r. 1547–1553)

MARY I

(r. 1553–1558)

ELIZABETH I

(r. 1558–1603)

House of Tudor

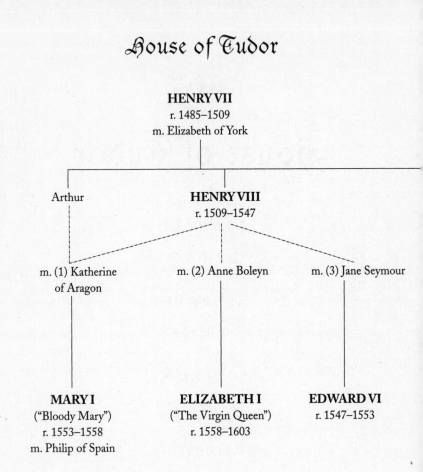

HENRY VII
r. 1485–1509
m. Elizabeth of York

Arthur

HENRY VIII
r. 1509–1547

m. (1) Katherine
of Aragon

m. (2) Anne Boleyn

m. (3) Jane Seymour

MARY I
("Bloody Mary")
r. 1553–1558
m. Philip of Spain

ELIZABETH I
("The Virgin Queen")
r. 1558–1603

EDWARD VI
r. 1547–1553

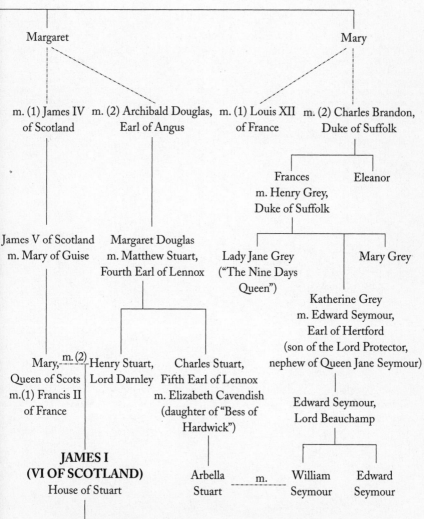

Introductory Chapter:

A Blending of Roses and the Beginning of
the Tudor Dynasty

The body count among England's elite was staggering: Three kings, a Prince of Wales, and numerous royal dukes were either murdered or executed, or died in battle during the epic struggle at the end of the fifteenth century that became known as the Wars of the Roses. It was essentially a vicious family feud between two branches of the Plantagenet royal dynasty—York (represented by the white rose) and Lancaster (represented in red)—over who would rule the island kingdom.

Emerging from this murderous clash was a relatively obscure member of the House of Lancaster, Henry Tudor, Earl of Richmond, who, in 1485, defeated the Yorkist King Richard III at the Battle of Bosworth Field, seized the crown, and established the House of Tudor as Henry VII.

Although the new king would be always be paranoid about potential rivals—and with good reason, as several imposters popped up during his reign and gained support as supposed members of the defeated House of York—the Wars of the Roses were effectively over. The restoration of peace and stability was symbolized by the marriage of Henry VII to Elizabeth of York, heiress of the rival royal house, and the birth of two sons secured the new dynasty. Only one, though, Prince Henry, was left to carry on the Tudor line after the sudden death of fifteen-year-old Arthur, Prince of Wales, in 1502.

Henry succeeded his father in 1509, two months before he turned eighteen. The late king had left a secure realm and a full treasury for his son, but the remote and suspicious monarch was never popular with his people, mostly because of his punishing tax policies. The accession of Henry VIII was therefore greeted with wild acclaim. "This day is the end of our slavery, the fount of our liberty," rhapsodized Thomas More; "the end of sadness, the beginning of joy."

Although More would one day join the scores of Henry's beheaded associates, his enthusiasm for the new reign was well founded. The new monarch embodied youthful vigor and hope for the future. A true Renaissance prince, he was athletic and strong, superbly educated, an able musician, and a gifted composer. Furthermore, Henry VIII looked like a model king.

"His Majesty is the handsomest potentate I ever set eyes on," reported the Venetian ambassador in 1515; "above the usual height, with an extremely fine calf to his leg, his complexion very fair and bright, with auburn hair combed straight and short, in the French fashion, his throat being rather long and thick. . . . He speaks French, English, and Latin, and a little Italian, plays well on the lute and harpsichord, sings from book at sight, draws the bow with greater strength than any man in England, and jousts marvelously. Believe me, he is in every respect a most accomplished Prince."

Almost as soon as he became king, Henry married his late brother's widow, Katherine of Aragon, who had been kept isolated and in near poverty by Henry VII after Arthur's death. It was as much an act of chivalry as it was of statecraft for the young monarch to rescue the sad princess and make her his queen. He was, he declared, "Sir Loyal Heart," and so he would be—until Katherine failed to give him a son, and he fell in love with a black-eyed temptress by the name of Anne Boleyn.

It was then that the dark and dangerous side of the king began to emerge. Queen Katherine was cruelly cast aside after two decades of marriage, while their daughter Mary—once Henry's "chieftest pearl"—was decreed to be a bastard. In order to marry Anne, King Henry defied the pope and declared himself Supreme Head of the Church in England, after which a savage bloodletting began for those who dared protest the new order. Monks were hanged still in their religious robes, while the head of Thomas More was impaled on a spike atop London Bridge.

Unfortunately for Anne Boleyn, the woman who inspired this religious revolution, the king quickly grew tired of her. She failed to give him the boy he wanted (only a daughter, Elizabeth), and, after she was falsely charged with adultery, her head was sliced off with a sword. Ten days later, Henry married wife number three, Jane Seymour, who earned the mercurial king's eternal devotion by bearing him the son he believed to be vital for the realm's future stability. With this prince, Henry was convinced the chaos of the Wars of the Roses would never be repeated.

But there was still plenty of blood to be spilled.

1

Henry VIII (1509–1547): Up the Stairs, Pulled by an Engine

The King was now overgrown with corpulency and fatness.

—EDWARD HALL

By 1540, Henry VIII had discarded his first wife, Katherine of Aragon, and beheaded his second, Anne Boleyn, on a false charge of adultery. He also married his third wife, Jane Seymour, who died right after giving Henry the son he had desired all along. Now—as the king grew monstrously obese— three more wives were in for the royal treatment.

Henry VIII was huge; a colossus who dominated not only his era but, as he grew heavier, his horse as well. The poor beast was on the losing end of the chunky king's decision to don his plus-sized armor, saddle up, and lead his English forces into battle against France in 1544. "It was no longer a glorious young prince who was to lead his Englishmen toward Boulogne," wrote Antonia Fraser, "but an unwieldy invalid who had to be winched aboard his horse with his armour cut away from his swollen leg."

Miserable as it must have been for the horse to have the obese monarch bouncing on top of it, so much worse it was for Henry's teenaged queen, Catherine Howard, when she found herself in the same position. Henry was pushing fifty when he married for the fifth time, a bloated tyrant with badly ulcerated legs that left the once vigorously athletic monarch largely immobile and subject to savage bouts of temper.

"The King was now overgrown with corpulency and fatness," reported the contemporary chronicler Edward Hall, "so that he became more and more unwieldy. He could not go up or down stairs unless he was raised up or let down by an engine." (The Duke of Norfolk also noted that Henry "was let up and down by a device," but there is no record of how the "engine" or "device" actually worked.)

Only his diminutive young queen seemed to make Henry happy. He called her his "blushing rose without a thorn" and couldn't keep his fat paws off her. "The King's affection was so marvelously set upon that gentlewoman," wrote Thomas Cranmer's secretary, Ralph Morice, "as it was never known that he had the like to any woman."

Young Catherine had vowed at her wedding to be "bonair [yielding] and buxom in bed," but that was no doubt difficult. King Henry was by this time so enormous that the Spanish chronicler reported "three of the biggest men that could be found could get inside his doublet." Little wonder, then, that Catherine risked everything and took on a lover of more pleasing dimensions; a man who could make *her* happy. Unfortunately, it cost the young queen her head.

Henry's fourth wife, Catherine's predecessor Anne of Cleves, had been spared the fifth queen's ordeals in bed because the king never deigned to sleep with her. "I like her not," Henry sniffed after meeting the German bride selected for him by his minister, Thomas Cromwell. It was the only politically arranged union of the king's long marital career, and after seeing Anne, he entered into this "unendurable bargain" with extreme reluctance. "My Lord," the king said to Cromwell on the morning of his wedding, "if it were not to satisfy the world, and my Realm, I would not do that I must this day for none earthly thing."

The king, who would be lusting after Catherine Howard later the same year, could not bear to consummate his marriage to Anne of Cleves. "I liked her before not well," he said the morning after his wedding, "but now I like her much worse." What had spared Anne the agony of Henry's sexual advances? He claimed her breasts sagged.

Instead of having the grunting monster flopping on top of her, as Catherine Howard would later, Anne had a much easier time of it. "When he comes to bed," she told her ladies, "he kisses me and taketh me by the hand, and biddeth me 'good night sweetheart' and in the morning, kisses me, and biddeth me 'Farewell, darling.'"

Anne of Cleves had been so exceedingly sheltered growing up that she actually believed this was what married couples did in bed. Had she known better, she might have been more grateful to Catherine Howard—her former lady-in-waiting—for taking her hefty husband off her hands. Henry quickly divorced her. Fortunately for Anne, it was an amicable split and she lived comfortably for the rest of her life as the king's "good sister."

Three years after marrying Anne of Cleves and Catherine Howard (both in 1540), Henry wed his sixth and final wife, Katherine Parr, whose job it was to nurse and comfort the ailing king. She just barely managed to survive him. Katherine dared dispute with the king on religious matters—never a good idea—but wisely humbled herself before the headsman did.

Henry VIII died on January 28, 1547. He was fifty-five, with a waist that measured about the same. It would take sixteen exceptionally strong yeomen of the guard to lower his enormous coffin into the tomb beneath St. George's Chapel at Windsor.

2

Edward VI (1547–1553): The Boy King

This whole realm's most precious jewel.

—KING HENRY VIII

Henry VIII was succeeded by his nine-year-old son, Edward, the child upon whom the late king had placed all his hope for the future of the Tudor dynasty. Though the reign of Edward VI was brief—just six years—it was packed with intrigue.

The little boy of nine sat without squirming throughout the seemingly endless coronation ceremony. Though tender of age, he was proclaimed not only England's sovereign but a divinely ordained savior, "a second Josiah"* who would see "idolatry destroyed, the tyranny of the bishops of Rome banished from [his] subjects, and images removed." Heightening the display of power and majesty, the boy king—propped up on pillows— shimmered in full royal regalia. Upon his head was a gold crown, made especially for his small size, adorned with rubies, diamonds, emeralds, and pearls. Before him bowed all the great nobles of the land, there to pay homage to the son Henry VIII had longed for, and who now claimed his inheritance as Edward VI.

* Josiah was an ancient king of Judah who came to the throne at the age of eight, destroyed pagan altars and images, and restored the true scripture to his people.

The ancient coronation ritual was believed to imbue the monarch with near mystical properties, but King Edward—God's chosen—was still a child and incapable of ruling on his own. His brief, six-year reign would be marked by intrigue and treachery as those closest to the boy tried to gain control over him and rule England in his name. Two of the king's uncles would lose their heads in various power struggles before Edward began to assert his own will, and, in the end, betray his own sisters.

Henry VIII was overjoyed when his third wife, Jane Seymour, delivered a baby boy on October 12, 1537. Two thousand rounds of ammunition were fired from the Tower of London in celebration, while church bells continuously pealed all across the city. For her tremendous reproductive success, Queen Jane became Henry's "entirely beloved," foremost among all his wives for giving him what he wanted most: a male heir to carry on the Tudor dynasty. The king had waited twenty-seven years for this momentous occasion, discarding two wives in the process and dissolving all ties to Rome. Given that, the death of Jane Seymour just two weeks after giving birth, while sad, was really of no consequence. It was the son who mattered, the child Henry declared to be "this whole realm's most precious jewel."

"There is no less rejoicing in these parts from the birth of our Prince, whom we hungered for for so long, than there was, I trow, at the birth of St. John the Baptist," Bishop Hugh Latimer wrote from Worcester. "God give us grace to be thankful."

The king became obsessed with Edward's health and safety and issued an exacting set of instructions for the care of his miraculous offspring. The prince was to be watched constantly, his food and clothing thoroughly tested. Doctors swarmed around the child, monitoring every nuance of his health, while access was strictly limited for fear of infection. Loitering any-where near the palace was prohibited. "If any beggar shall pre-sume to draw near the gates," Henry warned, "then they be appointed to be grievously punished to the example of others."

Despite the fastidious environment in which he was raised, Edward seems to have had a happy and robust early childhood. "My Lord Prince's grace is in good health and merry," reported Lady Byron, the head of Edward's household. "His grace danced and played so wantonly that he could not stand still, and was as full of pretty toys as ever I saw in my life."

Edward had a carefully selected group of playmates that in-cluded his close friend and confidant Barnaby Fitzpatrick and a girl named Jane Dormer, with whom the prince seemed quite taken. "My Jane," he called her. "His inclination and natural disposition was of great towardness to all virtuous parts and princely qualities," Jane later wrote, "a marvelous sweet child, of very mild and generous condition."

The future king had a close relationship with his half sisters, Mary and Elizabeth—daughters of Katherine of Aragon and Anne Boleyn, respectively—as well as with his father's sixth wife, Katherine Parr, whom he called his "most dear mother." It was Queen Katherine who brought all of Henry VIII's children closer to him, and who encouraged Edward in his studies. The curriculum was extremely rigorous and included, as Edward wrote, "learning of tongues, of the Scriptures, of philosophy and the liberal sciences."

The prince excelled in all his scholastic endeavors. He was, in fact, a child prodigy, but he could also be a bit of a prig. In one letter to Katherine Parr, for example, Edward wrote that his sister Mary—twenty years his senior—needed to be pro-tected "from all the wiles and enchantments of the evil one," and begged the queen to persuade her "to attend no longer to foreign dances and merriments which do not become a most Christian princess." The boy was eight at the time.

Though the prince enjoyed close family connections with his sisters and stepmother, the most important figure in his life, his father, was also the most remote. Edward held the king in awe and was desperately grateful for any instance of fatherly affection. Henry was always concerned about his son's well-being, but from afar, and tried to fill the void created by his absence with baubles.

"You have treated me so kindly, like a most loving father, and one who would wish me always to act rightly," Edward wrote to the king. "I also thank you that you have given me great and costly gifts, as chains, rings, jewelled buttons, neck-chains, and breast-pins, and necklaces, garments, and very many other things; in which things and gifts is conspicuous your fatherly affection towards me; for, if you didn't love me, you would not give me these fine gifts of jewellery."

Father and son never really knew each other, and before Edward turned ten, Henry VIII was dead. Now the new king's maternal uncles, Edward and Thomas Seymour, would vie with each other to gain control over their royal nephew.

Henry VIII's will specified that a regency council should rule with equal say during his son's minority. Yet as soon as the king breathed his last, Edward Seymour managed to subvert his brother-in-law's wishes. With a combination of shrewd backroom maneuvering and outright bribery, he managed to secure all power for himself. Seymour became Lord Protector—a king in all but name. He "governs everything absolutely," reported the imperial ambassador Van der Delft.

Soon enough, the Protector was so intoxicated with power that he began to see himself as royal. One of his first acts as de facto sovereign was to make himself Duke of Somerset (the title by which he will be referred to henceforth). That elevation was followed by his adoption of a coat of arms closely resembling those of his late sister Queen Jane. Somerset even had the temerity to address the French king as his brother, a presumption that earned him a sharp rebuke from across the Channel.

Like most kings, Somerset believed that his role had been divinely ordained. "Thou, Lord, by thy providence hast called me to rule," he said in a prayer after becoming Protector; "make me therefore able to follow thy calling."

Seething in the shadows during his older brother's rapid ascent was Thomas Seymour, an erratic but charming rascal, bursting with ambition. Though he had been given the office of Lord Admiral, and all the land and income that accompanied it, Seymour wasn't satisfied. He wanted a share in his brother's power, to be appointed governor of their young nephew, the king. "Why was he [Somerset] made Protector?" Seymour fumed. "It was not the King's will that dead is that any one man should have both the Government of the King . . . and also the Realm."

Thwarted in his aim to be young Edward's governor, Seymour sought advantage elsewhere. He set his sights on Henry VIII's widow, Queen Katherine Parr, with whom he had shared a love affair before Henry decided she would become his sixth wife. Now that Katherine was free from the ill-tempered ogre she had dutifully attended, she was ready for some real passion. Thomas Seymour, on the other hand, was ready for an influential ally.

The couple wed in secret, without Somerset's permission, which was dangerous. So to insulate himself from his brother's wrath, Seymour convinced his pliable young nephew the king to write a letter to Katherine, essentially urging her to marry Seymour and promising his protection.

"Wherefore ye shall not need to fear any grief to come, or to suspect lack of aid in need," King Edward wrote to his stepmother; "seeing that he [Somerset], being mine uncle, is so good in nature that he will not be troublesome . . . if any grief shall befall, I shall be a sufficient succor."

Somerset was incensed not only by his brother's blatant defiance of his authority but because he had no recourse, given the king's promise of protection. Even Edward felt his uncle's anger, noting in his journal that "the Lord Protector [Somerset] was much offended." In time, Seymour would give his brother Somerset even more cause for grief.

Exacerbating the tension brewing between the Seymour brothers were their wives, who, one observer noted, "raised so much dust at last to put out the eyes of their husbands." Somerset's impossibly proud spouse, Anne—"more presumptuous than Lucifer," as one court observer described her—loathed Katherine Parr, whom she had once served as lady-in-waiting. The Duchess of Somerset insisted that she, as the Protector's wife, now had precedence over the widowed wife of Henry VIII. Katherine disagreed, and on one occasion commanded Anne, or "that Hell," as she called the duchess, to carry her train. This Anne flatly refused to do, for, as the nineteenth-century historian William Camden put it, "It was unsuitable for her to submit to perform that service for the wife of her husband's younger brother."

The showdown between the duchess and the dowager queen was in fact a declaration of war. "If Master Admiral [Seymour] teach his wife no better manners," Anne snorted, "I am she that will." For her own part, Katherine wrote to her husband, Thomas, and announced that she had prayed for the duchess's "short dispatch."

Katherine no doubt had similar prayers for the Duke of Somerset, who she believed had usurped her expected role as regent during King Edward's minority. In retaliation for her presumption, Somerset refused to deliver to the queen the jewels Henry VIII had left her—including her wedding ring. Still, Katherine urged her husband not to overreact to his brother's ill treatment of her. "With all heart not to unquiet yourself with any of his unfriendly parts," she counseled, "bear them for the time, as well as you can." But when Somerset began leasing her dower lands without her approval, Katherine was feeling a little less benevolent. "My Lord your brother hath this afternoon made me a little warm [angry]," she wrote to Thomas. "It was fortunate we were so distant, for I suppose else I should have bitten him."

Thomas Seymour saw an opportunity to gain more control over his nephew while his brother was occupied elsewhere fighting the Scots. Money was the means he used to ingratiate himself with the king, offering himself as a bountiful contrast to Somerset, who was apparently quite stingy with the purse. "My uncle of Somerset dealeth very hardy with me," Edward was heard to say, "and keepeth me so straight that I cannot have any money at my will."

Seymour's largesse was a welcome addition to the young king's allowance, but it wasn't enough to bend him to his uncle's will. After Somerset returned from Scotland, Seymour tried to force through Parliament a bill that would make him Edward's governor, and he wanted the king to sign it. Citing protocol, Edward refused. He would do nothing without Somerset's permission.

Undaunted, Seymour continued to pressure his nephew, tempting the king with more money and dangling before him the prospect of more personal power. He even tried to shame the boy, calling him "a beggarly king," beholden to Somerset for whatever crumbs he deigned give. Edward buckled but ultimately remained resolved. "The Lord Admiral [Seymour] shall have no bill signed or written by me."

Without the king's cooperation, Seymour became increasingly desperate, and delusional. He convinced himself that he could gain enough support to seize power by force, boasting, as Henry Grey, Marquis of Dorset, reported, that "he had as great a number of gentlemen that loved him, as any nobleman in England."

To finance his ambitions, Seymour embarked on a number of

illegal schemes, such as a racketeering deal he conducted with the very pirates he was supposed to be fighting in his post as Lord Admiral. He also established a connection with William Sharington, under-treasurer of the Bristol mint and an accomplished counterfeiter, who simply forged the money Seymour needed.

Some of the Lord Admiral's plans were even more maniacal. Despite his advantageous marriage to Katherine Parr, for example, he tried to seduce the king's fifteen-year-old sister, Elizabeth, who was then living in his household. The queen caught Seymour embracing the young princess and sent Elizabeth away. But when Katherine died soon after giving birth to the couple's daughter Mary, Seymour renewed his pursuit of Elizabeth, which not only put her in grave peril (see Chapter 5) but added to the impression that his ambitions had grown wildly out of control.

"For God's sake take heed what you do," the Earl of Southampton warned. "You may say what you will that you mean well and mind all for the king, but in deed you shall show yourself his greatest enemy. . . . You may begin a faction and trouble but you cannot end it when you will."

By this time, though, Thomas Seymour was beyond all reason. On January 16, 1549, he tried to kidnap the king. He came as close as Edward's bedchamber at Hampton Court, but upon unlocking the door, he was surprised by the boy's pet spaniel. In a panic, he shot the barking animal, which alerted the king's guard. While his terrified nephew looked on, his dead dog beside him in the doorway, Seymour tried to explain that he was merely checking on the king's security and obviously meant him no harm. The council believed otherwise, however, and the next day Seymour was taken away to the Tower.

While he was being held there, the evidence of his misdeeds mounted. "He was a great rascal," Sir William Paget confided to the imperial ambassador. Thirty-three charges were eventually laid against the Lord Admiral and presented to the king.

"We do perceive," King Edward declared in a scripted speech, "that there are great things objected and laid to my Lord Admiral mine uncle—and they tend to treason—and we perceive that you require but justice to be done. We think it reasonable, and we will that you proceed according to your request."

A bill of attainder was passed in Parliament, and Seymour was sentenced to death. With a barely legible scrawl, Somerset signed his brother's death warrant. He was said never to have been the same afterward. On March 19, 1549, Thomas Seymour was beheaded upon Tower Hill. Less than three years later, on the same site, Edward Seymour, Duke of Somerset, would meet the same fate.

Somerset's reputation suffered mightily from the execution of his brother. He was openly derided as "a blood-sucker" and "a ravenous wolf," and it was commonly believed, as one observer wrote, that "the blood of his brother the Admiral cried against him before God." Seymour's death, though, was merely the beginning of Somerset's problems. Slithering in to engineer his downfall was John Dudley, a man historian A. F. Pollard described as "the subtlest and most daring of the English disciples of Machiavelli."

Conditions in England were dire at the time of Thomas Seymour's execution, and getting worse. Somerset had not only embroiled the kingdom in a ruinous war with Scotland but showed himself to be hopelessly ineffective in the face of a series of rebellions that arose over the radical changes taking place in religion and the enclosure of common lands. Thousands of lives were lost in the uprisings, while Somerset's position was fatally weakened.

"No improvement is observed in the keeping of order or the administration of justice," reported the imperial ambassador

Van der Delft. "The people are all in confusion, and with one common voice lament the present state of things."

The chaos and disorder in the realm that made Somerset so vulnerable proved to be a boon for Dudley, who organized the coup that ousted his rival from power. The king's uncle was charged with twenty counts of treason, stripped of his title, and sent to the Tower. But he would not face the headsman—yet. Young Edward had already seen one uncle executed; he would not sanction the death of another.

"We must return good for evil," Dudley said, addressing the council. "And as it is the king's will that the Duke should be pardoned, and it is the first matter he hath asked of us, we ought to accede to His Grace's wishes."

Dudley appeared to acquiesce, but as Sir Richard Morison said of him, "He had such a head that he seldom went about anything but he conceived first three or four purposes beforehand." He certainly recognized that his rise to power would be best accomplished by closely aligning himself with the king's wishes. Thus, Somerset's life was spared and he was restored to the council, though with significantly diminished influence. Dudley appeared to embrace the broken man but nevertheless remained determined to destroy him.

While personally lacking in any strong religious outlook, Dudley nevertheless synchronized himself with the king's beliefs, which tended toward the fanatical. Henry VIII had taken the audacious step of breaking with Rome and establishing himself as head of the Church in England. But he was still relatively conservative and retained many Catholic doctrines. Not so his son. Edward VI was a radical Protestant who gloried in the English Reformation. "In the court there is no bishop, and no man of learning so ready to argue in support of the new doctrine as the king," the imperial ambassador reported. The contemporary author John Foxe referred to Edward as "this godly imp," in his *Actes and Monuments,* a widely read and vastly in-

fluential book that spurred much of the anti-Catholic sentiment in England.

King Edward was still young, but he immersed himself in
religious matters and came to see himself as the one chosen by
God to deliver his kingdom from the grave errors perpetuated
for so long by the pope—or, as the king called him, "the true
son of the devil, a bad man, an Antichrist and abominable
tyrant." He would personally see England purified of all popish
abominations, which included wholesale destruction of ancient
religious art and treasures. "Edward was more than a keen participant in the ideas of the reformed religion," wrote historian
Chris Skidmore; "he was becoming an integral character in the
shaping of the religious atmosphere at court, and therefore the
nation at large."

Given the king's zeal, there was little room for dissent—
even from Edward's beloved sister Mary. Her tenacious adherence to the old religion created an ever-widening rift between
the royal siblings, one that would eventually cause Edward to
reject Mary's right to succeed him.

"So far as lies in me, I will be to you a dearest brother, and
overflowing with all kindness," the nine-year-old king had
written to Mary after the death of their father. As it turned out,
that bounty of brotherly love was entirely contingent upon
Mary's obliging him.

Somerset had allowed Mary to quietly practice her faith, but
after his downfall, King Edward began to insist that she con-
form to the dictates of the new faith. Mary refused. She believed the boy king was being led by wicked counselors who
had made him a cipher for their extreme agenda. Edward,
however, disabused her of that notion with a letter written in
his own hand. *He* was the king and would no longer tolerate
her disobedience.

"We have suffered it until now," Edward wrote in January
1551,

with the hope that some improvement might be forthcoming, but of none has been shown, how can we suffer it longer to continue? It is our duty to watch over the welfare of each one of our subjects as each ought to watch over himself. You would be angry to see one of the servants of your household, of those nearest to you, openly disregarding your orders; and so it is with us, and you must reflect that in our estate it is most grievous to suffer that so high a subject should disregard our laws. Your near relationship to us, your exalted rank, the conditions of the times, all magnify your offence. It is a scandalous thing that so high a personage should deny our sovereignty; that our sister should be less to us than any of our other subjects is an unnatural example; and finally, in a troubled republic, it lends colour to faction among the people.

Though the king was only thirteen at the time, he insisted that he would have known at age six when a subject was breaking the law, and that despite his youth, he had the same authority Henry VIII had, "without diminution of any sort, either culled from the Scriptures or drawn from universal laws." Edward concluded his missive with an ominous warning to Mary: "Our natural love for you is great without doubt; therefore do not seek to diminish it."

Mary was stunned by the force of Edward's letter, writing back to the king that his words caused her "more suffering than any illness even unto death." Still, she underestimated his fervor for religious reform. Mary acknowledged that Edward was "indeed gifted with understanding far beyond that possessed by others at your age," but for all that he remained a child. She begged her brother to suspend all judgment on spiritual matters "until you reach riper and fuller years, and then with better knowledge and understanding Your Majesty will exercise your freedom to decide."

Mary then went to court to plead her case in person but

found her brother unmoved. "I had suffered her mass against my will," the king wrote in his diary, but now he "could not bear it. . . . Her example might breed too much inconvenience."

The stalemate between siblings nearly became an international incident when the Holy Roman Emperor, Charles V, threatened to invade England in order to preserve his maternal cousin Mary's right to hear mass. The king's counselors, frightened by the prospect of a war they could ill afford, urged the king to relent a little for the sake of peace and security. Edward remained adamant, however, declaring that he would "spend his life, and all he had, rather than agree and grant to what he knew certainly to be against the truth." The emperor backed down; Edward never did.

While King Edward was in the process of subduing his sister, John Dudley was plotting to destroy the king's uncle Somerset once and for all. The master manipulator had already assumed the highest offices in government, capping his climb by creating himself Duke of Northumberland—a reflection of the considerable power he now possessed. He had also won Edward's total confidence by flattering the boy, encouraging him to exercise more royal authority, and especially by presenting himself as a passionate religious reformer. Now only Somerset stood in his way.

Though Somerset had been allowed to resume his place on the council, Northumberland (as Dudley was now called) deliberately provoked and marginalized him to such an extent that the former Protector sought to ally himself with the religiously conservative faction of peers and counselors, including the king's sister Mary. It was a perfect trap. Though there is some evidence that Somerset and his allies plotted to bring down Northumberland, the extent of their plans remains murky. What is certain, though, is that Northumberland pounced, manufacturing evidence that Somerset had plotted to kill him and capture the king.

Somerset was tried and, though acquitted of treason, condemned for the felony of unlawful assembly. His nephew the king—probably under the influence of Northumberland—was convinced of his guilt and seemed indifferent to his fate. "Let the law take its course," Edward reportedly remarked. He signed his uncle's death warrant, and when the execution was carried out on January 22, 1552, he had very little to say about it in his journal: "The Duke of Somerset had his head cut off upon Tower Hill between eight and nine o'clock in the morning."

The apparent lack of family feeling the young king showed over his uncle's violent demise would be even more evident when he moved against his sisters.

Edward VI is often thought of as a sickly boy who barely made it through his six-year reign. In fact, though, he was quite vigorous, with a love of tennis, hunting, and other sports. It was not until January 1553 that the fifteen-year-old king began to ail significantly.

"He does not sleep except when he is stuffed with drugs," one medical observer reported on May 28. "The sputum which he brings up is livid, black, fetid and full of carbon; it smells beyond measure. . . . His feet are swollen all over."

With his body failing, King Edward was determined to preserve the religious revolution inaugurated during his reign. He cut his Catholic sister, Mary, out of the succession, and even his Protestant sister, Elizabeth, as well.* The crown would descend instead upon his Protestant cousin Lady Jane Grey—granddaughter of Henry VIII's younger sister Mary Tudor (see Tudor family tree, pages 2–3)—who was quickly married that May to Northumberland's son Guildford. The daughters of Henry VIII, stripped of their birthright and declared bastards, were to "live in quiet order, according to our appointment."

---

* Both Mary and Elizabeth were declared "illegitimate and not lawfully begotten" in Edward's "Devise for the Succession," and thus unfit to inherit.

It was an act "both remarkable and revolutionary," wrote Chris Skidmore. "Edward was abandoning his family, turning against the traditional laws of inheritance and his late father's wishes. Instead, he would create a new dynasty, one founded upon the one true faith."

Having completed this betrayal of Mary and Elizabeth, Edward VI died on July 6, 1553, mostly likely of tuberculosis. One queen succeeded him as his disease-wracked corpse moldered unburied; another was in for the fight of her life.

3

Lady Jane Grey (1553):
The Nine Days Queen

She is now called Queen, but is not popular.
—BAPTISTA SPINOLA

Although she was called "queen," Lady Jane Grey was never anointed as such, nor recognized by the majority of the people.

As King Edward VI lay gasping his final breaths, the Duke of Northumberland scurried to seize power. He had already forced the marriage of his son Guildford to the king's designated successor, Lady Jane Grey. Now he tried to coax the legitimate queen, Edward's sister, Mary, back to London. The duke sent word that Mary's place was by her dying brother's side. But it was a trap, for while Northumberland's words were soothing, his intent was lethal. "It is to be feared that as soon as the king is dead they will attempt to seize the princess," reported the imperial ambassador.

Mary heeded the warning about the duke's plans for her destruction. Instead of going to attend to her brother at Greenwich, she headed north to her estate at Kenninghall, barely escaping before her home was raided by Northumberland's son Robert. The duke was incensed, declaring that Mary had "gone towards the provinces of Norfolk and Suffolk, being the coast opposite Flanders, with intent to involve the kingdom in troubles and wars, and bring in foreigners to defend her pretensions to the crown."

While one queen fled Northumberland's clutches, another squirmed miserably within them. Poor Jane Grey had no desire to rule England, or right. "Her nightmare lay in her awareness that she had become the prisoner of a power-hungry, unscrupulous junta, led by the man whom she feared above all others," wrote biographer Alison Plowden. The frightening father-in-law who had been foisted upon her would now complete his unscrupulous rise to power by seeing her crowned.

The teenaged girl was horrified to find her parents, once tyrannical figures in her life,* now kneeling in obeisance among other powerful personages. This seemed to make real her inescapable fate. Queen Jane was then taken to the Tower, where English monarchs traditionally held court before their coronations. Baptista Spinola, a Genoese merchant, recorded the scene:

Today I saw Lady Jane Grey walking in a grand procession to the Tower. She is now called Queen, but is not popular, for the hearts of the people are with Mary, the Spanish Queen's [Katherine of Aragon's] daughter. . . . She walked under a canopy, her mother carrying her long train, and her husband Guildford walking by her, dressed all in white and gold, a very strong boy with light hair, who paid her much attention. The new Queen was mounted on very high chopines [shoes with a specially raised cork sole] to make

---

* Jane once confided to a tutor her miserable situation at home: "For when I am in the presence of either Father or Mother, whether I speak, keep silence, sit, stand or go, eat, drink, be merry or sad, be sewing, playing, dancing, or doing anything else, I must do it as it were in such weight, measure and number, even so perfectly as God made the world; or else I am so sharply taunted, so cruelly threatened, yea presented sometimes with pinches, nips and bobs and other ways . . . that I think myself in hell."

her look much taller, which were concealed by her robes, as she is very small and short. Many ladies followed, with noblemen, but this lady is very heretical [Protestant] and has never heard Mass, and some great people did not come into the procession for that reason.*

Reaction to the news of Jane's accession had indeed been decidedly cool, though not because she was Protestant. Mary was simply the rightful queen. "No one present showed any sign of rejoicing" when Jane was proclaimed, an imperial envoy reported, "and no one cried 'Long Live the Queen!' except the herald who made the proclamation and a few archers who followed him." Any dissension was ruthlessly crushed by Northumberland's henchmen. One young barman named Gilbert Pot was arrested "for speaking of certain words of Queen Mary, that she had the right title." He was then set upon a pillory and had his ears lopped off.

Jane herself was painfully aware of how illegitimate her rule was, and that she was Northumberland's puppet. Even so, since she had been used for her Tudor bloodline, she was not about to share power with her nonroyal spouse. "I sent for the earls of Arundel and Pembroke," Jane later wrote to Queen Mary, "and said to them, that if the crown belonged to me I should be content to make my husband a duke, but would never consent to make him king."

---

* Spinola also left a vivid description of the teenaged usurper: "This Jane is very short and thin, but prettily shaped and graceful. She has small features and a well-made nose, the mouth flexible and the lips red. The eyebrows are arched and darker than her hair, which is nearly red. Her eyes are sparkling and reddish brown in color. I stood so near her grace that I noticed her color was good but freckled. When she smiled she showed her teeth, which are white and sharp. In all a gracious and animated figure. She wore a dress of green velvet stamped with gold, with large sleeves. Her headdress was a white coif with many jewels."

This decision of Jane's, which seems to have dominated most of her brief two-week reign, infuriated not only Guildford Dudley, with all his kingly pretensions, but also his mother, the grasping Duchess of Northumberland, who, Jane wrote, "persuaded her son not to sleep with me any longer as he was wont to do." After that, she related, "I was compelled to act as a woman who is obliged to live on good terms with her husband; nevertheless I was not only deluded by the Duke and the Council, but maltreated by my husband and his mother."

While Queen Jane was preoccupied with her pouty husband and nasty in-laws, Queen Mary was a fugitive with few prospects. Even the envoys of her powerful ally and cousin, Emperor Charles V, believed her cause to be hopeless. The Duke of Northumberland seemed invincible.

"Dudley had with him some three thousand mounted men and foot soldiers, thirty cannon from the Tower, and as many cartloads of ammunition," wrote Mary's biographer Carolly Erickson. "He controlled the capital, the government, the treasury, and the queen. No commander was superior to him in experience or skill; he seemed to have every advantage."

But, for all that, the people hated him. To most he was a wicked upstart, mad with power. Mary, on the other hand, was Henry VIII's own daughter—a princess who had endured much pain and heartbreak, and who was now being denied her birthright by a monster. In a steady procession, people began to rally to her banner. It was a spontaneous eruption of support by a people unwilling to see their rightful queen displaced.

Mary had been reminded by the council that she had been "justly made illegitimate and uninheritable to the Crown Imperial of this realm," and warned not to bother the loyal subjects of "our Sovereign Lady Queen Jane." Now Northumberland was preparing to answer her impudence.

It was Jane Grey's father, the Duke of Suffolk, who was originally charged with subduing the growing movement around

Mary and capturing her. Upon learning this, however, Jane burst into tears and begged that her father remain with her in London. The task then fell to Northumberland and his sons. "Since ye think it good," the duke said to the council, "I and mine will go, not doubting of your fidelity to the Queen's majesty which I leave in your custody."

Northumberland was wily enough to know that the men around him were all driven by self-interest, and that by leaving London he was exposing himself to betrayal should events turn in Mary's favor. Thus, he reminded them that he and his companions were risking their lives "amongst the bloody strokes and cruel assaults" of the enemy with the trust that the council would protect their interests at home. He warned anyone who might violate that trust and "leave us your friends in the briars and betray us" that he could in turn destroy them. More important, it would be a damnable betrayal of the sacred oath of allegiance they had sworn "to this virtuous lady the Queen's highness, who by your and our enticement is rather of force placed therein [upon the throne] than by her own seeking and request." The duke then concluded by praying that the council "wish me no worse speed in this journey than ye would have to yourselves."

As Northumberland's force prepared to leave London to "fetch in the Lady Mary . . . to destroy her grace,"* the rightful queen of England was rallying her supporters at Framlingham Castle, a stronghold she possessed near the Suffolk coast. It was a vivid display of royal might as Mary rode among the thousands gathered in her name, stirring them into battle. "Long live our good Queen Mary!" they shouted. "Death to traitors!"

It was far from the reception Northumberland received. "The people press to see us, but not one sayeth God speed us,"

---

* As recorded in the diary of a London merchant by the name of Henry Machyn.

the duke noted to a companion as they rode through the village of Shoreditch. In addition to the lack of popular support for his mission, Northumberland was faced not only with dissension among his own ranks but with desertion as well. Then came the crowning blow to his cause: A fleet of seven warships he had sent up the coast to prevent Mary from escaping now switched to her side. "After once the submission of the ships was known in the Tower," wrote an eyewitness, "each man then began to pluck in his horns."

The betrayal Northumberland had feared became real as he received "but a slender answer" from the council on his request for reinforcements. As town after town came out for Mary, the men who had sworn allegiance to Jane less than two weeks earlier abruptly switched sides. On the afternoon of July 19 they publicly proclaimed Mary queen, prompting a spontaneous eruption of joy in the city.

"As not a soul imagined the possibility of such a thing," one eyewitness reported, "when the proclamation was first cried out the people started off, running in all directions and crying out: 'The Lady Mary is proclaimed Queen!'"

While people celebrated wildly in the streets, Lady Jane was all but abandoned in the Tower. Even her father walked away, but not before ripping down the royal cloth of estate that had hung over her chair. Meanwhile, Northumberland surrendered in Cambridge without a struggle. He was arrested by one of his own confederates, the Earl of Arundel, who only a week before had sworn to die for him.

"I beseech you, my lord of Arundel, use mercy towards me, knowing the case as it is," Northumberland said.

"My Lord," answered Arundel, "ye should have sought for mercy sooner; I must do according to my commandment."

The once mighty duke was pelted with stones and insults by the outraged populace as he was led to the Tower in chains. "A dreadful sight it was," wrote the imperial envoy Simon Renard, "and a strange mutation for those who, a few days before, had seen the Duke enter London Tower with great pomp and magnificence when the Lady Jane went there to take possession, and now saw him led like a criminal and dubbed traitor."

With her mortal enemy now locked away, Queen Mary rode triumphantly into London among cheering crowds. She was dressed to dazzle in purple velvet, adorned with pearls and precious stones. And though she bore the marks of bitterness and deprivation that had stolen her youth, she was prepared to be merciful to her enemies.

Northumberland would, of course, have to die for his high crimes, which he did after making a dramatic repudiation of the Protestant faith he had espoused, but Lady Jane would be spared. The so-called Nine Days Queen swore to Mary in a long letter that she had never willingly participated in Northumberland's plans: "For whereas I might have taken upon me that of which I was not worthy, yet no one can ever say either that I sought it . . . or that I was pleased with it."

Though Jane remained in the Tower, it was expected that she would be released before long. After all, her father was free after having been forgiven for his part in Northumberland's conspiracy, and her mother enjoyed high favor in the court of her cousin the queen.

All seemed well until Mary made a momentous decision that would rock the kingdom, destabilize her throne, and destroy Jane Grey.

4

Mary I (1553–1558): Bloody Mary's Burning Desire

This marriage renders me happier than I can say.
—QUEEN MARY I

Queen Mary I became the first woman to rule England in her own right after defeating the Duke of Northumberland and his puppet, Jane Grey, in 1553. The Catholic queen's five-year reign was a disaster, most notably because of her fierce persecution of Protestants, which has blighted her reputation ever since. Even her marriage was a failure.

Shortly before she became infamous as Bloody Mary, England's first queen regnant was a blushing bride. She had come to the throne in 1553, after enduring decades of appalling abuse and neglect. Her father had cruelly discarded her mother, Katherine of Aragon, and terrorized Mary as a young woman for refusing to acknowledge herself as a bastard and him as Supreme Head of the Church in England. Then, under the reign of her fanatically Protestant half brother, Edward VI, she was threatened for practicing her Catholic faith and, in the end, deprived of her rightful place in the succession. Now, a year after her triumphant accession, the woman who once described herself as "the unhappiest lady in Christendom" was absolutely giddy with anticipation.

The queen's betrothed was her younger cousin Philip of

Spain, son of Emperor Charles V. Mary had been reluctant about the match at first, fearing not only the reaction of her xenophobic subjects to a foreign prince but Philip's reaction to her. She was pushing forty and was totally inexperienced with the opposite sex. Philip, on the other hand, was eleven years younger and known for his way with the ladies. It took some gentle coaxing from the emperor, in whom she put all her trust, before the queen was convinced. Once she was, Mary became like a giggly schoolgirl. All her hopes and dreams were now focused on Philip, the dashing prince who she believed would not only help her bring England back to the pope in Rome but would satisfy her deepest longings for love.

The queen told the emperor's representative, Simon Renard, that he "had made her fall in love with [Philip]," then added jokingly that "his Highness might not be obliged to him for it, though she would do her best to please him in every way."

One person stood in the way of the queen's happiness, however, and that was Lady Jane Grey. Mary had forgiven her young cousin for accepting the crown, and was even prepared to release her from the Tower. But then a rebellion broke out in opposition to the queen's proposed marriage to Philip, and Jane's father, the Duke of Suffolk, was one of the ringleaders. The rebels were decisively crushed, but Simon Renard made it clear to the queen that the emperor would never allow his son to come to England while Jane Grey still lived as the focus of future uprisings. "Let the Queen's mercy be tempered with a little severity," Charles V said. And so on February 12, 1554, the Nine Days Queen, not yet seventeen years old, lost her head.*

---

* Jane was given the opportunity to save her life if she would convert to Catholicism, but the girl who had been so shocked by the last-minute conversion of her father-in-law, the Duke of Northumberland, resolutely maintained her own strong Protestant faith. On the scaffold, before she laid

Popular opposition to the queen's marriage was not quelled by Jane's death. Spain was a hated enemy, and it was unthinkable to many that Mary would import a Spanish prince to rule over them. The Speaker of the House of Commons even dared remonstrate with the queen personally on the matter, but to no avail. Mary had sworn she would wed Philip, and she would never retreat from that vow.

As the queen's excitement grew to bursting, the prince of Spain finally came to England in the middle of July 1554. Several days before the wedding at Winchester Cathedral, Mary met him for the first time. She was delighted by what she saw, running up to Philip and kissing him when he entered the room. Clearly he had lived up to the dignified portrait by Titian that had so far been the queen's only contact with the man who was to rule England by her side.

Philip treated Mary with perfect decorum when he met her, but his gentlemen were quite disappointed by her appearance. Years of care and worry had taken their toll. "The queen is not at all beautiful," one of Philip's companions wrote. "Small, and rather flabby than fat, she is of white complexion and fair, and has no eyebrows." As biographer Carolly Erickson noted, Mary "looked exactly what she was: Philip's maiden aunt."

The Venetian ambassador was a little bit kinder in his assessment of the queen's appearance:

> She is of low rather than of middling stature, but, although short, she has not personal defect in her limbs, nor is any part of her body deformed. She is of spare and delicate frame, quite unlike her father, who was tall and stout; nor does she resemble her mother, who, if not tall, was

---

her head on the block, she reiterated that she looked to be saved "by none other mean, but only by the mercy of God in the merits of the blood of his only son Jesus Christ."

nevertheless bulky. Her face is well formed, as shown by her features and lineaments, and as seen by her portraits. When younger she was considered, not merely tolerably handsome, but of beauty exceeding mediocrity. At present, with the exception of some wrinkles, caused more by anxieties than by age, which makes her appear some years older, her aspect, for the rest, is very grave. Her eyes are so piercing that they inspire not only respect, but fear in those on whom she fixes them, although she is very shortsighted, being unable to read or do anything else unless she has her sight quite close to what she wishes to peruse or to see distinctly. Her voice is rough and loud, almost like a man's, so that when she speaks she is always heard a long way off. In short, she is a seemly woman, and never to be loathed for ugliness, even at her present age, without considering her degree of queen.

Winchester Cathedral, stripped of much of its ornate magnificence by Henry VIII, was temporarily restored to some of its former glory for the queen's wedding. Rich tapestries and cloth of gold were hung. On either side of the altar were two canopied chairs for the bride and groom (which can still be seen today). Mary's gown was of black velvet studded with precious stones, over which she wore a mantle of gold cloth matching that worn by Philip. The queen, one observer wrote, "blazed with jewels to such an extent that the eye was blinded as it looked upon her."

After the wedding a sumptuous feast was held at the bishop of Winchester's palace. The newlyweds then retired to lodgings specially prepared for them. "What happened that night only they know," one of the Spanish guests wrote. "If they give us a son our joy will be complete."

That would never happen, but before Mary was forced to reconcile herself to being barren, among other future woes, she was simply a smitten new wife. The queen wrote to her father-in-law, Charles V, after the wedding to thank him "for allying me with a prince so full of virtues that the realm's honor and tranquility will certainly be thereby increased. This marriage renders me happier than I can say, as I daily discover in the King my husband so many virtues and perfections that I constantly pray God to grant me grace to please him, and behave in all things as befits one who is so deeply embounden to him."

Philip was somewhat less enamored with his bride. "To speak frankly with you," his confidant Ruy Gómez wrote home to Spain, "it will take a great God to drink this cup." Nevertheless, Philip made the best of it. "He treats the queen very kindly," Gómez reported, "and well knows how to pass over the fact that she is no good from the point of view of fleshy sensuality. He makes her so happy that the other day when they were alone she almost talked love talk to him, and he replied in the same vein."

Several months after the wedding Mary believed she was pregnant, the joy of which was matched by her kingdom's reunion with Rome. With her husband by her side, and a baby in her belly (or so she thought), Mary began to burn heretics. Hundreds of men and women, many of them poor and uneducated, suffered agonizing deaths at the stake, while the queen solidified her place in English history as Bloody Mary.

During Easter Week, 1555, Queen Mary went into confinement at Hampton Court in anticipation of her delivery, which was expected early in May. The palace was a hive of activity in preparation for the arrival of the precious heir. "I warrant it should be a man child," Charles V declared confidently. But the due date came and went, followed by fresh calculations by the queen's doctors that she would deliver in June. Still no baby. As Mary became increasingly more anxious and depressed, people began mumbling that she may not have been pregnant at all. English diplomats searched for explanations for the delayed delivery as their queen was held to increasing ridicule in foreign courts. Another due date passed in July, by which time the doctors and midwives had ceased making calculations. Still, the Venetian ambassador, for one, continued to hold out hope that a miracle would "come to pass in this, as in all her majesty's other circumstances, which the more they were despaired of according to human reasoning and discourse, the better and more auspicious did their result then show itself."*

By the end of August there were few believers left; Philip departed for the dominions in Flanders that he was about to inherit from his father. Mary wept as she watched him go. She believed at first that her husband would soon return to her, but as his letters tapered off, and rumors of his philandering began to reach her, she despaired.

As the months went by, Mary became increasingly desperate, even pleading with her father-in-law, the emperor, to make Philip come back. "I beg your Majesty to forgive my boldness," she wrote, "and to remember the unspeakable sadness I experience because of the absence of the king." Sadness sometimes gave way to anger, as on the occasion when the queen ordered a portrait of her wayward husband removed from the council chamber, kicking it on the way out. Then there was the resignation that Philip would probably not be coming back. According to one report, the queen "told her ladies, that she had done all possible to induce her husband to return, and as she found he would not, she meant to withdraw utterly from men,

---

* It is possible that Queen Mary had a rare condition known as pseudocyesis, or false pregnancy. Not only do those who suffer from the disorder fervently believe they are pregnant, but they have a variety of symptoms to make it seem so, such as cessation of menstruation, abdominal enlargement, nausea and vomiting, breast enlargement, and food cravings. The condition baffles scientists, but some have suggested that pseudocyesis occurs in patients who desperately want to become pregnant. This would certainly fit Mary Tudor, who fervently prayed for an heir to maintain the Catholic restoration.

and live quietly, as she had done the chief part of her life before she was married."

As it turned out, Philip did return to England, but only briefly, and not to reconcile with Mary (though there was intimacy, and yet another false pregnancy). He needed her as an ally in a war he was fighting against France. The queen agreed to help her husband, but all she got in return was the devastating loss of Calais, the last of England's once numerous territories in France. Philip had broken her heart, but, she said, they would find Calais lying upon it when they opened her up after her death.

Bitter and abandoned, with all her hopes for a Catholic dynasty in ruins, Queen Mary I was finally forced to endure the inescapable fact that her hated half sister, Elizabeth, would be the one to succeed her.

5

Elizabeth I (1558–1603):

Perils of a Princess

My Lord, these are shameful slanders.

—Princess Elizabeth, later Queen Elizabeth I

She was Gloriana, perhaps the greatest of all England's kings and queens. But before Elizabeth I came to the throne and presided over that magnificent era bearing her name, she was a princess in almost constant peril. It was only with her formidable intelligence, and a little luck, that the young Elizabeth managed to survive—barely.

In one of fate's odd twists, Elizabeth Tudor enjoyed the most security of her early life during the reign of her father, Henry VIII. Sure, he was a monster who had her legally declared a bastard after beheading her mother, Anne Boleyn, but mostly the king ignored his precocious redheaded daughter and left her to her books. That kind of benign neglect had its benefits in those dangerous times, and Elizabeth grew up to revere her "matchless and most benevolent" father. After his death in 1547, though, she came under much more intense scrutiny, which nearly proved lethal.

The orphaned princess, just thirteen, was sent to live in the household of her fourth and final stepmother, Katherine Parr, who, after she managed to survive her marriage to Henry VIII,

wed the man she had always wanted: the dashing Thomas Seymour, Lord High Admiral of England and uncle to the new
king, Edward VI.

Queen Katherine had always treated Elizabeth with loving
kindness, but her new husband's interest in the girl might gen-
erously be described as predatory. Half-dressed, Seymour
would steal into Elizabeth's bedchamber first thing in the
morning, rouse the teenager with tickles, slap her rear end, and
attempt to kiss her. The princess was at first flattered by the attentions of the older, extremely charismatic man. But adoles-
cent infatuation gave way to probity. To avoid being vulnerable,
Elizabeth was forced to wake up earlier and dress fully before
Seymour burst into her room. Still, he persisted, and with
Katherine Parr's apparent acquiescence. In one bizarre incident, the queen even held Elizabeth down while Seymour cut
her dress to shreds.

Perhaps Katherine genuinely believed that her husband was
being playfully paternal with their young charge. He was, after
all, gregarious by nature. But her attitude changed abruptly
after she reportedly discovered her husband and stepdaughter
in an embrace. Pregnant and sick at the time, Katherine sent
Elizabeth away with a stern warning about the dangerous effects of scandal. She also promised the mortified girl that she
would report to her if her reputation had already been compro-
mised in any way.

A deeply chastened Elizabeth assured her stepmother in a
letter from her new residence that she was "replete with sorrow
to depart from your Highness, especially seeing you undoubt-
ful of health; and albeit I answered little, I weighed it more
deeper when you said you would warn me of all evilness that
you should hear of me; for if your Grace had not a good opinion of me, you would not have offered friendship to me that
way at all, meaning the contrary."

Though the breach with Katherine Parr was quickly healed,

the episodes with Seymour would come to haunt Elizabeth and taint her with treason. After he was arrested and imprisoned for having tried to kidnap King Edward (see Chapter 2), Elizabeth was left to answer the charge that he had conspired to marry her. The danger was acute, especially if the princess was found to have cooperated in Seymour's scheme. And all the more distressing, her devoted governess, Kat Ashley, who had been like a mother to her, and her servant Thomas Parry were sent to the Tower as co-conspirators. Anything Elizabeth said while being interrogated could put the lives of these beloved companions in danger as well.

Sir Robert Tyrwhitt, sent by the council to question Elizabeth, was pleased to report that she was "marvelously abashed, and did weep very tenderly a long time," upon hearing of Ashley and Parry's imprisonment. But behind those tears was the fierce determination and superior intelligence that would thwart and frustrate Tyrwhitt throughout his relentless interrogation.

"She hath a very good wit, and nothing is gotten of her but by great policy," Tyrwhitt conceded. Nevertheless, he remained convinced that he could break the princess. By using "gentle persuasion," he reported that he had already coaxed Elizabeth into admitting that her cofferer, Thomas Parry, had returned from a financial meeting with Thomas Seymour and had discussed the *possibility* of the Lord Admiral's marrying her.

Despite all his threats and cajoling, that was about all Tyrwhitt could get from Elizabeth or her servants. "I verily do believe," he confessed in frustration, "that there hath been some secret promise between my lady [Elizabeth], Mistress Ashley and the cofferer, never to confess to death." The interrogator was reduced to informing Elizabeth of the rumors then in circulation that she was in the Tower and pregnant with Seymour's child. The princess's composure temporarily broke upon hearing this; her honor was at stake.

"My Lord, these are shameful slanders," she wrote furiously to Seymour's brother, Somerset. "For the which, besides the great desire I have to see the King's Majesty, I shall most heartily desire your Lordship that I may come to court after your first determination, that I may show myself as I am."

Elizabeth's plea to vindicate herself publicly was ignored. Meanwhile, Tyrwhitt continued his assault, to no avail. "I . . . have practiced with my lady's grace by all means and policies to cause her to confess more than she hath already done," he lamented, "wherein she doth plainly deny that she knoweth any more than she hath already opened to me."

Having been outwitted by the crafty teenager, Tyrwhitt settled on a new policy. If Kat Ashley could be made to talk, that would shatter Elizabeth and "make her cough out the whole." As it turned out, Mrs. Ashley had long fantasized about a marriage between her royal charge and the charming Seymour, rhapsodizing about it endlessly. "If all the Council did agree, why not?" she had asked Elizabeth in the period following Katherine Parr's death. "For he's the noblest man unmarried in this land." Parry, too, shared in the chatter after his meeting with Seymour to discuss Elizabeth's finances. Now, in the dankness of the Tower, all their dangerous discussions were exposed.

Parry had sworn he "had rather be pulled with horses" than reveal any secrets. But confronted with very real terrors, he broke down and signed a detailed confession. "False wretch!" Kat Ashley cried when Parry and his confession were brought before her. She had languished in a grim dungeon—"so cold . . . and so dark"—but had said nothing. Now she had little choice but to tell what she knew as well, including details of those embarrassing morning romps in Elizabeth's bedchamber. She admitted that she had frequently discussed Seymour with Elizabeth, and "hath wished both openly and privily that they two were married together."

A triumphant Tyrwhitt presented the signed confessions to Elizabeth and reported that she was "much abashed and half breathless" upon reading them. Humiliating as some of the revelations were, though, Elizabeth was quick to recognize that they weren't damning. Nowhere was she implicated in Seymour's plot to marry her, and all Kat Ashley had to say about a potential union was merely foolish chatter, not evidence of criminal intent. The council was forced to agree. Only Tyrwhitt remained convinced that Elizabeth and her servants were holding back. "They all sing one song," he wrote to the Protector, "and so I think they would not do unless they had set the note before."

In the end only Thomas Seymour forfeited his life. Elizabeth, on the other hand, managed to survive her brother's brief reign with only her birthright taken away. But she came close to losing much more than that when her sister, Mary, became queen in 1553.

Elizabeth was right by her sister's side when Mary triumphantly rode into London to claim her crown after Northumberland's defeat. But it wasn't long before the new queen's deep-seated resentments toward her sister began to aggressively spew forth. It was Elizabeth's mother, Anne Boleyn, who had, after all, supplanted Mary's own mother, Katherine of Aragon, and who had viciously abused Mary, threatening at one point to poison her or "marry her to some valet." And when Elizabeth was born, Mary was deprived of her rank as princess, declared a bastard, and relegated to a lowly status within her exalted half sister's household. Her protests were met with Anne Boleyn's order to "box her ears as a cursed bastard."

The numerous indignities Mary had endured as a young woman were now heaped upon Elizabeth, whose rank at court was often superseded by lesser royals, like her cousin Margaret,

Countess of Lennox.* The queen even questioned whether Elizabeth was really her sister, noting cattily that she had "the face and countenance of Mark Smeaton," the musician executed as one of Anne Boleyn's alleged lovers, "who was a very handsome man."

Fueling Mary's animosity toward Elizabeth was Simon Renard, the ambassador of the queen's cousin Emperor Charles V. Renard perceived Elizabeth and her Protestant base of support as a threat, and was quick to exploit Mary's innate suspicions about her sister's loyalty. Elizabeth was "clever and sly," he insisted, and possessed "a spirit full of enchantment." Her very presence at court was dangerous, given that she "might, out of ambition or being persuaded thereto, conceive some dangerous design and put it to execution by means which it would be difficult to prevent." Mary hardly needed convincing.

To placate the zealously Catholic queen, Elizabeth adopted a submissive posture and requested instruction in her sister's faith so that she "might know if her conscience would allow her to be persuaded." Mary was at first delighted by Elizabeth's apparent willingness to convert, but soon she saw how half-hearted it really was. Before her first mass, Elizabeth complained loudly all the way to church that her stomach ached, Renard reported, "wearing a suffering air."

Mary was furious that her sister would prevaricate on a matter as essential as faith, and grew even more hardened in her mistrust. The queen confided to Renard "that it would burden her conscience too heavily to allow Elizabeth to succeed [her on the throne], for she only went to mass out of hypocrisy, she had not a single servant or maid of honor who was not a heretic, she talked every day with heretics and lent an ear to all

* Margaret Tudor's daughter by her second husband, Archibald Douglas, Earl of Angus (see Tudor family tree, pages 2–3).

their evil designs, and it would be a disgrace to the kingdom to allow a bastard to succeed."

Given her sister's hostility, Elizabeth requested permission to leave court and retire to the country. While she was away, a massive rebellion broke out in opposition to the queen's proposed marriage to Philip of Spain. London was nearly taken over before the rebels were finally subdued. How much Elizabeth knew about the plot to place her on the throne remains a mystery, but as far as Mary was concerned, she was the prime mover. The queen ordered her sister back to London. Elizabeth refused, claiming she was too ill to travel. This only served to heighten Mary's suspicions, and Elizabeth was practically dragged back. Swollen and pale, she arrived in London on February 22, 1554, less than two weeks after the execution of her cousin Lady Jane Grey. "It was Renard's fervent hope," wrote biographer Anne Somerset, "that Elizabeth would shortly suffer the same fate."

Despite the intensive interrogations of the uprising's leaders, no evidence against Elizabeth emerged. Still, she was ordered to the Tower as the investigation continued. The queen was convinced of her sister's culpability in the attempted coup and determined to prove it. Elizabeth's character, Mary told Renard, "was just what she had always believed it to be."

Before she was escorted away to the place where her mother had met her doom, Princess Elizabeth begged leave to write her sister, permission for which was reluctantly given by the two peers charged with her removal. It was a letter upon which Elizabeth was certain her life depended. In it, she swore to the queen that she had "never practiced, counseled, nor consented to anything that might be prejudicial to your person in any way, or dangerous to the state by any means. And therefore I humbly beseech your Majesty to let me answer afore yourself."

Two specific allegations had been laid against Elizabeth: that she had corresponded with one of the rebel leaders,

Thomas Wyatt, and also with the king of France. Both charges she hotly denied. "As for the traitor Wyatt," Elizabeth declared, "he might peradventure write me a letter, but on my faith I never received any from him. And as for the copy of my letter sent to the French King, I pray God confound me eternally if ever I sent him word, message, token or letter, by any means. And this truth I will stand in till my death."

Elizabeth appealed to Mary to remember her promise—delivered as Elizabeth prepared to remove herself to the country—that she would never condemn her "without answer and due proof, which it seems that I now am." And she reminded the queen of a situation with which they were both very familiar—that of the Seymour brothers and their lethal conflict during the reign of Edward VI.

"I have heard of many in my time cast away for want of coming to the presence of their Prince," Elizabeth wrote, "and in late days I heard my Lord of Somerset say that if his brother had been suffered [allowed] to speak with him he had never suffered; but persuasions were made to him so great that he was brought in belief that he could not live safely if the Admiral lived, and that made him give consent to his death."

As historian David Starkey noted in his study of Elizabeth's struggle, Simon Renard was persuading Mary of the threat her sister posed the same way Somerset had been turned against his brother. Indeed, Renard had just written to Charles V: "If [the council] do not punish [Elizabeth] now that the occasion offers, the queen will never be secure."

Elizabeth was quick to minimize the Seymour parallels. "Though these persons are not to be compared to your Majesty," she wrote, "yet I pray to God the like evil persuasions persuade not one sister against the other, and all for that they have heard false report, and the truth not known."

Queen Mary was utterly unmoved by her sister's plea. Her throne, indeed her very life, had been threatened by the rebellion, and now her hatred for Elizabeth was implacable. She refused to see her sister and was angered that the time given to Elizabeth to write her letter had delayed her imprisonment.

On March 18, 1544, in the midst of a drenching rain, Elizabeth Tudor was conveyed by boat to the Tower. Upon arriving, she refused to disembark, glaring defiantly at those who would dare force her. Then suddenly she stood, made her way to the steps leading into the forbidding complex, and declared dramatically, "Here landeth as true a subject, being prisoner, as ever landed at these stairs." With that, she plopped down on the cold, wet flagstone and refused to budge. "It is better sitting here than in a worse place," she answered in response to the pleas for her to come out of the rain. When the affecting scene reduced one of her servants to tears, Elizabeth asserted fiercely that she sat not out of fear or despair but in protest of the injustice she endured. The princess proclaimed that "she knew her truth to be such that no man would have cause to weep for her." She then rose and swept inside—her Tudor pride intact.

For nearly seven weeks Elizabeth lingered within the Tower walls, constantly in fear that any minute she would be taken away and beheaded. Yet despite her most earnest wishes, Mary could find no way to legally kill her sister. The council and judges were not prepared to take such a drastic step. Furthermore, no evidence against Elizabeth was uncovered, and Wyatt even exonerated her on the scaffold before his execution.

Yet while there was no reason to keep Elizabeth in the Tower, Mary was not willing to let her go. Instead, she would be kept under house arrest at a crumbling manor the queen owned in Woodstock, near Oxford. Sir Henry Bedingfield, who had been placed in charge of the princess, arrived to escort her there, accompanied by one hundred soldiers. The strength of this force led Elizabeth to believe that the time had come for her to die. Anxiously she asked "whether the Lady Jane [Grey's] scaffold were taken away or no?" The response that she was merely being moved to Woodstock did little to soothe the young woman's worry. There was still the fear of assassination.

After leaving the terrors of the Tower, Elizabeth was warmly welcomed by the common people on her way to Woodstock. The princess had always been held in high regard, now all the more so for having survived the persecution of her increasingly unpopular sister. Large crowds gathered in London to wish her well on her journey, while enthusiastic villagers along the route tossed fragrant herbs and other goods into her litter, shouting, "God save Your Grace!" as she passed.

But once she arrived at Woodstock, the popular acclaim Elizabeth enjoyed on the way was replaced by the maddening restrictions of her home confinement. Far from being the assassin she had feared, Bedingfield was instead a rigid bureaucrat fixated on following Mary's instructions precisely. In the name of the queen, he made Elizabeth's life hell. She was kept isolated from the outside world, with very little personal freedom—even to possess the Bible of her choice.

In exasperation, Elizabeth wrote a howling letter of protest to her sister. Gone was the humble obsequiousness she had shown the queen in her plea before being remanded to the Tower. Now she had the temerity to address Mary throughout as "You," a gross breach of etiquette, and insisted upon reaffirming her innocence. The queen was not pleased. She reiterated the grounds for her suspicions about Elizabeth and reminded her sister that she had been treated with "more clemency and favour . . . than [those] in like matters hath been accustomed." Mary then stated that in the future she did not wish to be "molested by such her disguise and colourable letters."

Bedingfield took his cue from the queen and made Elizabeth's life even more miserable. She would no longer be allowed to write the council, a ban, Elizabeth insisted, that was contrary to her basic rights and that left her "in worse case than the worst prisoner in Newgate." In such a state, she continued,

"I must needs continue this life without all hope worldly, wholly resting to the truth of my cause."

Redemption for Elizabeth came from the unlikeliest of sources: Philip of Spain, the same king who would one day launch the Spanish Armada against her. His protection was based solely on self-interest, for if his wife, Mary, should die childless, he would need Elizabeth as an ally. With that in mind, Philip encouraged the queen to bring her sister to court and treat her gently. Mary agreed, but most reluctantly. Her ill feelings had not abated at all.

Elizabeth waited for three weeks at Hampton Court before Mary finally deigned to meet with her. The queen had hoped that the suspense and anxiety leading up to the interview would make Elizabeth crack, but the Tudor princess was made of sterner stuff than that. She bowed humbly before her sister, whom she had not seen in a year, but conceded nothing. Mary was livid. "You will not confess your offence but stand stoutly in your truth," she growled in her deep, almost manly voice. "I pray God it may so fall out."

The rest of the interview went no better, with Mary insisting that Elizabeth would proclaim to the world that she had been unjustly punished. "I must not say so, to you," Elizabeth answered.

"Why then, belike you will to others," Mary retorted.

"No," said Elizabeth, "I have borne the burden and must bear it. I humbly beseech Your Majesty to have a good opinion of me, and to think me to be your true subject, not only from the beginning hitherto, but forever, as long as life lasteth."

Far from satisfied, Mary dismissed her sister "with very few comfortable words." Elizabeth remained at court, isolated, while the drama of the queen's false pregnancy played out. Then she was permitted to retire to her childhood home at Hatfield.

Though the queen seethed over her inability to move against

Elizabeth, she remained absolutely determined that Anne Boleyn's daughter would never succeed her. It would be an abomination, wrote the Venetian ambassador, for Mary "to see the illegitimate child of a criminal who was punished as a public strumpet on the point of inheriting the throne with better fortune than herself, whose descent is rightful, legitimate and legal."

Yet as much as the queen chafed at the prospect of Elizabeth's one day wearing the crown, the inevitability of it became increasingly apparent. Mary proved barren and, in the wake of her fanatical persecution of Protestants, deeply unpopular. Almost as a coda to her disastrous five-year reign, Calais was lost in an ill-advised war. Sick, tired, and in despair, Mary I died quietly on November 17, 1558.

When the news of her sister's demise arrived at Hatfield, Elizabeth fell to her knees. "This is the doing of the Lord," she gasped, "and it is marvelous in our eyes." The Elizabethan age had begun.

6

Elizabeth I (1558–1603):
A Clash of Queens

> The poor foolish woman will not desist until she
> loses her head.
>
> —CHARLES IX OF FRANCE

The reign of Elizabeth I was a triumph, a golden age in which the last Tudor monarch pursued policies of moderation and maintained relative peace within her kingdom. However, the queen's own tranquility was shattered by her cousin, Mary, Queen of Scots, who arrived in England as a fugitive from her own subjects and spent the next two decades as virtual prisoner there—all the while plotting against Elizabeth's life.

She may have been Henry VIII's daughter—"the lion's cub," as she called herself—but she was Anne Boleyn's as well. And that made Queen Elizabeth I a bastard in the minds of Europe's Catholic powers, who refused to recognize the validity of the late king's second marriage. Mary, Queen of Scots, was among those monarchs who rejected her cousin Elizabeth's right to rule, claiming the English crown for herself as Henry VIII's nearest relative.* Of course such blatant designs on her throne

---

* She was the granddaughter of Henry VIII's sister, Margaret Tudor, who had married James IV of Scotland. Thus, she was actually Elizabeth's first cousin once removed (see Tudor family tree, pages 2–3).

were bound to arouse the wrath of Elizabeth, who, after years of danger and deprivation, held her sovereignty most dear. The result was an escalating conflict between the two queens that would have in the end devastating consequences for both of them.

By the time Elizabeth came to the throne in 1558, when she was twenty-five, her cousin and future rival, Mary Stuart, had been queen of Scotland for nearly sixteen years—her entire life, really, since she inherited her father James V's crown when she was just six days old. The young monarch had spent little time in her own kingdom, however, having been sent to France as a child of five to be raised there as the future bride of Henry II's son, the dauphin Francis, whom she wed when she was fifteen. A year after her marriage, Mary became queen consort of France when her father-in-law was killed in a freak jousting accident and her husband succeeded him as Francis II.

It was while in France that Mary began to aggressively assert her claim to the English crown—a pretension encouraged first by Henry II and then by her maternal uncles from the powerful, fanatically Catholic House of Guise, who controlled Francis II. She had the audacity to incorporate the royal arms of England into her own coat of arms, which Elizabeth found galling enough. But even more egregious was Mary's refusal to ratify the Treaty of Edinburgh, which, among other provisions, called for the Scottish queen to relinquish her claim to the English throne and to acknowledge Elizabeth's right to it.*

In retaliation for her younger cousin's impudence, Elizabeth refused Mary's request for safe passage through England as she

---

* Catholic France had long held sway in Scotland, especially under the regency of Mary's mother, a member of the House of Guise, who ruled while her daughter, the Queen of Scots, was away in France. The Treaty of Edinburgh came about after Protestant forces in Scotland, with the aid of England, finally ejected the French in 1560.

prepared to return to her native kingdom after the untimely death of Francis II in 1560.* It was an intemperate response to what should have been a basic courtesy, and it reflected poorly on the English queen. Mary, in an interview with England's ambassador to France, Sir Nicholas Throckmorton, made the most of Elizabeth's rudeness. "It will be thought very strange amongst all princes and countries that she should first animate my subjects against me," Mary scolded, "and now being a widow to impeach me going into my own country."

The Queen of Scots then concluded the interview with a melodramatic declaration: "I trust the wind will be so favorable that I shall not need to come on the coast of England . . . for if I do then . . . the Queen your mistress shall have me in her hands to do her will of me and if she be so hard-hearted as to desire my end, she may do her pleasure and make sacrifice of me."

Elizabeth, however, was eager to put the unpleasantness of the safe-passage debacle behind her and extend her hand to her cousin and fellow sovereign. They were now neighbors, after all, and peace between them was far preferable to discord. Accordingly, Elizabeth wrote to Mary, asking her to accept her friendship and "bury all unkindness." Past disagreement would be forgotten, she assured her, and the queens would "remain good friends and sisters," since "you shall see we require nothing but justice, honor and reason."

Mary seemed responsive to Elizabeth's overtures, but there remained that pesky Treaty of Edinburgh lurking as a barrier to friendship. The Queen of Scots still refused to ratify it unless it was modified to at least designate her as Elizabeth's heir. That, however, was not something the English queen was prepared to do. In fact, the idea of naming her successor was abhorrent to

---

* Francis II was only sixteen, and had reigned less than two years, when he succumbed to an ear infection that abscessed in his brain. His widowed wife, Mary, was just shy of her eighteenth birthday.

her. She was well aware from her own experience as her sister's heir how rebels and malcontents rallied in her name.

"I know the inconstancy of the people of England," Elizabeth told Mary's secretary of state William Maitland, "how they ever mislike the present government, and have their eyes fixed upon that person that is next to succeed."

Mary's Catholic faith, as well as her close proximity, would make her particularly dangerous as the designated heir to the Protestant Elizabeth. Therefore, the English queen remained adamant that "the succession of the crown is a matter I will not mell [meddle] in."

Elizabeth believed that a face-to-face meeting with Mary would get them beyond the impasse over the succession issue. The Queen of Scots was delighted by the idea. Not only was she intensely curious about her cousin (as Elizabeth was about Mary), but she was convinced that her celebrated charm would win over the English queen as it had so many others.

William Maitland was not so sure. According to the English ambassador in Scotland, Thomas Randolph, Maitland feared his young queen would be out of her depth in any negotiations with the wily Elizabeth, for "he finds no such maturity of judgment and ripeness of experience in high matters in his mistress, as in the Queen's Majesty, in whom both nature and time have wrought much more than in many of greater years."

Despite Maitland's reservations, Mary was ecstatic over the prospect of seeing Elizabeth in person. "I see my sovereign so transported with affection, that she respects nothing so she may meet with her cousin," Maitland reported ruefully, "and needs no persuasion, but is a great deal more earnestly bent on it than her counselors dare advise her."

Elizabeth's counselors were no more enthusiastic about a meeting than Mary's were. France was on the brink of a religious civil war prompted by the aggression of Mary's ultra-Catholic uncle (and Elizabeth's sworn enemy), the Duke of

Guise, toward the nation's Protestant or Huguenot minority, and it was felt that the queen's attention should be focused on helping her fellow religious across the Channel. Elizabeth disagreed. Unless the situation in France broke down irretrievably, she would meet her cousin as planned.

The two queens exchanged expensive gifts in anticipation of their summit in the north of England. Mary sent Elizabeth a ring with a diamond shaped like a heart, saying "that above all things I desire to see my good sister and next that we may live like good sisters together." Elizabeth, for her part, sent Mary a huge, rocklike diamond.

Plans for the encounter were well under way when Elizabeth received the news that peace efforts in France had failed and the nation was now embroiled in a savage religious war. With the Duke of Guise poised to seize control of the kingdom, there could be no question now of Elizabeth leaving London. The meeting would have to be canceled. When Mary received the queen's decision "it drove her into such a passion as she did keep her bed all that day," reported Sir Henry Sidney, who had traveled to Scotland with the news. And though Elizabeth assured her cousin that they would meet at a more fortuitous time, they never did.

It was bad enough that Elizabeth still had to worry about a neighboring queen with designs on her throne. Worse, however, would be a *married* queen, with a husband powerful enough to enforce her claims. And the widowed Mary was giving every indication that she was ready to wed again. Such a desire was lost on Elizabeth, who, despite all the pressure for her to marry and produce an heir, was absolutely determined to remain single.* (Thus she became known as the Virgin Queen.)

* The queen's aversion to marriage was rooted not only in the lethal connotations it held for her—with the violent demises of, among others, her

The Queen of Scots tried to reassure her cousin that her intentions were nonthreatening. "I shall be guided by your wishes," she wrote soothingly, "and shall be careful not to marry any man of so high a rank that my position, my well-beloved sister, will overshadow yours." Meanwhile, though, Mary was in negotiations with Philip II of Spain (Elizabeth's former brother-in-law) to marry his son Don Carlos. Sure, the prince was a lunatic, with a streak of the sadist in him, but he had the power of Catholic Spain behind him.

Aware of the Scottish queen's machinations, Elizabeth made an inspired—some said outrageous—offer to Mary. The queen told Maitland "that if his mistress would take her advice and wished to marry safely and happily, she would give her a husband who would ensure both . . . one who had implanted so many graces that if she [Elizabeth] wished to marry him she would prefer him to all the princes of the world." And that husband would be Robert Dudley, one of Elizabeth's favorite courtiers, who was also whispered to be her lover.* In fact,

---

mother, Anne Boleyn, and her stepmother, Catherine Howard, both of whom had been beheaded—but also in her reluctance to share any of her power with a husband. As Sir James Melville put it so succinctly to Elizabeth: "Your Majesty thinks that if you were married you would be but Queen of England, and now you are both King and Queen. I know your spirit cannot endure a commander."

* Elizabeth and Dudley were strong intimates who had known each other since childhood. In fact, they were both imprisoned in the Tower of London during the reign of Bloody Mary (Dudley having risen up with his father, the Duke of Northumberland, to put his sister-in-law Jane Grey on the throne). There is no question that the queen adored Dudley, whom she immediately made Master of the Horse upon her accession, and flirted with him outrageously, always dangling before him the possibility of marriage. But it is highly improbable that she slept with him (or any of her other favorites). Elizabeth's honor meant far too much for her to ever risk losing it in a sexual affair, where shameful pregnancy was always a possibility—particularly in the absence of effective birth control.

many believed Dudley had killed his wife, Amy, so that he might marry the queen.*

It was a brilliant proposal as far as Elizabeth was concerned. She could reward her rejected suitor Dudley with a valuable consolation prize—the queen of Scotland—and at the same time ensure that Mary had a husband loyal to his English sovereign, one who could neutralize the Scottish queen's ambitions.

In Scotland, however, the idea landed with a thud. "Is that conforming to her [Elizabeth's] promise to use me as her sister?" the indignant Queen of Scots asked Thomas Randolph. "And do you think it may stand with my honor to marry a subject?" Don Carlos of Spain was the prize as far as Mary was concerned—certainly not the English queen's insulting offer of her Master of the Horse, even if Elizabeth did try to sweeten his appeal somewhat by elevating Dudley to Earl of Leicester.

Elizabeth warned Mary that the Spanish match would cause her to "judge that no good is intended toward us," but it was Philip II who finally scotched the proposed union with his imbecilic son, leaving the Scottish queen with few prospects but Dudley.

Though Elizabeth had earlier dangled the prospect of naming Mary her heir if she cooperated by marrying Dudley, it proved to be an illusionary enticement. Whenever Mary's representatives sought tangible assurances that would secure their queen's position, a key condition for Mary, Elizabeth always managed to wiggle away without making any promises. The stalemate drove the Queen of Scots to despair, and in a tearful outburst to the English ambassador she vented her feelings: "I accuse not your mistress, though she be loath to give unto me my desire in that which perchance any would be loath to do; but, so long a time to keep me in doubt, and now to answer me

---

* A coroner's inquest absolved him of any wrongdoing in his wife's death.

with nothing, I will find great fault, and fear it shall turn to her discredit more than to my loss."

The queen "wept her fill," as Randolph reported, then she did something entirely unexpected: She took a husband of her own choice—a Catholic so close to the English throne that his claim combined with Mary's made them a formidable pair indeed. He was the Scottish queen's first cousin Henry Stuart, Lord Darnley,* a spoiled, grasping lightweight who happened to be incredibly handsome. Mary was smitten from the moment she met him. "Her Majesty took very well with him," reported Sir James Melville, "and said that he was the properest and best-proportioned long man that ever she had seen."

Nothing could dissuade the queen from her single-minded ambition to marry her cousin—not the objections of her own Protestant subjects, and certainly not those of the English queen. Mary made it quite clear that she was tired of Elizabeth's "overlordship" and said that for too long she had been "trained with [Elizabeth's] fair speeches and beguiled in her expectations." Now she had found a man she loved, and insisted she would have him.

Thomas Randolph, the English ambassador, wrote despairingly of the Scottish queen's headlong behavior. He actually liked and respected Mary but now found her "so altered with affection towards the Lord Darnley that she hath brought her honour in question, her estate in hazard, her country to be torn in pieces. . . . The Queen in her love is so transported. . . . What shall become of her, or what life with him she shall lead, that already takes so much upon him as to control and command her, I leave it to others to think."

As it turned out, Mary's marriage was an epic disaster. Not

---

* Darnley was Margaret Tudor's grandson by her second marriage, to Archibald Douglas, Earl of Angus, which made him, like Mary, Queen Elizabeth's first cousin once removed. (See Tudor family tree, pages 2–3.)

only did it provoke rebellion in her kingdom, but Darnley himself was a crushing disappointment—behind his good looks was a swaggering weakling with a penchant for booze and brothels, who quickly earned Mary's total contempt. "He could not be persuaded upon to yield the smallest thing to please her," Randolph reported. "What shall become of him, I know not, but it is greatly to be feared that he can have no long life among this people." Indeed, he would not.

Mary's hatred of her husband culminated with his involvement in the brutal murder of her Italian secretary, David Rizzio, whose close relationship with the queen made Darnley insanely jealous. Less than a year later, Darnley was killed in his turn—assassinated, some said, with the queen's complicity. Though Mary professed to be horrified by her husband's violent demise, she did nothing to find or apprehend those responsible for it. Her cousin Elizabeth was appalled by her inaction.

"I cannot but tell you what all the world is thinking," the English queen wrote. "Men say that, instead of seizing the murderers, you are looking through your fingers while they escape; that you will not punish those who have done you so great a service, as though the thing would never have taken place had not the doers of it been assured of impunity."

Elizabeth went on to assure Mary that she did not believe the monstrous accusations and wished her cousin "all imaginable good, and all blessings which you yourself would wish for." Thus, the queen continued, "for this very reason I exhort, I advise, I implore you deeply to consider of the matter—at once, if it be the nearest friend you have, to lay your hands upon the man who has been guilty of the crime—to let no interest, no persuasion, keep you from proving to everyone that you are a noble Princess and a loyal wife."

But far from arresting the chief suspect in Darnley's murder—James Hepburn, Earl of Bothwell—the Queen of

Scots married him. The blustery Lord Bothwell, who had served as a close advisor to the queen, was, according to one contemporary description, "high in his own conceit, proud, vicious and vainglorious above measure, one who would attempt anything out of ambition." Just six weeks after Darnley's death, Bothwell staged an abduction of Queen Mary and allegedly raped her. Then, after securing a quick divorce from his wife, he and the queen were wed.

Elizabeth was utterly revolted by her cousin's actions. Randolph reported that she had "great misliking of that Queen's doing, which now she doth so much detest that she is ashamed of her." For a woman who believed as fervently as Elizabeth did in the divinely ordained nature of majesty, who sacrificed so much personal happiness for the welfare of her own kingdom, Mary's base behavior was inexcusable—a monstrous betrayal of monarchy. Nevertheless, she would never countenance the dethroning of an anointed queen, as the rebellious Protestant lords in Scotland planned to do with Mary, replacing her with her infant son, James. It was, Elizabeth declared, "a matter hardly to be digested . . . by us or any other monarch."

"Elizabeth was outraged by the notion that a queen could be divested of her regal dignity as if it were no more than a tattered old cloak," wrote her biographer Anne Somerset, "and felt that by accepting so profane a concept, she herself would be eroding the very foundations of Kingship."

On June 15, 1567, the Queen of Scots was taken prisoner by her own subjects after a standoff between her forces and those of the dissident Scottish lords.* Instead of celebrating the downfall of a rival who had threatened her since her accession,

* Mary agreed to give herself up if Bothwell would be allowed to escape. After fleeing Scotland, he was eventually captured and imprisoned in Denmark, where his confinement was apparently harsh enough to drive him insane. And in that sad state he died in 1578.

Elizabeth was horrified by the fate of a fellow sovereign. Majesty was at stake, and that made the English queen impervious to the advantages of a defanged Scottish queen—at least for a time. She was determined to defend not so much Mary the woman, whose behavior put her almost beyond redemption, but Mary the anointed monarch.

"Now for your comfort in such adversity as we have heard you should be in . . . we assure you, that whatsoever we can imagine meet to be for your honour and safety that shall lie in our power, we will perform the same," Elizabeth wrote to Mary; "that it shall well appear you have a good neighbour, a dear sister, a faithful friend; and so shall you undoubtedly always find us and prove us to be indeed towards you."

To ensure Mary's safety and the preservation of her rights, Elizabeth sent Sir Nicholas Throckmorton to Scotland with a stern warning to the rebel lords that if they deposed their queen, "we will make ourselves a plain party against them, to the revenge of their Sovereign, for example to all posterity."

Yet despite Elizabeth's threats, the Scottish lords forced their queen's abdication on July 24, 1567, and continued to keep her captive. Mary was twenty-five at the time and had just miscarried the twins she had conceived with Bothwell. Five days later, her thirteen-month old son was crowned King James VI.

The English queen was incensed when she received the news and, according to her chief advisor, William Cecil, "increased in such offence towards these Lords that in good earnest she began to devise to revenge it by war." Angry though she may have been, Elizabeth was still a practical politician who soon recognized the need to deal with the new regime in Scotland—a Protestant government that was, after all, far friendlier to her than Mary had been. So, while the queen maintained outward demonstrations of outrage over her cousin's treatment, she quietly allowed her representatives to deal with the Scottish lords behind the scenes. James Stuart, Earl of Moray, the illegitimate half brother of the deposed Queen of Scots who now served as regent for her son, James VI, perceptively noted that "although the Queen's Majesty seems not altogether to allow the present state here," he was certain "but she likes it in heart well enough."

Such was the situation when, on May 2, 1568, Mary Stuart managed to escape her castle prison with the assistance of Moray's younger half brother George Douglas, who, it was said, "was in a fantasy of love with her." The fallen queen then gathered an army of supporters and confronted her half brother Moray's forces outside of Glasgow. The ensuing Battle of Langside was a bitter defeat for Mary, who was forced to flee the field and spend the next three days as a hunted fugitive before finally crossing into England, where she found herself a most unwelcome guest.

Mary came to England fully expecting her cousin's assistance in regaining her throne. "I am now forced out of my kingdom and driven to such straits that, next to God, I have no hope but in your goodness," she wrote to Elizabeth. "I beseech you, therefore my dearest sister, that I may be conducted to your presence, that I may acquaint you with all my affairs."

To receive Mary was highly problematic, however. That would signal tacit approval of the refugee queen's behavior and thus obligate Elizabeth to help restore her to her throne. The English queen was inclined at first to help her cousin, but her counselors convinced her that aiding Mary would not only alienate the friendly Protestant regime in Scotland but open the way for an enemy to regain power. And even in her diminished state, Mary remained a dangerous adversary who had *still* not renounced her claim to Elizabeth's crown.

Almost as dangerous as Mary Stuart's restoration was her continued presence in England, where, besides enticing disaffected Catholics to her cause, she could invite foreign intervention as well. Indeed, she seemed to be plotting almost from the time of her arrival. In a note smuggled to the Spanish ambassador, she wrote, "Tell your master [Philip II] that if he will help me, I shall be queen of England in three months, and mass shall be said throughout the land."

The former Queen of Scots was proving to be a most vexing problem for Elizabeth. She could not keep her cousin too closely confined for fear of retaliation from the Catholic powers in Europe, nor could she allow her to roam free and cause untold havoc within the realm. It was Mary's half brother, the regent Moray, who offered a solution of sorts when he produced the so-called Casket Letters—a series of missives purportedly written by Mary to Bothwell in which she implicated herself in Darnley's murder.

The Duke of Norfolk advised Queen Elizabeth that the letters described "such inordinate love between Mary and Bothwell, her loathsomeness and abhorring of her husband that was murdered, in such sort as every good and godly man cannot but detest and abhor the same."

Mary, on the other hand, insisted that the letters were forgeries (as have some historians), but she refused to defend herself before a commission that had been gathered by Elizabeth to examine her case. It was beneath her dignity as a queen, she maintained, to answer to men with no authority over her. Thus, without her cooperation, the commission closed with the verdict that nothing had been proven.

It was a victory for Elizabeth. Mary was publicly disgraced by the Casket Letters, freeing the English queen from any obligation to help her. At the same time, the inconclusive verdict allowed her to avoid actually condemning her cousin while giving her an excuse to hold Mary under more restraint as the cloud of suspicion lingered. Still, as Cecil warned Elizabeth, "the Queen of Scots is and always shall be a dangerous person to your estate."

Mary Stuart justified Cecil's alarm time and time again, involving herself in any number of plots to depose Elizabeth and place herself on the English throne. "The poor foolish woman will not desist until she loses her head," declared Mary's former brother-in-law, Charles IX of France, when she was found complicit in one of the more serious conspiracies against the English queen.* "She will certainly bring about her own execution. If she does so, it will be her own fault."

Prescient as Charles's remark would later prove, the last thing Elizabeth wanted was to execute her cousin. Mary had flown to her realm "as a bird that had flown to her for succor from the hawk," as the queen put it, and no matter how pernicious her cousin's plotting, she could not consider the judicial killing of another queen. It was her continued adherence to this principle that would cause Elizabeth so much agony years later when she was confronted with the most diabolical of all Mary's schemes against her.

———

Averse as she was to killing her cousin, Elizabeth showed no such reluctance in keeping Mary under increasingly close confinement until, in 1585, she was sealed off from the world entirely at a fortified manor house called Chartley, under the vigilant eye of Sir Amias Paulet. The austere jailor took great pride in the security measures he devised to keep the former

---

* The plot centered around the scheming of a Florentine banker by the name of Roberto di Ridolfi, a fanatic Catholic with close contacts to both Pope Pius V and Philip II of Spain. The aim of the Ridolfi Plot, as it came to be called, was to have Elizabeth assassinated and replaced on the throne by Mary. The Queen of Scots was implicated in the scheme when it was exposed, as was Elizabeth's cousin, Thomas Howard, fourth Duke of Norfolk, who was to wed Mary and rule by her side. Elizabeth reluctantly signed Norfolk's death warrant, but she absolutely refused to move against her fellow queen.

Queen of Scots utterly isolated, ensuring that no secret correspondence could ever be smuggled in. "I cannot imagine how it may be possible for them to convey a piece of paper as big as my finger," Paulet boasted.

But despite all Paulet's precautions, Sir Francis Walsingham, Elizabeth's secretary of state and so-called spymaster, still feared that Mary would find a way to communicate with her allies and foment trouble. Therefore, he wanted her to be able to send and receive correspondence in a controlled way so that he could better monitor her schemes. To that end he used a shady character by the name of Gilbert Gifford, described by one acquaintance as "the most notable double and treble villain that ever lived." Gifford had been in Paris, where he agreed to be a courier for Mary's agent there, but upon his return to England he was apprehended and used by Walsingham to serve the secretary's own purposes.

Gifford was sent to the French embassy, where most correspondence intended for Mary was sent in the hopes that the ambassador could find the means to deliver it. There he announced that he had found a way to surreptitiously slip correspondence into Chartley and offered to act as courier. The ambassador agreed to test Gifford's system, and soon enough Mary was thrilled to receive a letter from him. In a return post, also smuggled out by Gifford, she urged the ambassador to trust the courier and rely on his system.

What Mary did not know was that each letter sent to her was first delivered to Walsingham's office, where it was opened, decoded, and examined for content, then meticulously resealed and sent north by messenger to a cooperative local brewer, who would hide it within the bunghole of a beer barrel he delivered to Chartley. There Mary's steward would retrieve it and then send out Mary's letters in the empty barrel, which started the whole process again in reverse. It was a lethally efficient system that would soon ensnare the Queen of Scots.

As it turned out, a Catholic priest named John Ballard had received assurances from the Spanish ambassador to France that Philip II would send troops to England if Queen Elizabeth was assassinated first. Armed with this encouragement, Ballard sought out Anthony Babington, a wealthy Catholic Englishman known to be sympathetic to Mary. Babington, in turn, gathered a group of trusted associates who would work together to kill Queen Elizabeth, then free Mary in anticipation of the Spanish invasion.

Inspired by this holy quest, Babington wrote to Mary, addressing her as "My dread sovereign and Queen," and informed her of the plan. One key element, he made clear, was the murder of Elizabeth: "For the dispatch of the usurper, from the obedience of whom we are by excommunication of her made free,* there be six noble gentlemen, all my private friends, who for the zeal they bear to the Catholic cause and your Majesty's service will undertake that tragical execution."

Mary's initial response to Babington was simply to let him know that she was considering his proposal and would reply as soon as possible. Walsingham's code breaker, Thomas Phelippes, was delighted upon deciphering the message, writing, "We attend her very heart at the next." Sure enough, within a week, Mary implicated herself entirely when she agreed to Babington's plan—including the killing of her cousin: "The affairs being thus prepared and forces in readiness both within and without the realm, then it shall be time to set the six gentlemen to work, taking order, upon the accomplishing of their design I may be suddenly transported out of this place."

A roundup of the conspirators ensued, followed by their

* In 1570, Pope Pius V issued the papal bull *Regnans in Excelsis,* which excommunicated "Elizabeth, the pretended Queen of England and the servant of wickedness" as a heretic, deprived her of her throne, and released her subjects from any allegiance to her.

brutal executions. While traitors were normally hanged until unconscious, then disemboweled and cut into quarters, some of the Babington plotters were still very much alert when they were castrated and gutted. The queen's wrath was dreadful indeed, except when it came to Mary. Killing her was still too horrible to contemplate. Nevertheless, there would have to be a trial.

Mary was taken to Fotheringhay Castle on September 25, 1586. At first she refused to appear before the gathered commissioners, insisting that "she was no subject [of Elizabeth's] and rather would die a thousand deaths than acknowledge herself a subject." The commission then carried a letter to Mary from Elizabeth. It was short and concise:

> You have, in various ways and manners, attempted to take my life, and to bring my kingdom to destruction and bloodshed. I have never proceeded so harshly against you, but have, on the contrary, protected and maintained you like myself. These treasons will be proved to you, and all made manifest. Yet it is my will, that you answer the nobles and peers of the kingdom as if I were myself present. I therefore require, charge and command that you make answer, for I have been well informed of your arrogance. Act plainly, without reserve, and you will sooner be able to obtain favor of me.

Mary agreed at last to appear, and the trial commenced on October 15. Though denied counsel, or the opportunity to inspect the evidence against her, she defended herself well. Still, the proof against her was overwhelming, and on October 25 the commissioners pronounced that she was guilty of the "compassing, practicing and imagining of Her Majesty's death."

Despite the verdict, and the subsequent calls for Mary's head in Parliament, Elizabeth could not bring herself to inflict the ultimate penalty. Her agony was evident in a candid speech she gave before a parliamentary delegation that came before her to plead for the Scottish queen's dispatch.

"And since it is now resolved that my surety [safety] cannot be established without a princess's end," the queen told the delegation, "I have just cause to complain that I, who have in my time pardoned so many rebels, winked at so many treasons, and either not produced them or slipped them over with silence, should now be forced to this proceeding against such a person." She openly wondered what would become of her reputation abroad "when it should be spread that for the safety of her life, a maiden queen could be content to spill the blood even of her own kinswoman?" And though she acknowledged the very real danger Mary posed—stating that she was not "so ignorant as not to know it were in nature a foolish course to cherish a sword to cut mine own throat; nor so careless as not to weigh that my life daily is in hazard"—she said "that many a man would put his life in danger for the safeguard of a king. I do not say that so will I, but I pray you think that I have thought upon it." The queen concluded by stating how grateful she was for the love and care the delegation had demonstrated toward her, but "as for your petition: your judgment I condemn not, nor do I mistake your reasons, but pray you to accept my thankfulness, excuse my doubtfulness, and take in good part my answer answerless."

Elizabeth did eventually relent and allow a public proclamation of Mary's sentence to be read, which resulted in an eruption of celebration across London. But she had yet to sign the death warrant, and there was little indication that she was prepared to do so. While her own subjects were clamoring for Mary's blood, pressure—especially from Scotland and France—was mounting at the same time for her to show mercy. Though King James VI had already abandoned his mother, he nevertheless pleaded for her life, and quite tactlessly at that, writing to Elizabeth that "King Henry VIII's reputation was never prejudged but in the beheading of his bedfellow [Anne Boleyn]." The French king, Henry III, another of Mary's former brothers-in-law, warned that he would "look upon [her execution] as a personal affront."

Elizabeth's recognition that neither king would be in a position to retaliate for Mary's execution alleviated some pressure, but a letter she received from the former Queen of Scots herself left her devastated. Mary wrote that she was glad for the "happy tidings" that she had come "to the end of my long and weary pilgrimage," and said that she wished to die in perfect charity with everyone. "Yet while abandoning this world and preparing myself for a better, I must remind you that one day you will have to answer for your charge, and for all those whom you doom, and that I desire that my blood and my country may be remembered in that time."

With her counselors becoming more and more vociferous about the dangers threatening with Mary's continual existence, Elizabeth desperately scrambled to find a solution without publicly executing her cousin. In one of the less savory acts of her long and proud reign, she tried to convince Paulet to do away with the Scottish queen privately. But the queen's jailor balked at the suggestion, writing that "his good livings and life are at her Majesty's disposition . . . but God forbid that I should make so foul a shipwreck of my conscience, or leave so great a blot to my poor posterity, to shed blood without law or warrant!"

"Elizabeth has been censored for seeking to rid herself of Mary underhand," wrote Anne Somerset, "but she had sound enough reasons for thinking it more seemly to proceed by stealth. . . . In her own eyes and those of God, nothing could alter the fact that the killing of a Queen was wrong, but since circumstances forced her to countenance such a deed, she took the view that an evil committed out of sight was less obnoxious than one performed brazenly before the world."

There was no escaping the fact that Mary's fate rested squarely with Elizabeth, and though she finally signed her cousin's death warrant, she still maintained the unrealistic hope that one of her servants would take the matter out of her hands. It was not to be, for on February 8, 1587, Mary, Queen of Scots, was led into the Great Hall of Fotheringhay Castle and there beheaded.*

Mary had paid the ultimate penalty, but it was Elizabeth who would suffer the consequences. She seemed stunned upon receiving the news of her cousin's execution. According to William Camden, the contemporary historian of Elizabeth's reign, "her countenance altered, her speech faltered and failed her and, through excessive sorrow, she stood in a manner astonished, insomuch that she gave herself over to passionate

---

* The execution of Mary, Queen of Scots, was an unusually gruesome affair. After she placed her head on the block, the headsman raised his axe and brought it down hard. The blow missed the queen's neck, however, and struck the back of her head instead. "Sweet Jesus," Mary was heard to mutter, before a second blow all but decapitated her. The remaining sinew was then severed by using the axe as a saw.

With the head finally off—but with the lips still moving, as they would for the next quarter of an hour—the executioner held it aloft before the gathered witnesses, shouting, "God save the queen." As he did so, the head suddenly fell to the floor and the executioner was left holding the auburn-colored wig Mary wore to cover her own hair, which had turned gray and was cut very short.

After this unnerving spectacle, the dead queen's pet dog, Geddon, crept out from beneath her petticoats, where he had been hidden, and came to rest between her shoulders and head, covered in his mistress's blood.

Finally, after her clothes and adornments were burned to prevent them from becoming relics, Mary's corpse was sealed in a coffin. But it was not sent to France for burial, as she had requested before her death. Instead, it lay moldering at Fotheringhay for months before at last being interred at Peterborough cathedral. (After Mary's son, James, became king of England he had his mother's body reburied with an elaborate monument at Westminster Abbey.)

grief, putting herself into a mourning habit and shedding abundance of tears." Then she viciously lashed out at her ministers. *They* had procured the Scottish queen's death, Elizabeth insisted; she had only signed the death warrant as a precaution. It was the justification the queen gave her fellow monarchs, but as the French ambassador so accurately observed, "This death will wring her heart as long as she lives."

PART II

House of Stuart

JAMES I (VI OF SCOTLAND)

(reigned 1603–1625)

CHARLES I

(r. 1625–1649)

COMMONWEALTH—NO MONARCHY

(1649–1660)

CHARLES II

(r. 1660–1685)

JAMES II

(r. 1685–1688)

WILLIAM III AND MARY II

(William: r. 1689–1702; Mary: r. 1689–1694)

ANNE

(r. 1702–1714)

House of Stuart

JAMES I (VI OF SCOTLAND)
r. 1603–1625
m. Anne of Denmark

Henry

Elizabeth
m. Frederich, Elector of Palatine

Sophia,
m. Ernest Augustus,
Elector of Hanover

CHARLES II
r. 1660–1685
m. Catherine of Braganza

GEORGE I
(House of Hanover)

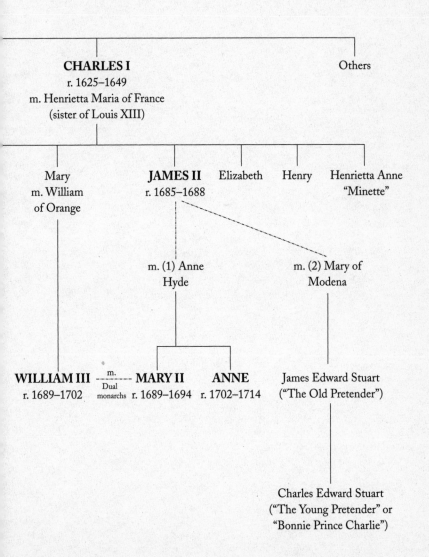

CHARLES I
r. 1625–1649
m. Henrietta Maria of France
(sister of Louis XIII)

Others

Mary
m. William
of Orange

JAMES II
r. 1685–1688

Elizabeth

Henry

Henrietta Anne
"Minette"

m. (1) Anne
Hyde

m. (2) Mary of
Modena

WILLIAM III
r. 1689–1702

m.
Dual
monarchs

MARY II
r. 1689–1694

ANNE
r. 1702–1714

James Edward Stuart
("The Old Pretender")

Charles Edward Stuart
("The Young Pretender" or
"Bonnie Prince Charlie")

7

James I (VI of Scotland) 1603–1625:

Kissing Cousins

Nourished in fear
—MARQUIS DE FONTENAY MAREUIL

James VI of Scotland, son of the executed Mary, Queen of Scots, succeeded his cousin Elizabeth I in 1603 and established the Stuart dynasty in England as James I. Thus the two kingdoms were ruled under one crown (although it would take another century before England and Scotland were officially joined to become the United Kingdom of Great Britain in 1707). Before ascending the English throne, James endured a very turbulent childhood in Scotland, where he reigned since he was just over a year old.

The christening of the infant Prince James at Stirling Castle seemed to bode well for a brilliant future. Representatives of the great European powers were gathered at the ceremony, bearing rich gifts. Charles IX of France, the child's godfather, sent a necklace of pearls and rubies. His godmother and cousin, Elizabeth I of England, whose throne James was destined to inherit, sent a gold baptismal font. The chapel at Stirling, where in 1543 the baby's mother, Mary, had been crowned queen of Scotland at just nine months old, glowed with torches, gilded cloth, and hopeful prayers for Scotland's future King James VI (and England's James I).

But all was not well at Stirling that December day in 1566.

The castle, rising high on a crag above the plains of central Scotland, had a dark history dating back centuries. It was there, among many bloody episodes, that James II had the corpse of the Earl of Douglas, whom he had just murdered, contemptuously tossed out of a window in 1452. And it was where the baby prince, whose baptism was being celebrated with feasts, masques, and fireworks, would grow up "nourished in fear," as the French ambassador the Marquis de Fontenay Mareuil later wrote.

Indeed, all the royal pomp and ceremony surrounding the christening was an illusion, masking seething hatreds and murderous conspiracies. The child's father, Henry Stuart, Lord Darnley, was not even present at the grand occasion. Instead, he remained holed up in his room at Stirling, estranged from his wife, the queen, who had grown to despise him, and nursing his many resentments.

When he married the Queen of Scots in 1565, Darnley had been given the title of king but none of the power he craved. Spoiled and weak, he bitterly resented the influence of David Rizzio, the queen's Italian secretary, and was lured into a plot to kill him. Queen Mary was six months pregnant with James when Rizzio was dragged away from her, screaming for his life, and stabbed more than fifty times before his mutilated corpse was dumped down a flight of stairs.

To be rid of the queen's upstart secretary was the main reason for Rizzio's murder, but Darnley also hoped that his wife would miscarry from the trauma of witnessing the violent demise, for he didn't believe the child she was carrying was his. Yet despite his father's evil intent, James survived. Years later, in a speech to the English Parliament after the failed Gunpowder Plot of 1605,* King James stated that his "fearful nature" could

* A group of disaffected Catholics intended to assassinate the king by blowing up the Palace of Westminster as James formally opened Parlia-

be traced "not only ever since my birth, but even as I may justly say, before my birth: and while I was in my mother's belly."

Darnley had fallen so low in the queen's estimation "that it is heartbreaking for her to think that he should be her husband," wrote Mary's secretary of state, William Maitland, "and how to be free of him she sees no out gait [way out]." It just so happened, however, only two months after the baptism of Prince James at Stirling, Mary did find a convenient way out of her miserable marriage. Darnley was found dead outside the house where he was staying, Kirk o' Field, which was destroyed in an explosion. Suspicions that the queen had been complicit in her husband's murder were only inflamed when she married the chief suspect, James Hepburn, Earl of Bothwell, only three months later.

Just before her ill-advised wedding, the queen went to see her baby son, James, at Stirling—some believed with the intention of snatching him away. It was the last time mother and child would ever see each other. Mary had sacrificed her credibility and the confidence of her people by marrying Bothwell. She was imprisoned and forced to abdicate in favor of her only son, who was crowned king in the Protestant church just outside the gates of Stirling Castle. He was thirteen months old.

Scotland was in chaos at the time of James VI's accession, torn by religious wars and savage rivalries among nobles. The young king was the pawn everyone wanted to control. He was not yet four when his uncle the Earl of Moray, then serving as regent, was assassinated and replaced by the boy king's paternal grandfather, the Earl of Lennox. The following year, during a clash at Stirling between the Catholic supporters of the king's

---

ment. Guy Fawkes remains the most notorious of the conspirators in the foiled plot, which is still commemorated every year in Britain with bonfires and celebrations.

deposed mother and reform Protestants, Lennox was slaughtered. James would later say that his conscious life began the
morning he saw his grandfather's bloody corpse being carried
past him through the castle gates.

Stirling Castle was effectively the boy's prison. He would
not leave it until he was eleven, as it was deemed too dangerous.
Between episodes of horror, like the violent death of his grandfather, the young king's life at the castle was dreary and loveless.
He slept in a bed of black damask, with black-bordered
pillows—not exactly the cheeriest of settings for a child all but
orphaned.

His chief tutor, George Buchanan, had a virulent hatred for
James's mother, now imprisoned in England by her cousin
Queen Elizabeth (see Chapter 6), and authored a tract that
condemned her as both an adulterer and a murderess. Inter-
spersed with lessons in languages, history, and mathematics
were Buchanan's unrelenting efforts to indoctrinate the king
against the deposed Queen of Scots. He was often abusive to
the boy, calling him "the true bird of the blood nest from which
he sprang."

On one occasion, as Buchanan was beating young James, the
wife of his guardian intervened. "How dare you?" the indignant
woman demanded. "How dare you lay your hands on the
Lord's anointed?"

"I have whipped his arse," Buchanan snarled back. "You can
kiss it if you like."

Miserable as life was at Stirling, it was there that King
James, aged thirteen, fell in love for the first time when his
much older cousin Esmé Stuart arrived from France. For the
pale boy, deprived of love or affection since infancy, legs de-
formed by rickets, this handsome, sophisticated Frenchman
was a dream—even if the dream was married, with four children, and well over two decades James's senior. "No sooner did
the young King see him," reported one observer, "but in that he

was so near allied in blood, of so renowned a family, eminent ornaments of body and mind, [he] took him and embraced him in a most amorous manner."

Having served as a gentleman of the bedchamber for the flamboyantly homosexual Henry III of France, the older man was well versed in the seduction of kings and was prepared to return all his younger cousin's amatory feelings.

"James grew up with a passionate desire to love and be loved in the romantic sense," wrote his biographer Antonia Fraser, "to worship something beyond himself, something fairer, more physically perfect than the stunted prodigy's body with which he had been endowed."

The king was certainly not shy about the physical expression of his feelings for Esmé, whom he dubbed Duke of Lennox. Sir Henry Woddrington noted how James was "persuaded and led by him, for he can hardly suffer him out of his presence, and is in such love with him, as in the open sight of people, often-times he will clasp him about the neck with his arms and kiss him."

The Scottish nobility, and particularly the Church (or Kirk, as it was called), were not quite as enamored of the Duke of Lennox as James was. Many believed he was an agent of the French government, sent to corrupt the king and restore Roman Catholicism to Scotland. The influence he had over the young monarch troubled them deeply, and Lennox was demonized from the pulpit.

One preacher denounced him for "raising of uproars in the Kirk, troubling of the common wealth, the introducing of prodigality and vanity in apparel, superfluity in banqueting and delicate cheer, deflowering of dames and virgins, and other fruits of the French court, and vexing of the commons of the country with airs." Worst of all, though, he "made the King the author of all these faults, and labored to corrupt him."

Elizabeth I of England was worried about the pernicious

influence of Esmé Stuart as well, convinced, she wrote, that he would "make some ready way, by colour of division and faction, to bring strangers, being Romanists, into the realm, for his party, and, consequently, by degrees, to alter religion, yea, in the end, to bring the person of the young King in danger."

A group of nobles took it upon themselves to seize King James and force him to dismiss his favorite. The Earl of Gowrie intercepted the king as he was hunting outside Perth and invited him to come back to his castle. The next morning, as James went to leave, he found the gates barred, his exit blocked. Realizing he was trapped, with no alternative but to obey, the young king burst into tears of anger and frustration.

"Better that bairns [children] should weep than bearded men," one of the king's captors said mockingly.

James was forced to expel Lennox from Scotland, and to write his love a letter of strong rebuke, accusing him of "inconstancy and disloyalty." Lennox responded before he left for France: "Whatever may befall, I shall always be your ever faithful servant, and although there might be still this misfortune, that you might wish to banish me from your good graces, yet in spite of all you will always be my true master, and he alone in this world whom my heart is resolved to serve."

Within a year, Esmé Stuart was dead. His last wish was that his embalmed heart be sent to James, which it was, without Lennox's widow ever knowing. The king lamented the loss of his first love in a poem in which Esmé is feminized and represented as a phoenix; "betwixt my legs herself did cast," seeking shelter from the savage attacks of envious nobles.

Esmé Stuart was no more, but he had awakened in James his lifelong passion for men. Being king, he did have to marry a woman to produce an heir. But he didn't have to like it. With disarming candor at the time of his marriage to Anne of Denmark, he wrote, "As to my own nature, God is my witness I could have abstained longer."

8

James I (VI of Scotland) 1603–1625:

Bewitched

My intention . . . is only to prove . . . that such
devilish arts have been and are.

—King James VI and I

King James VI and I expressed many of his most firmly held beliefs in the
books he wrote. For example, he promulgated the divine right of kings in
The True Law of Free Monarchies *and* Basilikon Doron
and railed against smoking in A Counterblaste to Tobacco. *Then*
there was Daemonologie, *in which the king encouraged the persecution*
of witches in Scotland. James was inspired, he wrote, by "the fearful
abounding, at this time and in this country of these detestable slaves of the
devil."

King James, famous for the Bible that bears his name, ignored
many of the injunctions contained in the good book—like the
one against sleeping with other men. He did, however, zealously heed one scriptural admonition found in Exodus: "Thou
shalt not suffer a witch to live."

After an extended sojourn in Denmark, where he may have
been educated about the dangers of witchcraft, the king returned
to Scotland in 1590 with a new queen and an appetite for burning witches. Given his feelings about marriage, and women in
general, it seems somehow fitting that the deeply misogynistic

monarch would, at the time of his nuptials, become a rabid witch hunter.

Scotland had largely avoided the witch persecutions that had swept Europe for centuries. But King James changed all that in the winter of 1590–91 when he encouraged a series of trials based on allegations that more than three hundred witches had gathered at various places and times to work treasonous spells against him. The king was convinced that these so-called servants of Satan conspired to kill him by raising rough seas on his voyage home from Denmark, concocting evil potions, and melting his waxen image while chanting curses.

The king was an enthusiastic participant in many of the trials—cross-examining some defendants, triumphantly heralding the tortured confessions of others, and exhorting juries to send them to the stake. He took particular interest in the case of Barbara Napier, a known associate of his enemy the Earl of Bothwell,* who claimed in her interrogation that she was pregnant. If in fact she was, she would be spared the death penalty if convicted. James, however, wanted to see her reduced to ashes.

"Try by the mediciners' oaths if Barbara Napier be with bairn [child] or not," the king instructed his minister John Maitland. "Take no delaying answer. If you find she be not, to the fire with her presently, and cause bowel [disembowel] her publicly."

James was indignant when the jury in the Napier trial failed to convict her. He was the Lord's anointed, and *he* said she was guilty. How dare they decide otherwise! It was bad enough that the king's sacred person had been endangered by the evil arts Barbara practiced, but as he said in a rebuke to the recalcitrant jury, the realm had been endangered as well.

---

* Not to be confused with the Bothwell who married James's mother after murdering his father.

The king insisted that he did not fear death personally. Rather, he was concerned for "the common good of this country, which enjoyeth peace by my life . . . as you may collect by mine absence, for if such troubles were in breeding whilst I retained life, what would have been done if my life had been taken from me?"

Lest anyone doubt the power of these evil women—witches who worshipped at the feet of Satan, then had sex with him—James attested to the fact that he, too, had been a skeptic. But, as detailed in a tract sanctioned by the king called *News of Scotland*, a witch by the name of Agnes Sampson took him aside and revealed "the very words which passed between the King's Majesty and his Queen at [Oslo] in Norway, the first night of their marriage, with their answer to each other: where at the King's Majesty wondered greatly, and swore, by the living God, that he believed that all the devils in hell could not have discovered the same, acknowledging her words to be most true, and therefore gave the more credit to the rest that is before declared."

The tract did not include the words the king spoke to his bride on their wedding night, though it's easy to imagine that, because she was not a man, poor Anne must have found his pillow talk wanting.

King James had worked hard to root out the witches who threatened his life and the peace of Scotland, consigning scores of them to the flames. Nevertheless, there were still some who persisted in their skepticism—including the English author Reginald Scot, who with his 1584 treatise *The Discoverie of Witchcraft* set out to methodically disprove the belief that Satan had human mistresses. The king responded with his own book, *Daemonologie*, in which he set out to educate the doubters and, as he wrote, refute "the damnable opinions of two principally in our age, whereof the one called Scot an Englishman, is not ashamed in publike print to deny, that ther can be such a thing as Witch-craft: and so maintains the old error of the Sad-ducees, in denying of spirits."

Written in the form of a dialogue and divided into three parts, *Daemonologie* was little more than a rehash of the witch lore that had been circulating in Europe for centuries: tales of humans who sell their souls to the devil and in exchange are given extraordinary powers—to fly through the air, raise storms, destroy crops, and generally cause great evil.

"My intention in this labour," James wrote, "is only to prove two things, as I have already said: the one, that such devilish arts have been and are. The other, what exact trial and punishment they merit."

The king provided a handy means to identify witches: "So it appears God hath appointed, for a supernatural sign of the monstrous impiety of the witches, that the water shall refuse to receive them in her bosom that have shaken off the sacred water of baptism, and wilfully refused the benefit thereof. Not so much as their eyes are able to shed tears (threaten and torture them as ye please) while they first repent (God not permitting them to dissemble their obstinacy in so horrible a crime) albeit the womenkind especially be able otherways to shed tears at every light occasion when they will, yea, although it were dissemblingly like the crocodiles."

Six years after the publication of this edifying bit of scholarship, in 1603, James inherited the throne of England. By then his interest in witchcraft was diminishing as he became increasingly focused on the parliaments that would bedevil him throughout his reign. Yet even without the king's personal attention, the persecution he launched in Scotland raged on for another century or so—a testament to the power of officially sanctioned superstition.

9

James I (VI of Scotland) 1603–1625:
Arbella Stuart: Too Close for Comfort

I must shape my own coat according to my cloth.
—ARBELLA STUART

As a great-great-granddaughter of Henry VIII's sister Margaret, Arbella Stuart had a viable claim to the crown, which, in the bloody politics of the day, put her in a very precarious position. It was a danger Arbella failed to heed.

King James VI of Scotland became King James I of England in a peaceful transfer of power when Queen Elizabeth died in 1603. His succession had by no means been assured, however. A rival for the crown was James's first cousin Arbella Stuart, a young woman proud of her "most royal lineage" and determined to forge her own destiny. "I must shape my own coat according to my cloth," she once declared, "but it will not be after the fashion of this world but fit for me." Arbella's royalty made her drive for independence extremely dangerous. And her failure to recognize this inescapable fact led to her doom. Along the way, though, she made some impressively bold strides.

Royal blood ran thick in Arbella Stuart as a descendant on her father's side of Margaret Tudor, Henry VIII's older sister (see Tudor family tree, pages 2–3). This "renowned stock," as Arbella called it, made her a very valuable commodity, and her family was determined to profit by it. Orphaned at a young age, she was left in the care of her maternal grandmother, Elizabeth, Countess of Shrewsbury (popularly known as Bess of Hardwick), "a woman of masculine understanding," as the antiquarian Edmund Lodge described her—"proud, furious, selfish and unfeeling." Perhaps she wasn't quite that bad, but Bess was indeed formidable. Four lucrative marriages in succession—the last to the Earl of Shrewsbury, one of the most prominent peers in England, as well as the keeper (for a time) of the captive Mary, Queen of Scots—made Bess one of the wealthiest and most powerful women in England. She had already married her daughter Elizabeth off to Margaret Tudor's grandson Charles Stuart (younger brother of Henry Stuart, Lord Darnley, the second husband of Mary, Queen of Scots), and now she was eager to see her "jewel," Arbella, become the next queen of England.

James VI had a better claim to the English crown than did his cousin Arbella. Both his parents (Mary, Queen of Scots, and Henry Stuart, Lord Darnley) were descendants of Margaret Tudor. But James was born and raised in Scotland, which made him, as a foreigner, potentially ineligible to inherit. Many believed, in fact, that Arbella Stuart would be the next to rule.

Elizabeth I made no effort to clarify the issue of the succession. In fact, the spinster queen had always been notoriously cagey on the subject. Naming an heir would, she once said, "require me in my life to set my winding sheet before my eye." Still, it looked like Elizabeth might be leaning toward Arbella when, in 1587, she called her young cousin to court for the first time—an invitation never extended to King James.

The first encounter with the mighty Elizabeth had to have been frightening for eleven-year-old Arbella. "This was the woman she had been raised to emulate, the one who held her fortune in her hands," wrote biographer Sarah Gristwood. "What is more, she curtseyed before the terrifying figure who, just five months before, had ordered the beheading of her royal aunt Mary [Queen of Scots], whose unburied body still lay stinking at Fotheringay."

Arbella was given all the honors due a royal lady of her rank, even the enviable opportunity of dining right beside the sovereign. She performed so well at court that she was able to write triumphantly that the queen "by trial pronounced me an eaglet of her own kind." Elizabeth did indeed seem impressed by Arbella. "Look to her well," she remarked to the wife of the French ambassador. "She will one day be even as I am."

Tantalizing as the queen's words were—an apparent endorsement of Arbella as her successor—nothing was ever quite as it appeared with Elizabeth Tudor. In fact, she was engaged in a game of diplomatic chess, and Arbella was a mere pawn—conveniently transformed into "a near cousin of her [Elizabeth's] own, whom she loves much, and whom she intends to make her heir and successor," as the French ambassador perceptively put it. Arbella was dangled as a potential bride in the European power market, as Elizabeth saw fit, then withdrawn. She was also used as a check on King James in Scotland: trotted out as the one who could easily displace him in line as the next potential English monarch should he grow too confident, or dare overreact to his mother's execution.

Blissfully unaware of these machinations, Arbella reveled in her starring role at Elizabeth's court. Her time there was fleeting, however, and when she was no longer diplomatically useful, she was sent back to the remote Derbyshire countryside, under the ever watchful eye of her domineering grandmother, Bess. As Arbella grew into adulthood, this increasingly suffocating existence at Hardwick Hall became intolerable. "The unfortunate lady has now lived for many years, not exactly as a prisoner, but, so to speak, buried alive," wrote the Venetian envoy.

Bess of Hardwick unintentionally offered a glimpse of her granddaughter's bleak existence—the one she helped create—

in a letter to Queen Elizabeth's chief minister, William Cecil, Lord Burghley: "Arbella walks not late; at such a time as she shall take the air it shall be near the house, and well attended on; she goeth not to anybody's house at all; I see her almost every hour in the day; she lieth in my bed-chamber." Little wonder, then, that Arbella was desperate to break away.

As Queen Elizabeth's reign drew to its close, Arbella made a frantic gambit to free herself from her grandmother's total domination and, quite possibly, to enhance her chances of inheriting the throne. She attempted to betroth herself to another royal cousin and possible candidate to become king, Edward Seymour, a direct descendant of Henry VIII's younger sister, Mary Tudor (see Tudor family tree, pages 2–3), and, incidentally, a great-grand-nephew of Henry's third wife, Jane Seymour. The union of these two royal lines would be a potent combination but, without the queen's consent, a treasonable one as well. And Elizabeth's wrath was legendary when it came to such matters, as Edward Seymour's grandmother Catherine Grey—sister of the ill-fated Jane Grey (see Chapter 3)—knew all too well. She had married Seymour's grandfather, also named Edward, without the queen's permission, and as a result, she and her husband were imprisoned in the Tower.*

It was the elder Seymour, knowing something of what a displeased queen was capable of, who wisely reported Arbella's

---

* Catherine's spouse, Edward Seymour, was the son of the Duke of Somerset, the Lord Protector, who was executed for treason during the reign of his nephew Edward VI (see Chapter 2). Catherine was already pregnant when she entered the Tower and had her son there. Then, apparently with the connivance of the Lieutenant of the Tower, Catherine and Edward managed to get together and produce another boy, much to Queen Elizabeth's displeasure. The enraged monarch permanently separated the couple when she sent her cousin away to live under house arrest. Catherine died of tuberculosis five years later, in 1568, after which Edward Seymour was released from the Tower.

potentially treasonous attempt to marry his grandson. But the reaction at court to her audacious maneuver was oddly subdued. Queen Elizabeth was fading, and Robert Cecil, who inherited his father's position as chief minister, was eager to keep things calm as he secretly orchestrated the succession of King James of Scotland. Arbella's foolish marital endeavors were officially attributed to unnamed "base companions," who, "thinking it pleasing to her youth and sex to be sought in marriage," led her astray.

Arbella was warned to "content herself to live in good sort with so dear a parent and so worthy a matron" as her grandmother. To the young woman trapped in Derbyshire, this might as well have been a death sentence. And, on the face of it, Arbella seems to have lost her mind.

Struck in what she called her "extraordinary yoke of bondage," Arbella began writing a series of rambling and very bizarre letters that made some question her sanity. She declared, for example, that her attempted betrothal to Edward Seymour was in fact a clever ruse on her part—a piece of "honest cunning," as she called it—to expose the plot the Seymours had hatched for Edward to marry *her*. "I thank God it fell out better than I and my dearest and best trusted could have devised or imagined though we have beat our brains out these three years," she wrote.

While this "revelation" may have been merely a weak attempt by Arbella to extricate herself from the Seymour marriage debacle, another pronouncement really did make it seem as if she had gone mad. Most people in their right mind would have been bathed in relief had the queen's government essentially winked at their treasonable activity, but Arbella seemed to be deliberately courting real danger when she announced that she was engaged to an anonymous suitor. "I may compare the love of this worthy gentleman (which I have already unrevocably accepted and confirmed) to gold which hath been so often purified that I cannot find one fault, jealousy only excepted," she wrote. At one point, when pressed, she claimed this mystery lover was none other than King James himself.

The frenzied writing and outrageous assertions bewildered government officials. "I think she hath some strange vapors to the brain," concluded Robert Cecil. Arbella herself suggested that her "scribbling melancholy," as she called it, was "a kind of madness." But was the madness real, or feigned?

Some historians say she was merely writing out her fantasies, a harmless exercise to amuse or comfort herself. Others have suggested that she suffered from porphyria, a malady often characterized by outbreaks of manic, unsettling behavior, and believed to have manifested itself occasionally in the British royal bloodline—most notably in King George III (see Chapter 21). Then there are those who propose that Arbella—far away from court and essentially imprisoned at Hardwick Hall—was desperate to keep the focus on herself as a contender, even if the attention she drew might be negative. If this was the case, she certainly succeeded.

Rumors of her (imaginary) engagement rocked the court and reportedly drove Elizabeth closer to her grave. It "is well known that this unexpected event has greatly disturbed the queen," the Venetian envoy reported, "for she has suddenly withdrawn into herself, she who was wont to live so gaily . . . so anxious is she that the rumours of this beginning of troubles should not spread beyond the kingdom, that she forbade either persons or letters to leave any of the ports."

Harsh interrogations of Arbella yielded nothing in the way of information regarding her phantom lover, just more puzzling behavior, including her refusal to eat. Bess of Hardwick, utterly exasperated by her granddaughter's shenanigans, begged the council to remove the young woman from her charge. "She is so wilfully bent," Bess wrote, "and there is so little reason in most of her doings, that I cannot tell what to make of it. A few more weeks as I have suffered of late will make an end of me."

No matter how much Arbella, and now Bess, hated it, she was stuck at Hardwick Hall and, because of her royalty, deprived of the essential freedom to choose her own destiny. "When it shall please Her Majesty to afford me those ordinary rights which other subjects cannot be debarred of justly," she wrote defiantly, "I shall endeavour to receive them as thankfully now as if they had been in due time offered."

The storms Arbella raised at Hardwick were stilled when Queen Elizabeth I breathed her last on March 24, 1603, and King James peacefully succeeded her. The onetime potential heir was suddenly no longer relevant. Still, she remained determined to "shape my own coat according to my cloth." And this time it would cost her everything.

———

King James was prepared to be magnanimous toward his former rival, proclaiming his desire "to free our cousin the Lady Arbella Stuart from that unpleasant life which she has led in the house of her grandmother with whose severity and age she, being a young lady, could hardly agree." Arbella was welcomed at court, with the precedence due her rank, and, at twenty-seven, given perhaps the greatest gift she could imagine: a home of her very own. Soon enough, though, trouble would find her.

Not long after James I was crowned, Robert Cecil uncovered a plot to kill the king and, with the help of Spain, put Arbella on the throne. One of the accused leaders of what became known as the Main Plot was that dashing figure from the Elizabethan court, Sir Walter Raleigh. But evidence presented against him at trial was largely insubstantial, and as the prosecution's case began to unravel, intimations of Arbella's involvement began to emerge. Fortunately, Robert Cecil quickly put a stop to them. "Here hath been a touch of the Lady Arbella Stuart, the king's own near kinswoman," Cecil declared at Raleigh's trial. "Let us not scandal the innocent by confusion of speech. She is innocent of all these things as I, or any man here: only she received a letter from my Lord Cobham [one of the accused conspirators] to prepare her, which she laughed at and immediately sent to the king. So far was she from discontentment that she laughed him to scorn."

Arbella was grateful for Cecil's defense but "by reason of these grave events, kept in a state of constant perturbation of mind," according to the Venetian envoy. And things were about to get much worse.

The court of King James became almost as much a prison for Arbella as her grandmother's Hardwick estate. It was an alien place for one who had been as exceedingly sheltered as she was, filled, as one contemporary described it, with "malice, pride, whoredom, swearing and rejoicing in the fall of others . . . so wicked a place as I wonder the earth did not swallow it up." Indeed, flagrant drunkenness and debauchery were the new order, led by a king reveling in the company of grasping male favorites. Intelligent women such as Arbella found little favor from the deeply misogynistic monarch, and even less access. Furthermore, Arbella lacked the financial resources necessary to play any meaningful role in a court that valued conspicuous consumption.

"She is not very rich," reported the Venetian ambassador, "for the late queen was jealous of everyone, and especially of those who had a claim to the throne, and so she took from her the larger part of her income, and the poor lady cannot live as magnificently nor reward her attendants as liberally as she would."

Worst of all, Arbella would still never be allowed to marry a man she favored without the king's consent. And it was unlikely that a sanctioned marriage would ever be forthcoming. "Any child of hers could still present a future threat to his dynasty," wrote Sarah Gristwood. "This reality dawned on Arbella only slowly. She must, by contrast, quickly have become aware that in the new court, forgetful of Elizabeth's example, there was less kudos than ever in her unmarried state."

So there she was, a royal lady "without mate and without estate," as one observer succinctly put it. But Arbella Stuart was not prepared to let life or love pass her by. On June 22, 1610, she did the unthinkable and secretly married the man of her choice. The fact that he was Edward Seymour's younger brother made the illegal match all the more reckless. Perhaps she was crazy after all, or coldly calculating. Or maybe she was just a fool in love. Whatever the case, James I would prove far less forgiving of his cousin's follies than Queen Elizabeth had been.

Word of the couple's engagement had reached the king and council before they married. After being closely questioned, both Arbella and William Seymour continued to deny any such arrangement. They were warned sternly to abandon any thought of getting married and seemed to comply, although Arbella, as was her way, did so only grudgingly. She spoke at length before the king and gathered nobles, "denying her guilt and insisting on her unhappy state," as the Venetian ambassador reported. Then, at the insistence of King James, she humbled herself before him and was restored to favor. Soon after, she joined the rest of the royal family in the ritual investiture of James's oldest son as Prince of Wales. It would be the last time Arbella would ever enjoy the king's benevolence; only a few weeks later she was secretly married.

Unlike Edward Seymour, whom Arbella had never met before seeking his hand in what appeared to be a political alliance, she did seem to love William Seymour—at least a little, even if he was more than a decade younger. "Love maketh no miracles in his subjects, of what degree or age whatsoever," she had once written. And though William's ardor was less obvious, there is evidence that he loved Arbella, too. Given his family's history, he was certainly smart enough to realize that there could be little political advantage in wedding his royal cousin—quite the opposite, in fact. And throughout the ordeal that came as a consequence of their illicit union, William remained steadfast in his devotion to his wife.

The marriage did not stay secret for long. After what would be a very brief honeymoon in each other's arms, William was hauled off to the Tower and Arbella into the custody of Sir Thomas Parry, chancellor of the duchy of Lancaster. Separation of the couple was deemed imperative lest any further intercourse result in a baby with the royally rich blood of both Margaret and Mary Tudor. The thought of that was enough to make King James shudder.

Arbella and William were reunited a month after their wedding, but only to face a joint interrogation. William denied at first that a marriage had ever taken place; Arbella, on the other hand, remained defiant. According to the Venetian ambassador, she "freely confessed it and excused the denial of her husband on the score of fear. She endeavoured to demonstrate that neither by laws divine nor human laws could she be prevented."

Clearly Arbella was oblivious at this point to the danger she faced. Certainly her living conditions with Thomas Parry gave no indication of trouble. His home on the Thames was pleasant enough, and Arbella was allowed one or two of her servants. However, the fate of the rest of her servants concerned her. They were like a second family of sorts. "There are divers of my servants with whom I never thought to have parted whilst I lived," she wrote to her uncle. "But since I am taken from them, and know not how to maintain either myself or them, being utterly ignorant how it will please his majesty to deal with me, I were better to put them away now, than towards winter. Your lordship knows the greatness of my debts and my unableness to do [anything] for them."

Arbella boldly signed the letter to her uncle "the poor pris-

oner your niece, Arbella Seymour," apparently quite proud of
her married name. She made the mistake of signing a petition
to the king the same way—a note of defiance that seemed to
reflect her woeful underestimation of how dire her circumstances really were. Several rough drafts of the petition indicate
the same thing. In one discarded version she wrote, "Restraint
of liberty, comfort, and counsel of friends and all the effects of
imprisonment are in themselves very grievous, and inflicted as
due punishments for greater offences than mine."

The final version of the petition was much more tactful, signature aside, and Robert Cecil reportedly admired the elo-
quence with which Arbella presented her arguments. King
James was decidedly less impressed, however, infuriated by the
signature and not persuaded by the content of the plea. He demanded to know "whether it was well that a woman so closely
allied to the blood royal should rule her life after her own
humor."

The king was no more amenable to intercessions on Arbella's behalf from his wife, Queen Anne of Denmark, "on
whose favor," Arbella wrote, "I will still chiefly rely." One of the
queen's ladies, Jane Drummond, reported to Arbella that
"when [the queen] gave your ladyship's petition and letter to
his majesty he did take it well enough, but gave no other answer than that ye had eaten of the forbidden tree."

Arbella's reaction seemed almost deliberately naïve: "I cannot rest satisfied till I may know what disaster of mine hindreth
his Majesty's goodness toward me, having such a mediatrix to
plead so just and honest a cause." Jane Drummond appeared to
understand the situation so much better: "The wisdom of this
state, with the example [of] how some of your quality in the
like case [Catherine Grey] has been used, makes me fear that
ye shall not find so easy [an] end to your troubles as ye expect,
or I wish."

Arbella seemed more realistic about her predicament when

she began pleading to the king with a degree of flattering deference she had not previously demonstrated. She referred to herself as His Majesty's "handmaid," his "most humble faithful subject and servant," and claimed that "the thought never yet entered into my heart, to do anything that might justly deserve any part of your indignation." But if she had made the king angry, she begged, "let it be covered with the shadow of your gracious benignity, and pardoned in that heroical mind of yours."

The king's wrath was not so easily soothed, however, especially after rumors of Arbella's pregnancy reached him. In fact, he only grew angrier. Arbella, the king declared in a warrant, "hath highly offended us in seeking to marry herself without our knowledge . . . and in proceeding afterwards to a full conclusion of a marriage with the self same person whom (for many just causes) we had expressly forbidden her to marry." Now she and William were going to pay. Seymour was sentenced to life in the Tower; Arbella to exile in Durham—"clean out of this world," she wrote despairingly.

"It is thought the king will send her even further," reported the Venetian ambassador, "and putting her out of the kingdom [to Scotland] he will secure himself against disaffection settling round her. Her husband is confined to the Tower for life and more closely guarded than heretofore; this has thrown him into extreme affliction, nor are there wanting those who bewail his unhappiness." Arbella wrote a tender letter to her imprisoned husband when she heard he was ailing. "Sir," she began formally:

> I am exceedingly sorry to hear you have not been well. I
> pray you let me know truly how you do and what was the
> cause of it, for I am not satisfied with the reason Smith
> [their messenger] gives. But if it be a cold I will impute it
> to some sympathy betwixt us having my self gotten a
> swollen cheek at the same time with a cold. For Gods sake

let not your grief of mind work upon your body. You may
see by me what inconveniences it will bring one to ...

... we may by God's grace be happier than we look for
in being suffered to enjoy ourselves with his Majesty's
favour. But if we be not ... I for my part shall think myself
a pattern of misfortune in enjoying so great a blessing as
you so little a while. No separation but that deprives me of
the comfort of you, for wherever you be or in what state so
ever you are, it sufficeth me you are mine. ... I assure you
nothing the state can do with me can trouble me so much
as this news of your being ill doth ... Be well, and I shall
account my self happy in being

> your faithful loving wife.
> Arb.S.

In the face of exile, with all its inherent dangers, Arbella appealed to the rule of law. She wrote to several judges protesting
that she was to be removed "far from these courts of justice
where I ought to be examined, tried, and then condemned or
cleared." She asked the judges that if they could not offer her
"the ordinary relief of a distressed subject," then to intercede so
she might still receive "such benefit of justice ... as both his
Majesty by his oath hath promised and the laws of this realm
afford to all others."

King James was not about to let legal niceties stand in the
way of his divine right to wrath. He would punish the way *he*
saw fit, not the courts. So, without the law to protect her, Arbella was reduced to writing frenzied letters to people she
barely knew. In one missive to an unnamed knight, she opened,
"Though you be almost a stranger to me," and continued by
begging him to help "a poor distressed gentlewoman ... out of
this great distress and misery and regain me his Majesty's
favour which is my chiefest desire." It was all to no avail.

Arbella swooned when the bishop of Durham and his men came to take her away. Then, refusing to budge, she left the men no choice but to carry her out on the mattress of her bed. The journey north was no smoother. A planned one-night stay in Highgate, for example, became six as Arbella fell ill (or pretended to). King James finally ordered her removed "by strength of men's hands," if necessary. Then, at Barnet, the party was forced to stop again as Arbella claimed she could go no farther. The king was naturally suspicious and sent a physician to examine her.

According to one report, the doctor found Arbella "very weak, her pulse dull and melancholy for the most part, yet sometimes uncertain; her water bad, showing great obstructions; her countenance very heavy, pale and wan; nevertheless, she was free from any fever or any other actual sickness, but of his conscience he protested that she was in no case to travel until God restored her to some better strength both of body and mind."

Whether by design or not, Arbella had won from the reluctant king an extended respite in Barnet. She did not waste the opportunity. With the help of her maternal aunt Mary Talbot, she began amassing money for an extraordinarily ambitious, if not impossible, plan: to free herself from the clutches of the bishop of Durham while her husband made a simultaneous escape from the Tower of London; then to sail away together to the Continent, where they would live forever free of the vengeful king. It almost worked.

On Monday, June 3, 1611, Arbella, disguised as a man and accompanied by her gentleman servant, slipped out of Barnet, headed for the town of Blackwall on the Thames. There she was to meet her husband after his own escape from the Tower. Because of her rank and station, and because she was supposedly sick, Arbella had not been held in close confinement. Escape was relatively easy, therefore. She just got on a horse and, riding like a man, took off.

William Seymour was held in similarly loose confinement at the Tower, where he was free to move about the complex and enjoyed a furnished suite of rooms above Traitor's Gate. And though his escape was certainly nerve-wracking enough—he might have been exposed at any moment—in the end it was really, like Arbella's, just a matter of walking away in disguise.

Yet despite the relative ease of their escapes, the plan was treasonous and exposed them to extreme dangers—torture and execution among them. Furthermore, freeing themselves was only the first step. They still had to connect at Blackwall, and that would prove agonizing.

Arbella arrived first, and with no sign of her husband, she waited. Hours went by and no William. He had been delayed and, because it was getting late, decided to go straight to the port of Leigh, where they were to board a ship to France. Arbella had no way of knowing this, however, and, after waiting in Blackwall until it became too dangerous to stay there any longer, sadly moved on to Leigh herself. There she and her small party found the boat that was to take them to Calais. William wasn't on it. Arbella was in despair, but with the winds turning, they had to be off. She didn't know that her husband had connected with another ship and had set sail as well. Only one of them would ever make it to France.

King James was wild with fury when he heard that the couple had slipped away. Not only had his authority been flaunted, but he believed his throne was at stake should Arbella ally herself with a foreign power. Catholics were rooted out as potential enemies, and Bess of Hardwick was arrested. A royal proclamation demanded the return of the fugitives who had committed "divers great and heinous offences," while foreign courts were alerted to the news in the most urgent terms. The chase was on.

"James always reacted with near-hysteria to the thought of any threat," wrote Sarah Gristwood—"a legacy of that youth of alarums, excursions and abductions, when the assassin's dagger was never far away. To his ever-fearful imagination, this was not a romantic escapade. It was a political threat—an enormity."

A small armada was sent to search for the runaways in the English Channel. Griffen Cockett, captain of the pinnace *Adventure*, spotted Arbella's ship off the coast of Calais, where she had insisted it stop to wait for William. The captain of her ship, a Frenchman by the name of Tassin Corvé, tried to run from the *Adventure*, but the winds were against him. Cockett opened fire, which, after some time, finally convinced Arbella to surrender. Still defiant, she was "not so sorry for her own restraint as she should be glad if Mr. Seymour might escape," reported Sir John Moore.

William Seymour did indeed escape, to Bruges. It was "a thing of no such consequence," Robert Cecil sniffed. Arbella was the real prize. And now she took her husband's place in the Tower—never to emerge again.

There was no heroic end to the story, no dramatic last stand from the woman who had defied the will of two monarchs. Held in rigid confinement, alone and all but abandoned, Arbella gradually gave up hope, took to her bed, and slowly faded away. Four years later, on September 25, 1615, she died, having refused to eat or drink. "Her death is deplored by a great number of the chief of the people," the Venetian envoy reported. "The king has not said a word about it."

10

Charles I (1625–1649): With His Head Held High

I would know by what power I am called hither.

—KING CHARLES I

The reign of Charles I, who succeeded his father, James I, in 1625, was marked by frequent clashes between the king and Parliament that culminated in civil war. Charles and his Royalist supporters were eventually defeated by Parliamentarian forces in 1649, after which the king was tried and executed for treason.

King Charles I had little in common with his father. Where James I had been rather crude, with a fondness for drink and pretty young men, Charles was dignified in every degree, a connoisseur of fine art, and completely devoted to his wife. Nevertheless, father and son did share one dominant trait: an exalted view of kingship. "The state of monarchy is the supremest thing upon earth," James I had rhapsodized, "for kings are not only God's lieutenants upon earth and sit upon God's throne, but even by God himself they are called gods." Charles I tenaciously adhered to this principle, and in the end it cost him his head.

History has not been kind to the second Stuart monarch, and with much cause. Charles was an exceedingly small man who brooked no opposition and reacted violently to any perceived intrusion upon his royal prerogative. His worldview was essentially medieval, with the king atop an ordered hierarchy where power trickled down. Parliaments, he believed, were merely instruments to carry out his will. In this Charles was woefully out of synch with the evolving political order, and his inability, or unwillingness, to recognize it had terrible consequences.

Though the precise causes of the bloody civil wars that ravaged Britain in the 1640s will forever be debated, the policies of Charles I certainly played no small part. Compromise was anathema to this king, and he was unwilling to listen to legitimate grievances over his arbitrary rule. To concede anything would be to diminish his high office and the established order. "I will rather die than yield to these impertinent and damnable demands," Charles wrote with characteristic obstinacy, this time in response to resistance to the religious policies he sought to impose in Scotland, "for it is all one, as to yield to be no King in a very short time." To defend his prerogatives, Charles I was willing to wage war in his own kingdom.

It might be argued, charitably, that Charles's stance was principled, grounded as it was in his belief that law and order in the realm depended upon a strong king and obedient subjects; that anything less would inevitably lead to anarchy. But he betrayed his own elevated view of monarchy by consistently reneging "on the word of a king." Whenever he was trapped, Charles simply lied to extricate himself and to regain the upper hand. This is what ultimately doomed him. Indeed, by the time compromise might have saved his life, the word of the king meant nothing.

Charles I was, in short, a bad king. Yet for all his many flaws, he managed to redeem himself when all was lost. A transformation took place during his trial and subsequent execution that actually made him great. "His death gave his life a tragic dignity," wrote historian Charles Carlton. "In dying he showed grandeur in place of meanness, resolve instead of vacillation, honesty where duplicity had often been the norm."

On January 20, 1649, King Charles, defeated in war and now a prisoner, was led into Westminster Hall to stand trial for treason. It was in this same hall, almost twenty-three years before, that the king sat regally upon his throne, attended by the nation's great nobles, as he prepared for his coronation. Now, facing the assembled tribunal alone, without counsel, he heard the charges against him.

The king, it was declared, had "caused and procured many thousands of this nation to be slain" in the civil wars. "All which wicked designs, wars, and evil practices of the said Charles Stuart have been and are carried on for the advancement and upholding of a personal interest of will, power and pretended prerogative to himself and his family, against the public interest, common right, liberty, justice and peace of the people of this nation." And for having caused the wars, the charges continued, Charles was "guilty of all the treasons, murders, rapines, burnings, spoils, desolations, damages and mischiefs" that arose from them.

The preordained verdict was death, for that was the only reason the court had been assembled in the first place. The veneer of a fair and open trial was merely a pretense for judicial murder. "I tell you we will cut off his head with the crown upon it," roared Oliver Cromwell, leader of the king's enemies in Parliament.

There was no precedent for putting a monarch on trial, and certainly no mandate. Such a thing was inconceivable for many who believed the king was the Lord's anointed and at the apex of an ordered society. Indeed, only a small faction of extremists in the House of Commons had called for the trial; the majority of members opposed had been forcibly debarred by the army. And the House of Lords had withheld its approval entirely. Ironically, then, a king charged with tyranny against his own people was himself being tried in an unrepresentative, entirely illegal proceeding.

Confronting what historian Michael B. Young described as

a "makeshift court . . . assembled to engineer his execution,"
Charles I managed to shine. He refused to legitimize the cha-
rade by offering a defense. Instead, he challenged the court's le-
gitimacy. "I would know by what power I am called hither," the
king said in refusing to answer the charges against him, as had
been demanded.

> I would know by what authority, I mean *lawful;* there are
> many unlawful authorities in the world; thieves and robbers
> by the highways. . . . Remember, I am your King, your *law-
> ful* King, and what sins you bring upon your heads, and the
> judgement of God upon this land. Think well upon it, I say,
> think well upon it, before you go further from one sin to a
> greater. . . . I have a trust committed to me by God, by old
> and lawful descent, I will not betray it, to answer a new un-
> lawful authority; therefore resolve me that, and you shall
> hear more of me. . . . Let me see a legal authority warranted
> by the Word of God, the Scriptures, or warranted by the
> constitutions of the Kingdom, and I will answer.

For once the king was taking a worthy stand. He knew he
was doomed, but by emphasizing the illegality of the proceed-
ings against him, he made a much broader appeal to the rule of
law. If a small, unrepresentative group of men could grab power
and subvert all legal authority to try him, then ultimately no
one was safe. Or, as Charles said it, "if power without law may
make laws, may alter the fundamental laws of the Kingdom, I
do not know what subject he is in England, that can be sure of
his life, or anything that he calls his own."

The king concluded:

> This many a day all things have been taken away from
> me, but that I call more dear to me than my life, which is my
> conscience, and my honour: And if I had a respect to my life

more than the peace of the Kingdom, and the liberty of the subject, certainly I should have made a particular defence for myself; for by that at leastwise I might have delayed an ugly sentence, which I believe will pass upon me. . . . Now, sir, I conceive, that an hasty sentence once passed, may sooner be repented of than recalled; and truly, the self-same desire that I have for the peace of the Kingdom, and the liberty of the subject, more than my own particular ends, makes me now at last desire . . . before sentence be given, that I may be heard . . . before the Lords and Commons. . . . If I cannot get this liberty, I do protest, that these fair shows of liberty and peace are pure shows, and that you will not hear your King.

Charles's eloquent arguments flustered the commission but did not deter it from its mission to kill him. Less than a week after convening, the court pronounced Charles guilty and condemned him to death. He tried to make a statement after the sentence was delivered but was silenced. "I am not suffered for to speak," he said as he was led away. "Expect what justice other people will have."

Some of the soldiers present in the hall spat on the king as he passed; others blew tobacco smoke in his face. "Execution!" they cried. "Justice! Execution!" Three days later they would be satisfied.

On the eve of his death, Charles met with two of his younger children, Elizabeth and Henry, who were essentially prisoners of Parliament.* The king sat the young ones on his lap and, in a highly emotional scene, gently counseled them. "You are not to grieve or torment yourself for me," he told his

---

* Their older brothers, the future kings Charles II and James II, had escaped to the Continent, along with their mother, Queen Henrietta Maria, and their youngest sister, Henrietta Anne.

thirteen-year-old daughter, "for it will be a glorious death I shall die, for it is for the laws and liberties of this land. I have forgiven all my enemies and I hope God will forgive them also. And you and all the rest of your brothers and sisters must forgive them. Tell your mother that my thoughts have never strayed from her and my love for her will be the same to the last."

Turning to his eight-year-old son, Charles explained what was going to happen the next day and quietly admonished the boy not to become a pawn of the forces aligned against the royal family. "They are going to cut off your father's head," he told Henry. "Mark, child, what I say, they will cut off my head and perhaps make you a king. But you must never be king while your brothers Charles and James are alive. For they will cut off your brothers' heads, when they catch them; and cut off your head too, at the last. And so I charge you: You must never let them make you King."

"I will be torn to pieces first," young Henry replied, trying hard to be brave.

Satisfied, Charles gave what little treasure he had left to the tearful children, kissed and blessed them, then finally bid them farewell.

The next day, the appointed day, was bitterly cold. The king asked for an extra shirt to wear, loath to be seen shivering on the scaffold and have that mistaken for fear. "I would have no such imputation," he said. "Death is not terrible to me; I bless my God I am prepared." A knock on the door signaled that it was time to leave St. James's Palace, where Charles had been confined during his final days, and walk the short distance to the execution site at Whitehall Palace.

The scaffold had been erected just outside the palace's Banqueting House, a superb edifice designed by Inigo Jones (and all that remains of the original palace). Walking through that grand structure, Charles passed under the ornate ceiling paintings by Rubens glorifying the Stuart dynasty. How poignant the irony, then, that the king who commissioned this vibrant celebration of monarchy, and long held court beneath it, was about to actually lay his head upon a chopping block just outside.

The day had become brilliantly sunny when Charles stepped through a window of the Banqueting House and onto the black-draped scaffold. There, in the center, he saw the block, with chains nearby to bind him in the event that he struggled and refused to submit to the axe. A cheap coffin was off to one side, ready to receive his remains. The king remained composed, but the low height of the block seemed to disconcert him. "It can be no higher, sir," one of the two hooded executioners said without explanation.

Charles was permitted to speak, but the large crowd gathered to witness the grisly spectacle was kept so far back from the scaffold that he realized he would not be heard. He opted instead to address the people directly around him. Removing a small piece of paper from his pocket that contained some brief notes, he remarked that he would have been happy to remain silent, "but I think it is my duty, to God first, and to my country, to clear myself both as an honest man, a good King, and a good Christian."

He went on to insist that he was not responsible for the civil wars that had ravished the country, and that the sentence he received was illegal. Nevertheless, he acknowledged that the injustice of his fate was proper punishment from God for having shamefully submitted earlier in his reign to Parliament's demand for the head of his loyal servant Thomas Wentworth, Earl of Stafford.* "God forbid that I should be so ill a Christian as not to say God's judgments are just upon me," the king said. "Many times He does pay justice by an unjust sentence. That is ordinary.

---

* The earl had been a key supporter of Charles I and his rights as monarch, which put him at odds with Parliament. The king had promised to protect

I will only say that an unjust sentence that I suffered for to take effect is punished now by an unjust sentence upon me."

Though he professed to forgive his enemies, Charles still emphasized what he saw as their dangerous lawlessness and defended his own view of the proper order. "For the people, truly I desire their liberty and freedom as much as anybody whatsoever," he maintained. "But I must tell you their liberty and freedom consists in having government—those laws by which their life and their goods may be most their own." And that government, he reasserted, was maintained by the monarch, as it had been for centuries.

"Sirs," he continued, "it is for this that I am now come here. If I would have given way to an arbitrary power, for to have all laws changed according to the power of the sword, I need not have come here. And therefore I tell you—and I pray God it not be laid to your charge—that I am a martyr of the people."

Having concluded his speech with an affirmation of his Christian principles, Charles prepared for death. "I go from a corruptible to an uncorruptible crown," he said to his confessor, "where no disturbance can be, no disturbance in the world." The king then proceeded to distribute the last of his possessions, after which he stood silently for a moment in prayer. Finally he removed his cloak, lowered himself down to the block, and, after a few seconds, stretched out his arms as a signal to the headsman. In a flash his head was severed and held up to the crowd. With that, one witness reported, the gathered people gave "such a groan as I have never heard before, and I desire I may never hear again."

Wentworth but was ultimately forced to submit to Parliament's demand for his head in 1641.

11

Charles I (1625–1649): A Grisly Afterlife

Their hands and sticks were tinged with his blood.
—Sir Roger Manley

The execution of King Charles I in 1649 was one of the most momentous events in British history. The monarchy was abolished and replaced by a republic, led by Oliver Cromwell. The Commonwealth, as the new regime came to be called, lasted until 1660. The postmortem ordeal of Charles I endured for much longer.

Even Charles I's most inveterate enemies were forced to admit that he died with admirable grace. But with the king's last breath came the end of anything that even remotely resembled dignity. His corpse was subjected to a ghastly series of ordeals, perpetrated over two centuries, that made the trial and execution preceding them seem almost sublime by comparison.

Right after raising the king's head to the moaning crowd that cold January day in 1649, the executioner slammed it down on the scaffold, bruising the face. Then, one witness wrote, "his hair was cut off. Soldiers dipped their swords in his blood. Base language upon his dead body." For a price, onlookers were invited to take ghoulish souvenirs of the execution. "His hair and blood were sold by parcels," reported Sir Roger Manley. "Their hands and sticks were tinged with his blood and the block, now cut into chips, as also the sand, sprinkled with his sacred gore, were exposed for sale."

The king's head and body were reunited in the cheap coffin that had been waiting on the scaffold to receive them, after which soldiers allowed paying members of the public to view the corpse. It was apparently a lucrative enough enterprise to prompt one soldier to remark, "I wish we had two or three more Majesties to behead, if we could but make such use of them."

When the unseemly show on the scaffold was at last concluded, Charles's body was brought back into the Banqueting House, through the same window the king had stepped out of to meet his doom. For several days the corpse was exposed to further view at Whitehall, during which time Oliver Cromwell, the leader of the revolution against the king, is said to have secretly visited it one night. "Cruel necessity!" he reportedly muttered before quietly slipping away.

Some believed they were looking upon the remains of a saint. Sir Purback Temple wrote of a companion who, "in a scoffing manner took me by the hand and said, 'If thou thinkest there is any sanctity or holiness in [the corpse] look here,' where I saw the head of the blessed martyr'd King, lie in a coffin with his body, which smiled as perfectly as if it had been alive."

On February 1 the body was finally embalmed. The surgeon retained for the task, Thomas Trapham, reattached the head with some thread and, with a true professional's respect for the dead, was later heard to remark that he had "sewed on the head of a goose." After being disemboweled and cleaned, the corpse was sealed in its coffin and transported to St. James's Palace, there to await burial instructions from Parliament.

Westminster Abbey—the resting place of many of Charles's relatives, including his parents—was rejected because it was deemed too close to Parliament's front door and apt to become an unwelcome shrine for Royalist pilgrims. They settled instead on St. George's Chapel at Windsor Castle—far enough away and fortified to keep the late king's supporters at bay.

The body, it was decreed, "should be privately carried to Windsor without pomp or noise." And so it was. The exact location for burial within the chapel was left unspecified, however. To find an available vault, those charged with the interment were forced to tap around the floor of St. George's with sticks until they found a hollow sound. They stumbled upon the burial chamber of King Henry VIII and his third wife, Jane Seymour, which, curiously, had been left unmarked. There Charles I would rest in anonymity next to his mighty predecessor (a bone of whose one participant in Charles's burial secretly snatched away as a souvenir). The king's sleep was not destined to be restful.

Charles II always intended to properly memorialize his father after being restored to the throne in 1660. "He spoke of it often," wrote the king's chief minister, Lord Clarendon, "as if it were deferred till some circumstances and ceremonies in the doing it might be adjusted." Charles even had the famed architect Sir Christopher Wren design a magnificent mausoleum. In the end, though, other priorities always interfered and Charles I's grave remained unmarked. It was only briefly disturbed in 1696 when one of Queen Anne's many stillborn children was added to the vault, the tiny coffin resting right on top of the child's great-grandfather.

A far more significant disturbance—a violation, actually—occurred a century later when, in 1813, space was being excavated in St. George's Chapel for the burial of King George III's sister, Princess Augusta, Duchess of Brunswick. Workers inadvertently knocked a hole in the wall of Charles I's adjacent crypt. Informed of the accident, King George's eldest son, then serving as prince regent, decided for some reason that his royal ancestor's coffin should be opened. Thus commenced the final, and perhaps most aggressive, assault on the dead king's dignity.

The prince regent, who would soon succeed his father as King George IV, was present at the disinterment, as was his personal physician, Henry Halford, who left a vivid account of the whole unseemly process. The black velvet pall that had been covering the late king's coffin since its original interment was stripped away. Then a square opening was cut into the upper part of the coffin to reveal the corpse wrapped in waxen cerecloth. The part of the cloth covering the king's face was cut away.

"The complexion of the skin of it [the face] was dark and discolored," Halford reported. "The forehead and temples had lost little or nothing of their muscular substance; the cartilage of the nose was gone; but the left eye, in the first moment of exposure, was open and full, though it vanished almost immediately: and the pointed beard, so characteristic of the period of the reign of King Charles, was perfect. The shape of the face was a long oval; many of the teeth remained; and the left ear, in the consequence of the interposition of the unctuous [oily] matter between it and the cere-cloth, was found entire."

The identification of the late king for the historical record was the ostensible reason for the disinterment. That should have been satisfied with the inscription on the coffin that read KING CHARLES. Since that was apparently not enough evidence, the features that clearly matched those of the king might have sufficed. But no, the prince regent wanted more. So, the head was lifted out of the coffin for closer examination; Thomas Trapham's "goose" stitches immediately unraveled. "It was quite wet, and gave a greenish red tinge to paper and linen which touched it," wrote Halford, taking great pains not to conclude that the liquid was blood, but believing it to be.

"The back part of the scalp was entirely perfect, and had a remarkably fresh appearance," Halford continued; "the pores of the skin being more distinct, as they usually are when soaked in moisture; and the tendons and ligaments of the neck were of considerable substance and firmness. The hair was thick at the back part of the head, and, in appearance, nearly black. A portion of it, which has since been cleaned and dried, is of a beautiful dark brown color. That of the beard was a redder brown. On the back part of the head it was more than an inch in length, and had probably been cut so short for the convenience of the executioner, or perhaps by the piety of friends soon after death, in order to furnish memorials of the unhappy king."

Then it was only left to examine the neck wounds to confirm that the corpse had indeed been decapitated. That, Halford wrote, "furnished the last proof wanting to identify King Charles the First."

Having resolved this great historical question, the intrepid researchers helped themselves to mementos of their quest: part of the king's beard, some hair from the back of his head, part of a neck vertebra, and a tooth. The coffin was then resealed and the vault closed.

Two decades later, the prince regent's brother, King William IV, ordered an inscribed marble slab placed on the floor over the tomb to identify at last the royal personages held within. Then, in 1889, the vault was opened one last time when the future King Edward VII ceremoniously deposited a small casket containing the body parts taken from Charles I seventy-five years earlier and returned to the Prince of Wales by the heirs of Sir Henry Halford.

After two centuries, the king was finally allowed to rest, albeit in pieces.

12

Charles II (1660–1685):

The Great Escape

We see the soldiers going up and down . . .
searching for persons escaped.
—King Charles II

Although Charles I was executed in 1649, the English Civil War didn't end until 1651, when the executed king's son, Charles II, having returned from exile to reclaim the crown, was defeated at the Battle of Worcester. Charles made a perilous escape to France after the battle and would remain in exile for another eight years.

Hidden among the leaves and branches of a large oak, the king of England could see enemy soldiers all around him. He might be discovered any minute, which would mean certain death, but after a long, terrifying night on the run, exhaustion began to overwhelm him. Resting his head on the lap of a faithful companion, the king soon fell asleep. It was a slumber with potentially lethal consequences. Any noise he might make would surely alert the soldiers lurking all around, but rousing him was dangerous as well; the startled sound of being jolted awake would betray him just as easily.

Few British monarchs ever faced the peril, or sheer adventure, that Charles II did after his crushing defeat at the Battle of

Worcester in 1651. For six weeks he was a fugitive in his own kingdom, with a bounty on his head worth far more than most Englishmen could hope to earn in a lifetime. Yet with a combination of guile and extraordinary luck, as well as the aid of a handful of faithful subjects, Charles managed to make a remarkable escape.

It had been nearly three years since his father's execution and Parliament's abolishment of the monarchy when Charles, aged twenty-one, returned from exile to claim his crown. With a force consisting mostly of Scots, the king without a country met Oliver Cromwell's army at Worcester on September 3, 1651. It was the last great clash of the English Civil War, "as stiff a contest as ever I have seen," Cromwell later said. Charles fought fiercely. "Certainly a braver prince never lived," one officer recalled, "having in the day of the fight hazarded his person much more than any officer of his army, riding from regiment to regiment." Despite the king's unwavering courage, however, it was clear by the end of the day that his cause was lost.

Charles managed to slip out the back of his headquarters just as Cromwell's men stormed in through the front, but he was still in grave danger. With his extraordinary height (at least for the time; he was just over six feet tall), swarthy complexion, and regal gait, he was hardly inconspicuous. Furthermore, the king was accompanied by remnants of his shattered army, which made his identity all the more apparent—"and though I could not get them to stand by me against the enemy [at Worcester]," Charles later said sardonically, "I could not get rid of them, now I had a mind to do it."

Under cover of night, the king and his companions made their way north through forest and bramble, venturing onto the main roads only when they had no alternative. At dawn they reached a home called Whiteladies, built on the ruins of a former Cistercian convent. The sympathetic owner provided the royal refugee with food and a warm fire, while Charles had his hair cut short and donned the clothing of a woodsman. As the sun continued to rise over Whiteladies, it was deemed unsafe for the king to remain there. Cromwell's men were thought certain to search the home, as indeed they later did.

Taking leave of his entourage, many of whom were later captured, Charles hid in a nearby wood with a local man named Richard Penderel. It was a miserable day, without food or water, during which the fugitive king was in constant danger of being captured. From his hiding place he could actually see Cromwell's soldiers on the adjacent road. It was only "by great good fortune it rained at the time," Charles recalled, "which hindered them, as I believe, from coming into the wood to search for men that might be fled thither." And what the king found "remarkable enough" was to later learn that it had only rained over the copse in which he was concealed and nowhere else, "this contributing to my safety."

By this time Charles had abandoned any hope of escaping to London, as he had originally planned, and settled instead on Wales, which was much closer—just across the Severn River. Creeping out of the woods that night, the king and Penderel started to make their way west through the countryside toward Wales. At one point they passed a mill, the owner of which suddenly appeared and demanded that they identify themselves. Rather than risk being exposed, Charles and Penderel opted to run. "Rogues! Rogues!" the miller shouted as he gave chase, running past his panting quarry who had hidden in some hedges.

Having evaded the miller, the pair made it to the home of a gentleman named Wolfe, who insisted he would not risk his neck harboring any man unless it was the king himself. After Penderel revealed Charles's identity—"very indiscretely, and without my leave," as the king later recounted—the stunned man fed them and put them up in his barn behind some hay, while Mrs. Wolfe endeavored to further disguise the king by smearing his face and hands with walnut juice.

While with Mr. and Mrs. Wolfe, Charles learned that crossing the Severn into Wales would be impossible because Cromwell had all the bridges blocked. There was now no choice but to turn back. In an effort to avoid the miller who had earlier confronted them, Charles and Penderel took a detour. But along this alternative route they came upon a small river that they would have to cross. Unfortunately, Penderel couldn't swim. Charles forded the river first and found it wasn't too deep. "Thereupon," he recalled with some pride, "taking Penderel by the hand, I helped him over." It was the first small service the king could offer his invaluable companion.

The pair returned almost to where they had started, arriving near dawn at an isolated hunting lodge leased by the Penderel family called Boscobel, a name derived from the Italian *bosco bello,* or "beautiful wood." There the most famous episode of Charles II's flight unfolded.

The king was welcomed at Boscobel with news that one of his most faithful supporters, Colonel William Carlis, was at the moment hiding in the woods outside. Charles quickly joined him, and together they climbed a large oak that would in time become the most renowned tree in the land. It was thick and bushy enough to conceal the two men but isolated enough from the other trees to give them a good view of the surrounding area.

"We see soldiers going up and down, in the thicket of the wood, searching for persons escaped," Charles recounted. "We seeing them now and then peeping out of the wood." And they could hear the soldiers as well, discussing among themselves what they would do with the "malicious and dangerous traitor," as Cromwell called Charles, once they found him.

All day long the king remained in the tree, his head resting on the lap of the faithful Carlis. Eventually he fell asleep, exhausted from the ordeal of the past few days. Carlis could hear the soldiers coming closer but was loath to wake Charles for fear that any sound the king might make as he was startled out of his slumber would betray their hiding place. It was not until evening that they felt safe enough to climb down.

That night at Boscobel Charles first heard of the enormous one-thousand-pound bounty Cromwell had put on his head. Carlis, however, was quick to reassure him: "If it were one hundred thousand pounds, it were to no purpose." As the Penderels tended to the king's blistered and bloody feet—a result of all the walking he had done in woodsman's shoes much too small for him—Charles asked for some mutton for supper. Perhaps in the warm glow of the evening he had forgotten where he was, and in what sorry state. Mutton was a luxury the Penderels could hardly afford, and even if they could, ordering such an extravagance from the butcher would certainly attract unwelcome attention. Once again, Carlis came through for his king. Stealing over to a neighboring property, he killed a sheep and brought it back. Charles helped with the preparation and jovially demanded to know who was the better cook, he or Carlis.

The king spent the night tucked into a tiny hiding place designed to shelter fugitive Catholic priests.* The accommodations were hardly spacious, but at least Charles was relatively safe. Still, he couldn't stay at Boscobel indefinitely, and despite the fact that he had been on the run for several days since the battle, he really hadn't gotten very far. Fortunately, a new avenue of escape was about to present itself.

News came to the king that a Royalist named Colonel Lane had obtained from the local parliamentary commander a travel

---

* Catholics were severely repressed at the time, and the shelter at Boscobel was part of a vast underground network. Charles came to sympathize with the Catholics' plight and is even believed to have converted on his deathbed.

pass, required of all Catholics, allowing his sister Jane to go to the port city of Bristol, accompanied by a servant. The purpose of the visit was for Jane to attend to a friend, Mrs. Norton, who was about to have a baby. This provided King Charles with an excellent opportunity. He could pose as Jane Lane's servant and, once in Bristol, escape on any number of ships bound for France.

The plan called for Charles to rendezvous with Jane and several others at Moseley Hall, the home of a member of the Catholic underground by the name of Thomas Whitgreave. Getting there would be dangerous, however, and Richard Penderel and his four brothers insisted on accompanying the king. They had already risked their lives harboring him, a crime that would have been punished by death, and now they were going to further expose themselves.

Still in disguise, Charles rode Humphrey Penderel's cart horse part of the way to Moseley Hall. It was a concession to his shredded feet, but a conspicuous one; the rest of the distance he would have to walk. In mock exasperation, the king complained that his mount was "the heaviest dull jade" he had even ridden, to which Humphrey Penderel quickly responded, "My liege, can you blame the horse to go heavily when he has the weight of three kingdoms [England, Scotland, and Ireland] upon his back?"

It had been agreed that only two of the brothers would accompany the king all the way to Moseley Hall; the others would return to Boscobel with the horse. Dismounting at the appointed place, the king eagerly set off for his destination without acknowledging the Penderels' remarkable service. Suddenly he stopped, turned around, and ran after them. "My troubles make me forget myself," he said humbly. "I thank you all."*

* The Penderels were richly rewarded upon Charles II's restoration, as were many of the others who had risked their lives in aiding him.

Terror descended on Moseley Hall after Charles arrived there to await his rendezvous with Colonel Lane and his sister Jane. "Soldiers!" a maid screamed. "Soldiers are coming!" Whitgreave, the owner of the home, whisked the king into a hiding place that had been created for fugitive priests. He then went outside nonchalantly to meet the soldiers, who immediately recognized him as a Royalist. They were about to arrest him, but Whitgreave convinced them that he had not participated in the recent Battle of Worcester, a fact verified by his neighbors.

Before meeting with the soldiers, Whitgreave had ordered that all the doors of the home be kept open to avoid any suspicion that he might be harboring someone inside. This seemed to have effectively misled the men, who left without searching the home—all except one, who slipped into the backyard and questioned the blacksmith working there. The soldier offered one thousand pounds for information as to where the king might be, but the blacksmith, either out of loyalty or actual ignorance of Charles's whereabouts, remained silent.

The trouble passed, and Charles and Jane Lane set out at last for Bristol. It was the first time since he fled Worcester that the king was able to ride out in the open—albeit disguised as a servant going by the name of Will Jackson. He played the part well, relying now more on his wits, and later recounted a scene along the way after the horse he and Jane were riding threw a shoe. In his role as servant, it fell to the king to take the horse to a blacksmith.

"As I was holding my horse's foot," Charles recalled with a touch of glee, "I asked the smith what news. He told me there was no news that he knew of, since the good news of the beating of the rogues of the Scots [the king's army at Worcester]. I asked him whether there was none of the English taken that joined with the Scots. He answered that he did not hear that the rogue Charles Stuart was taken; but some of the others, he said were taken, but not Charles Stuart. I told him, that if that rogue were taken he deserved to be hanged, more than all the rest, for bringing in the Scots. Upon which he said that I spoke like an honest man, and so we parted."

After reaching the Norton home near Bristol, it was essential that the king maintain a low profile as he might be recognized by members of the household—particularly since he had spent time around Bristol during the Civil War of his father's reign. Even the Nortons were not to know his identity. Jane Lane helped facilitate the deception by announcing that her servant was very ill and needed to go straight to bed. "And the truth is," Charles later said, "my late fatigues and want of meat had indeed made me a little pale."

Despite all the precautions, the king was recognized by the Nortons' butler, a man named Pope. Fortunately he was loyal and Charles decided to trust him. "I am extremely happy to know you," Pope said, "for otherwise you might run great danger in this house. For though my master and mistress are good people, yet there are at this time one or two in it that are very great rogues, and I think I can be useful to you in anything you will command me."

Pope proved very useful indeed. When told that Charles's associate Lord Wilmot would be arriving at the Norton home to meet with the king, the butler warned Charles that Wilmot would be easily recognized there. He offered to intercept Wilmot and smuggle him into the home under cover of night. Pope also agreed to make discreet inquiries about ships leaving Bristol for France, a mission that proved disappointing when he discovered that nothing suitable would be available until at least a month later. That was too long for the king to safely remain in the area, so Pope suggested he move to the village of Trent on the southern coast, where he could hide at the home of Colonel Francis Wyndham, a staunch Royalist, while waiting for an opportunity to escape England by sea. Charles would travel the forty miles or so to Trent still disguised as Jane Lane's servant Will Jackson.

The day before they were set to leave, the plan nearly unraveled when Mrs. Norton delivered a stillborn baby. Since the official reason for Jane Lane's visit to Bristol was to be with her friend, it would undoubtedly arouse suspicions if she were to leave abruptly just when Mrs. Norton needed her most. Charles devised a brilliant solution. That night at dinner he arranged for Pope to deliver a fake letter advising Jane that her father was gravely ill and that she and her servant would have to return home immediately. Everyone in the Norton household would of course understand the urgency of her departure, and the next morning she and the king set off for Trent.

Charles arrived safely at Colonel Wyndham's house, but early in his stay he encountered a rather unsettling scene in the village. Bonfires roared and bells tolled in some kind of celebration. The king, holed up in the house and eager for some excitement, sent a maid to find out what the fuss was all about. She returned with a report that a government soldier had come to Trent bragging that he had personally killed the king at Worcester and that the buff coat he was wearing had been stripped from Charles's corpse. The eruption of joy that followed the soldier's bogus revelation made it painfully apparent to the king that he was not among friends. "Alas!" he said. "Poor people."

After witnessing this disheartening celebration of his apparent demise, Charles's spirits were lifted considerably when he learned that a ship had been found to carry him to France. Stephen Limbry owned a small coasting vessel and agreed to pick up the king at midnight, September 22, on the shore of the nearby village of Charmouth. Giddy with anticipation, Charles and his party arrived at the appointed time. Hours went by, however, and there was no sign of Limbry. Had they been betrayed? With dawn approaching, and the king in increasing danger, it was decided that he and Wyndham would take the

London road to the town of Bridport and wait at an inn there while the other members of his party tried to discover what had happened to Limbry. (As it turned out, Limbry's wife had discovered his mission and, fearful of the consequences should he be caught helping the fugitive king, locked him in his room.)

Approaching Bridport, Charles and Wyndham were horrified to find the town crawling with government troops gathered to subdue the last Royalist stronghold of Jersey. Wyndham begged the king to turn around, but that would mean they would miss the planned rendezvous with the rest of the group, who had gone in search of Limbry. Charles decided that the best option was the boldest. "We found the yard very full of soldiers," the king recalled. "I alighted, and taking the horses thought it best way to go blundering in amongst them, and led them through the middle of the soldiers into the stable; which I did, and they were very angry with me for my rudeness."

The stableman looked closely at the king. "Sure, Sir," he said, "I know your face?" This, Charles remembered, "was no very pleasant question to me." He deflected it by asking the stableman about himself, where he had lived and worked. The answers gave the king the cover he needed. The man told Charles that he had worked in the stables of one Mr. Potter during the Civil War. "I thought it best to give the fellow no further occasion of thinking where he had seen me," Charles said, "for fear he should guess right at last; therefore I told him, 'Friend, certainly you have seen me then at Mr. Potter's, for I served him a good while, above a year.'" This seemed to satisfy the stableman, who suggested they go for a pot of beer together. The king politely declined, claiming he had to serve his master dinner, but he promised to join him the next time he was in Bridport, three weeks hence.

Meanwhile, a soldier in Charmouth had become suspicious after observing the royal party awaiting Limbry's boat. He alerted his commanding officer, Captain Macy, who immediately launched a search for the king. Only minutes after Charles left Bridport, Macy and his men stormed into town. Following the scent there, Macy raced up the London road toward Dorchester—the same road the king had planned to take before deciding at the last minute to return to Trent and await news of another ship. Charles had barely entered the path to Trent, which diverged off the London road, when Macy and his men roared past on their way to Dorchester. The event was celebrated by Royalists for years afterward and became known as the Miraculous Divergence.

It would take another three weeks of anxious waiting and the threat of capture before a ship was finally found to take the king to France. His arrival there was bittersweet, for though he had eluded his enemies in England, he was still without a crown. Oliver Cromwell's power was entrenched, and it would be another eight and a half years before Charles was invited back to rule.

The diarist John Evelyn described the king's glorious entry into London upon his restoration in 1660, with the

> triumph of above 20,000 horse and foot, brandishing their swords and shouting with inexpressible joy; the ways strewed with flowers, the bells ringing, the streets hung with tapestry, fountains running with wine, the Mayor, Alderman and all companies in their liveries, chains of gold and banners: lords and nobles clad in cloth of silver, gold and velvet: the windows and balconies well set with ladies: trumpets, music and myriads of people flocking even so far as from Rochester. . . . It was the Lord's doing, for such a restoration was never mentioned in any history, ancient or modern, since the return of the Jews from the Babylonian captivity.

Safe and secure on his throne, King Charles never tired of recounting his harrowing adventures, though many a courtier grew weary of hearing about them.

13

Charles II (1660–1685): Old Rowley

A king is supposed to be the father of his people,
and Charles certainly was father to a good many of
them.

—GEORGE VILLIERS, SECOND DUKE OF BUCKINGHAM

*The majority of Parliamentarians who controlled England after the execution
of King Charles I were Puritans who sought to impose their austerity on the
nation at large. Celebratory holidays such as Christmas were suppressed, and
theaters banned outright. It wasn't until Charles II was invited back to rule in
1660 that the repressive decade of Puritan rule was replaced by a more colorful period known as the Restoration. King Charles, or the Merry Monarch,
as he was called, certainly represented well this era of relaxed morality.*

Monarchs have always kept mistresses, but the reign of Charles
II is often remembered as being far more licentious than most,
perhaps because after a decade of repressive Puritan rule, the
vigor with which Charles pursued his affairs offered such a
vivid contrast to the dour days of Cromwell.

The king simply loved the ladies—lots of them—and did so
with unabashed enthusiasm. In the process he sired scads of
bastards, a dozen or so, by seven or eight women, prompting
the Duke of Buckingham to quip, "A king is supposed to be the
father of his people, and Charles certainly was father to a good
many of them."

Charles II set the tone for his colorful court, and was often the target of the irreverent wits who thrived there. In one bit of verse, for example, the Earl of Rochester made reference to the equipment with which the Merry Monarch satisfied his fleet of paramours:

> *Nor are his high desires above his strength,*
> *His scepter and his prick are of a length.*

The affable king added to the chorus by making fun of himself. He had been given the nickname Old Rowley, after a famous stallion renowned for having sired an impressive progeny. One day, upon hearing a maid of the court singing a bawdy ballad comparing the king to the stud horse, Charles knocked on her door. "Who's there?" the startled woman asked. With that the king popped his head in and cheerfully announced, "Old Rowley himself, madam, at your service."

King Charles valued the women in his life and treated them well—too well, in fact, heaping upon them riches he could hardly afford. Yet despite the serious drain on his finances, the king considered his mistresses a worthy investment. "He enjoyed their company," wrote biographer Antonia Fraser, "not only for the purposes of making love to them, but to talk to them, to have supper with them, to be entertained by and to entertain them."

Women were essential to Charles II, and he started with them quite young. The Earl of Clarendon wrote disapprovingly of Charles's saucy nurse, Mrs. Wyndham,* who took her charge's virginity when he was fourteen and celebrated the conquest with untoward familiarity. She was "a woman of great rudeness and a country pride," Clarendon wrote snappishly,

---

* Sister-in-law to Colonel Francis Wyndham, who sheltered Charles after his disastrous defeat at the Battle of Worcester (see Chapter 12).

who "valued herself much upon the power and familiarity which her neighbours might see she had with the Prince of Wales [Charles's rank at the time], and therefore upon all occasions in company, and when the concourse of the people was greatest, would use great boldness towards him." Her greatest crime, according to Clarendon, was racing across a crowded room and planting a sloppy wet kiss on the young prince.

Even during the darkest days of his exile, Charles sought female companionship. In fact, the very year his father was executed, his Welsh mistress, Lucy Walter—a "brown, beautiful, bold but insipid creature," as the diarist John Evelyn described her—delivered the first of Charles's many illegitimate children, a boy named James.* Unfortunately, Lucy became a little too loose with her favors, which was thus an embarrassment to Charles—a double standard indeed. "Advise her, both for her sake and mine, that she goes to some place more private than the Hague [where Charles spent some time in exile at the court of his sister and brother-in-law, the prince and princess of Orange]," Charles instructed his friend Lord Taaffe, who had also slept with Lucy, "for her stay there is very prejudicial to us both."

Lucy left for England with her son and was promptly arrested upon her arrival. Eager to humiliate the king-in-exile, Cromwell soon released Charles's "lady of pleasure and the young heir," as he derisively called them, and had them shipped back to the Continent. There Lucy continued her sexual adventures and proved herself an entirely unfit mother. "He [James] cannot be safe from his mother's intrigues wheresoever he is," reported Charles's servant Daniel O'Neale. "It is a great pity so pretty a child should be in such hands as hitherto have

---

* James, who was given the title Duke of Monmouth by his doting father, led a rebellion against his Catholic uncle James II in 1685 and was beheaded as a result.

neglected to teach him to read or to tell twenty, though he hath a great deal of wit and a great desire to learn."

Charles was determined to wrest control of his son away from his estranged mistress, though this would prove difficult while he remained in exile without much money and even less power. In one mortifying scene, an agent of the king's tried to snatch the boy away from his mother, who ran screaming into the streets of Brussels and nearly caused a diplomatic incident.

Eventually, Lucy was forced to give up young James. The boy was sent to Paris, where, under the watch of Charles's mother, Queen Henrietta Maria, the egregious gaps in his education would be filled. Lucy Walter followed her son but died shortly afterward, reportedly of venereal disease.

By this time, Charles had taken up with a new love, a dazzling companion who accompanied the king back to England in 1660 to finally claim his crown, and who would become the most powerful of all his mistresses. Her name was Barbara Villiers Palmer, a tall, voluptuous beauty, with violet-blue eyes and a sensuous mouth that practically begged to be kissed. Beneath that magnificent exterior, though, was a greedy, ruthlessly ambitious virago—the "curse of our nation," as John Evelyn called her. Barbara absolutely controlled the enchanted king, and, in so doing, drained his treasury.

Samuel Pepys lamented in his diary how blinded Charles was by lust (even while the diarist himself harbored a secret passion for Barbara, "whom I do heartily adore")* and defied all wise counsel if it interfered with his carnal desires: *"Cazzo dritto non vuolt consiglio,"* Pepys wrote, citing the Italian proverb: A man with an erection heeds no advice.

---

* Pepys reported seeing Barbara's lacey petticoats hanging to dry in the Privy Garden at Whitehall and wrote that "it did me good to look upon them." On another occasion he became so excited hearing a salacious story about her "that I spent in my breeches."

Barbara, who became Countess of Castlemaine,* was the uncrowned queen of Charles's court, housed in sumptuous apartments at Whitehall Palace and indulged in every desire by the captivated king, whom she ruled with a potent mixture of hedonism and a violently explosive temper.

Given how much she loved power, the countess was not at all pleased when Charles married his real queen, Catherine of Braganza, in 1662. Her determination to retain her hold over the king provoked what became known as the Bedchamber Crisis.

Poor Catherine had no idea what awaited her when she arrived from Portugal. The twenty-three-year-old bride had been exceedingly sheltered at her father's Catholic court, spoke no English, and had little to recommend her to Charles except for a fat dowry. She was, wrote Evelyn, "low of stature, pretty shaped, languishing and excellent eyes, her teeth wronging her mouth by sticking a little too far out, for the rest sweet and lovely enough."

All seemed well, at first. Catherine found her new husband reasonably attentive (although, in a rare instance for Old Rowley, he was unable to consummate the marriage the first night, "for I was so sleepy"). And the king appeared happy with his new bride, writing to the Earl of Clarendon shortly after her arrival, "I cannot easily tell you how happy I think myself, and must be the worst man living (which I think I am not) if I am not a good husband."

Alas, the good husband had a mean mistress. Just as the king and queen settled into Hampton Court for their extended honeymoon, Barbara swooped into the palace to deliver her latest child by Charles. Even worse, she bullied the king into

---

* As a sop to Barbara's cuckolded husband, Roger Palmer, Charles created him Earl of Castlemaine, though it was clear that the power of the title rested with his wife. Palmer could only bear the humiliation for a time, and after

appointing her a lady of the queen's bedchamber. It was a monstrous insult to Catherine, who, sheltered though she was, knew exactly who the Countess of Castlemaine was. She angrily scratched the mistress's name off her list of ladies. Then, after actually meeting Barbara, she went into a rage so intense that it left her nose bleeding. "It is said here that she is grieved beyond measure," Charles's sister Henrietta Anne (known as Minette) wrote from France, "and to speak frankly I think it is with reason."

Confronted with either an unhappy wife or an unhappy mistress, Charles chose Barbara, which began an ugly quarrel with the queen. Catherine threatened to leave England, only to be told she needed the king's permission to do so. She was isolated at court, her Portuguese retinue sent away. When the king's chief minister, Clarendon, tried to intervene on the queen's behalf, Charles rebuked him: "Whosoever I find to be my Lady Castlemaine's enemy in this matter, I do promise on my word to be his enemy as long as I live."

Harmony was eventually restored when Queen Catherine realized that the hysterics were best left to Barbara. She learned to graciously accept the king's infidelities, and he came to honor her genuine goodness. Indeed, Catherine did what few women were able: She won Charles's heart. His devotion to her was evident when she became dangerously ill in 1663 and the king went into a frenzy of anxiety—even if he did manage to steal away from the queen's sickbed to sleep with Barbara.

Catherine of Braganza prevailed with what Charles praised as her "simplicity, gentleness and prudence," while Barbara was soon confronted with a rival more formidable than the queen. Her name was Frances Stewart, and she was one of Catherine's

---

Barbara delivered the second of the five children she would have with the king, he finally separated from her for good.

ladies-in-waiting and, according to Charles's sister Minette, "the prettiest girl in the world and the most fitted to adorn a court." She was not only younger and more beautiful than Barbara* but infinitely more virtuous, unwilling to trade her chastity for reward or advancement. This made La Belle Stewart, as she came to be called, a rare creature in the Restoration court. Her guileless unavailability drove King Charles crazy with desire, his incessant pining documented in some (rather clunky) verse he wrote:

> *Oh then, 'tis O then, that I think there's no hell*
> *Like loving, like loving too well.*

Barbara was made frantic by the king's diverted attentions and tried to refocus him by using the innocent young Frances as erotic lure. On one occasion she arranged a mock marriage between herself and the younger woman, ostensibly for fun. That night, as the unwitting Frances slept, Barbara set up a lesbian tableau for the king's pleasure. But the king only had eyes for La Belle Stewart, whose virtue remained unassailable despite her sovereign's single-minded pursuit. So desperate was the chase that Charles's friends formed the "Committee for the Getting of Mistress Stewart for the King," while he had his unobtainable love immortalized in an engraving as Britannia. It was with this image, adorned with helmet and trident, that Frances Stewart came to preside over British coinage for the next three centuries.

The king's relentless pursuit ended abruptly, not because he finally captured his elusive quarry but because Frances Stewart did the unthinkable and eloped with someone else. Charles was livid. "You may think me ill-natured," he wrote to his sister

---

* Pepys called Frances Stewart "the greatest beauty I ever saw I think in my life; and if ever woman can, doth exceed my Lady Castlemaine."

Minette, "but if you consider how hard a thing 'tis to swallow an injury done by a person I had so much tenderness for, you will in some degree [understand] the resentment I use toward her." Charles did manage to emerge from his petulant snit and, after Frances recovered unscarred from smallpox, was big enough to write, "I cannot hinder myself from wishing her very well."

The removal of Frances Stewart as a rival did little to revive Barbara's diminishing status as the king's favorite mistress. Her epic tantrums and relentless greed had grown intolerable, and Charles was ready to be rid of her. "Madame," he said as he dismissed her, "all that I ask of you for your own sake is, live so for the future as to make the least noise you can, and I care not who you love." As parting gifts Barbara was given the title Duchess of Cleveland as well as Henry VIII's magnificent palace Nonsuch, which she promptly ordered dismantled and sold for scrap.*

There was one last ferocious scene as Barbara tried to have the king acknowledge a sixth child she claimed was his. Charles had already accepted paternity of five of Barbara's children, but this latest, a girl, he refused to recognize as his. The child appeared to be the result of one of Barbara's other liaisons, perhaps with John Churchill, the future Duke of Marlborough.

"God damn me, but you shall own it!" Barbara screeched. "I will have it christened in the Chapel at Whitehall and owned as yours . . . or I will bring it into Whitehall Gallery and dash its brains out before your face!"

"I did not get this child," Charles calmly replied.

"Whoever did get it," Barbara cried, "you shall own it."

He never did.

Barbara was replaced by a bawdy actress, plump and dim-

---

* Nothing remains of the palace on-site, although some pieces of it were recovered and are now in the British Museum.

pled, named Nell Gwynn—"a bold merry slut," as Pepys called her—who thoroughly charmed the king. Though she lacked the social standing and education of some of the other royal mistresses, Nell's earthy sensuality and quick wit made her one of Charles's most treasured companions. She would remain so for nearly two decades, until his death in 1685.

Nell called the king "My Charles the Third," as she had already been with two lovers bearing the name, and in her utterly unaffected way, she would call out to him, "Charles, I hope I shall have your company tonight, shall I not?" And in contrast to Barbara, she was refreshingly free of a political agenda—a fact celebrated in a bit of popular verse:

> Hard by Pall Mall lives a wench call'd Nell.
> King Charles the Second he kept her.
> She hath got a trick to handle his prick,
> But never lays hands on his scepter.

Politics may have meant little to Nell, but money was another matter. Like Barbara, she spent it lavishly. She also resented her lack of rank. Charles adored her, but he never deigned give her a title (with its many accompanying perks) as he had some of his other mistresses. Still, Nell did manage to obtain for her son by Charles a proper title. According to one account, she called out to the boy in front of the king, "Come here, you little bastard, and say hello to your father." When Charles objected to the child's being referred to as such, Nell quickly responded, "Why, Your Majesty has given me no other name to call him by." Soon enough, the boy was made Baron Headington and Earl of Burford, as well as Duke of St. Albans sometime later.

Nell reserved some of her most scorching wit for one of her rival mistresses, Louise de Keroualle, Duchess of Portsmouth, whose pretense just begged to be punctured. When, for example, Louise went into mourning for the death of some supposedly grand relation, Nell did the same in honor of her own imaginary relative, whom she called "the Great Cham of Tartary." In any exchange of barbs, Louise was always left sputtering and looking stupid. Once, when Nell was dressed in an uncharacteristically lavish dress and dripping with jewelry, the duchess cracked, "Nelly, you are grown rich, I believe, by your dress. Why, woman, you are fine enough to be a queen."

"You are entirely right," Nell shot back, "and I am whore enough to be a duchess."

Louise was hated by the British people for being French, Catholic, and an excessive drain on the treasury. One time, Nell was mistaken for the despised duchess as she rode along in her carriage. As an angry mob circled and grew menacing, Nell popped her head out of the carriage and, with typical aplomb, declared, "Good people, this is the *Protestant* whore!"

It was just such a scene that demonstrated why Charles II was so devoted to this particular mistress, even if he never gave her the rank she wanted. On his deathbed the king was heard to plead with his brother, "Let not poor Nelly starve."

14

James II (1685–1688):

A Fool and His Crown

My own children have deserted me!

—KING JAMES II

Upon the death of Charles II in 1685, the throne passed to his brother James II, who would reign less than four years before being ousted by his daughter and son-in-law in 1688. James maintained a court-in-exile in France as a guest of his cousin Louis XIV until his death in 1701.

James II suffered from a malady that proved fatal to his reign: He was, as Lord Montagu put it so succinctly, "a wilful fool"— an obstinate believer in his royal prerogative, without the intelligence to exercise it properly. "He has all the faults of the King his father [Charles I]," observed the French ambassador Paul Barrillon, "but he has less sense and behaves more haughtily in public." Indeed, the only lesson James seemed to have gleaned from the fate of his father was to become even more unyielding when challenged. And though, unlike Charles I, he managed to keep his head, his political stupidity cost him his crown. Worse, it was his two daughters, Mary and Anne, along with his nephew William, who snatched it from him.

James ascended the throne peacefully after the death of Charles II in 1685, which was rather surprising given all the controversy that surrounded him during his brother's reign. He had converted to Catholicism—a mortal sin in the minds of most Englishmen—and, aggravating the fact, he made no effort to conceal it. (Curiously, though, James's zealous embrace of his new faith did nothing to diminish his lusty appetite for ugly mistresses.*) So outraged was the reaction to James's undisguised Catholicism that King Charles was forced to exile his brother for a number of years. There were even several attempts in Parliament to have James excluded from the succession. Though these ultimately failed, Charles, always wise to political realities, as well as his brother's foibles, predicted nothing but disaster when James inherited. "My brother will lose his throne for his [Catholic] principles," the king declared, "and his soul for a bunch of ugly trollops."

Charles had been remarkably prescient. Almost as soon as James came to the throne he began to squander the goodwill that accompanied his succession by pressing his pro-Catholic agenda. For example, he appointed Catholic officers to head regiments of an expanded standing army, which was against the law. Parliament objected and was prorogued, never to sit again during the king's reign.

In an era of violent religious divides, James refused to recognize the deep antipathy toward his adopted faith that had developed in the English psyche since Henry VIII's split from Rome a century and a half before. Almost every literate home contained a copy of John Foxe's *Actes and Monuments*, which detailed the horrors of "Bloody" Mary Tudor's efforts to stamp out heresy in England by burning Protestants alive. And every year people riotously celebrated Guy Fawkes Day, marking the

---

* One of James's mistresses, Catherine Sedley, was apparently bewildered by his attraction to her. "It cannot be my beauty because I haven't any," she said, "and it cannot be my wit because he hasn't enough of it to know that I have any."

failure of a Catholic plot to blow up Parliament during the reign of James I.

Many Englishmen associated Catholicism with arbitrary rule—a belief reinforced by the persecution of Protestants in France by the absolute monarch Louis XIV, James II's cousin and ally. Now their king was demonstrating the same tendencies by subverting the law to achieve what many believed was his ultimate aim: the destruction of the established Anglican Church and a reunification with Rome.

The tension between the king and his subjects was well illustrated in July 1687, when James—on his knees—welcomed the papal nuncio, Count d'Adda. Charles Seymour, Duke of Somerset, had refused to present d'Adda at court because, he said, it was against the law to recognize the pope's representative. "Do you not know I am above the law?" the king asked loftily, to which Seymour replied, "You may be, sire, but I am not."

One factor did mitigate the fears about James's Catholic despotism: His two daughters by his first wife, Anne Hyde, were his only heirs, and both were staunchly Protestant. "I must tell you that I abhor the principles of the Church of Rome as much as it is possible for any to do," the younger daughter, Anne, wrote to her sister, Mary, "and I as much value the doctrine of the Church of England."

Both women had been raised Protestant at Charles II's insistence to counter the criticism arising from his brother's avowed Catholicism. James had not been pleased. He wanted his daughters instructed in his own faith, but as he wrote in his memoirs, he did not attempt it because "they would have immediately been quite taken from [me]." That didn't mean he didn't try to convert them later, though, especially after he became king. His elder daughter and heir, Mary, had married her cousin William of Orange (the son of James's sister Mary) and lived with him in the Netherlands. From across the English Channel, James bombarded her with religious tracts he hoped would open her eyes to his faith. The princess of Orange was not persuaded by his proselytizing, however.

"I have found nothing in all of this reading but an effort to seduce feeble spirits," she wrote, "no solid reasoning, and nothing that could disturb me in the least in the world, so much that the more I hear of this religion the more pleased I am with my own, and more and more thanks have I to render to my God for His mercy in preserving me in His true faith."

The Protestant succession seemed secure, but the comfort that came from that was shattered in 1687 when it was announced that the king's second wife, the Catholic queen Mary Beatrice of Modena, was pregnant. If she had a son, he would succeed James and a Catholic dynasty would be entrenched. This was too terrible to contemplate, and, wrote the Tuscan ambassador Terriesi, "it would be impossible to describe the passion of those who do not desire [the birth of a son]."

Few, it seemed, were more distraught than the king's daughter Anne. "No words can express the rage of [Anne] at the Queen's condition," Terriesi reported. "She can dissimulate it to no one, and seeing that the Catholic religion has a prospect of advancement, she offers more than ever, both in public and in private to show herself hostile to it, and [to be] the most zealous of Protestants, with whom she is gaining the greatest power and credit at this conjunction."

A concentrated and cynical campaign to discredit the queen's pregnancy began almost as soon as it was announced. Anne led the charge. "It is strange to see how the Queen's great belly is everywhere ridiculed, as if scarce anybody believed it to be true," wrote Anne's maternal uncle Henry Hyde, second Earl of Clarendon. "Good God, help us!"

Certainly Anne did not have to dig very deep to reach the venomous bile she unleashed in calling into question her stepmother's pregnancy. She already loathed the queen, despite the fact that Mary Beatrice had always treated her well. "She pretends to have a great deal of kindness to me," Anne wrote to her sister, "but I doubt it is real, for I never see any proofs of it, but rather the contrary."

Among the many faults Anne found with Mary Beatrice was her belief that the queen had pushed James toward his Catholic extremism. "She is a very great bigot in her own way," Anne wrote, "and one may see by her that she hates all Protestants." (This coming from the woman who declared, "The Church of Rome is wicked and dangerous, and directly contrary to Scriptures, and their ceremonies—most of them—plain, downright idolatry.")

Poor Mary Beatrice probably had no idea just how much her stepdaughter hated her. Anne made certain of that. "I am resolved always to pay her a great deal of respect," she wrote to her sister, "and make my court to her, that she may not have any just cause against me." Now, with her great façade of friendliness, Anne was prepared to destroy the queen by cultivating the innuendo surrounding what she called Mary Beatrice's "false belly." She actively encouraged doubt with her sister, Mary, in the Netherlands:

> For, me thinks, if [the pregnancy] were not [a deception], there having been so many stories and jests made about it, she should, to convince the world, make either me or some of my friends feel her belly; but quite contrary, whenever one talks of her being with child she looks as if she were afraid one should touch her. And whenever I happen to be in the room as she is undressing, she has always gone into the next room to put on her smock. These things give me so much just cause for suspicion that I believe when she is brought to bed, nobody will be convinced it is her child, except it prove a daughter. For my part, I declare I shall not, except I see the child and she parted.

Mary, who had always enjoyed a warmer relationship with her stepmother—just three and half years her senior*—was at first rather complacent upon hearing the news of the queen's pregnancy. "I rendered thanks to God that this news did not trouble me in any fashion," she wrote in her journal. Although Mary would be supplanted as her father's immediate heir if a son was born, she was perfectly content to be William's wife, the princess of Orange, and really had no desire to be queen of England anyway. But then came Anne's letter, which, Mary wrote, "gave me just reason to suspect there had been some deception."

On June 10, 1688, Queen Mary Beatrice gave birth to a son, James Francis Edward Stuart, the prince who would one day be known as the Old Pretender (see Chapter 19). Rumors immediately shifted from a false pregnancy to a substitute child. And though King James had no way of knowing it at the time, the doubts aroused by the birth of his heir heralded the end of his reign.

The king's daughter Anne, always ready to promote vicious tales, now spread the story that another child had been secretly brought into the birth chamber and presented as the newborn prince. She had not been present at the queen's delivery (some historians believe she stayed away deliberately lest she be called to verify the birth) and shortly after wrote to Mary: "My dear sister can't imagine the concern and vexation I have been in, that I should be so unfortunate to be out of town when the Queen was brought to bed, for I shall never now be satisfied whether the child be true or false. It may be it is our brother, but God only knows, for she never took care to satisfy the

---

* The two were more like sisters. James married Mary Beatrice when she was just fifteen and introduced his child bride to his elder daughter by saying, "I have brought you a new play fellow." Mary Beatrice called Mary her "dear Lemon," and wrote, "I love her as if she were my own daughter."

world, or give people any demonstration of it. . . . After all this, 'tis possible it may be her child, but where one believes it, a thousand do not. For my part, except they do give very plain demonstrations, which is almost impossible now, I shall be of the number of unbelievers."

Mary soon joined the ranks of the skeptics as well. "One hears every day things so strange that it is impossible to avoid having very strong suspicions," she wrote. At first the princess of Orange had insisted that prayers be said for the baby in her chapel, but these gradually tapered off as Mary's conviction grew that the child being called the Prince of Wales was in reality a changeling.

Queen Mary Beatrice certainly noticed a puzzling coolness coming from the stepdaughter she loved so much. "You have never once in your letters to me taken the least notice of my son," she wrote to Mary. Several weeks later, after a stilted response, the queen wrote again: "Even in this last letter, by the way you speak of my son; and the formal name you call him by, I am further confirmed in the thought I had before, that you have for him the least indifference. The King has often told me, with a great deal of trouble, that often as he has mentioned his son in his letters to you, you never once answered anything concerning him."

Neither Queen Mary Beatrice nor King James was aware that such poisonous tales were being told about the birth of their child. They were horrified when they learned the truth. James was shocked that anyone would believe him so wicked that he "would debar [my] own daughters from the right of succeeding [me], to give [my] kingdoms to a suppositious son." The king declared that he would rather "die a thousand deaths than do the least wrong to any of my children."

Whether or not people actually believed a baby had been substituted was irrelevant. The suspicion served as the perfect pretext to toss the autocratic Catholic king off his throne. A group of leading nobles, known as "the Seven," issued a secret invitation to James's son-in-law and nephew, Mary's husband, William, to invade England and restore the rule of law. The prince of Orange was prepared to answer the call. And though it pained her deeply to have to move against her own father, Mary unreservedly supported her husband. She had come to firmly believe that the birth of the Prince of Wales was indeed a fraud—part of a Catholic conspiracy to subvert the Protestant succession and destroy the established church in England.

"The consideration of all this," she wrote, "and the thought that my father was capable of a crime so horrible and that, humanly speaking, there was not any other means to save the Church and State than that my husband should go to dethrone him by force, are the most afflicting reflections and would not be supportable without the assistance of God and a firm and unshakeable confidence in Him."

James was doomed. His subversion of the law to promote his faith had so damaged the Catholic cause that even the pope supported William's invasion. As the prince of Orange prepared his fleet, word of his plans excited the English populace. They waited anxiously for the "Protestant wind" that would carry William's fleet east to the English coast. "The wind, which had been hitherto west, was east all this day," John Evelyn wrote happily on October 14, 1688, the king's birthday. "Wonderful expectation of the Dutch fleet."

The inevitability of his nephew's invasion settled on King James, after his desperate reversals of policy achieved nothing. He now became fixated on the large weather vane that stood atop the Banqueting House of Whitehall Palace, waiting for the dreaded west wind. Yet despite the dreary forecast, James still held out hope that his older daughter was innocent of any complicity in her husband's plans.

"I easily believe you are embarrassed how to write me, now that the unjust design of the Prince of Orange's invading me is so public," he wrote to Mary in October, after her failure to respond to a previous letter. "And though I know you are a good wife, and ought to be so, yet for the same reason I must believe you will be still as good a daughter to a father that has always loved you so tenderly, and that has never done the least thing to make you doubt it. I shall say no more, and believe you very uneasy all this time, for the concern you must have for a husband and a father. You shall still find me kind to you, if you desire it."

James never heard back from his daughter. Less than a month after James sent his letter to Mary, William's Dutch armada—the largest invasion force ever launched against England—landed near the port of Plymouth. The king, once so stubbornly resolute in pushing his own agenda, now crumbled. Fearing disloyalty among his army, he refused to engage William at Salisbury, where his forces had been strategically placed. "What a rejection of leadership," wrote biographer Maurice Ashley. "What an excuse for cowardice!"

Instead of fighting William, James fled back to London. What he found there was devastating: His daughter Anne had defected to the enemy.* "God help me!" he cried. "My own children have deserted me."

Realizing all was lost, and haunted by the fate of his father, James arranged for the escape of his wife and son to France. Then he too stole away in disguise—tossing the Great Seal of England into the Thames as he went. But the king was recognized before boarding the ship that was to carry him away and was brought back to London a prisoner. It was only a brief detainment, though, as William allowed his father-in-law to escape once again. His was to be a bloodless coup.

---

* "You have my wishes for your good success in this so just an undertaking," Anne had written to her brother-in-law William of Orange before the invasion. She later greeted him upon his arrival festooned with orange ribbons.

James's supporters had warned him that to leave his kingdom was to abdicate his rights as monarch, but the broken man was determined. "If I do not retire I shall certainly be sent to the Tower," he said, "and no king ever went out of that place but in his grave."

Hearing of her father's ignoble departure, Princess Anne was "not in the least moved," according to her uncle the Earl of Clarendon, "but called for cards and was as merry as she used to be." When the earl reproved his niece for her apparent insensitivity, he reported that Anne answered that "it was true she did call for cards then because she was accustomed to play, and that she never loved to do anything that looked like affected restraint."

"And does your Royal Highness think that showing some trouble for the King your father's misfortunes could be interpreted as an affected restraint?" her exasperated uncle remonstrated. "Such behavior lessens you much in the opinion of the world, and even in that of your father's enemies."

Clarendon's lesson was lost on his niece: "She was not one jot moved."

15

William III (1689–1702) and Mary II
(1689–1694): Joint Sovereigns

> He was to conquer enemies, and she was to gain
> friends.
>
> —GILBERT BURNET

After the flight of James II in 1688, his nephew William of Orange de-
manded that he be given full rights as sovereign, along with his wife, Mary,
who, as James II's daughter, was closer in the line of succession. Parliament
agreed, in exchange for William's acceptance of the Bill of Rights, which ex-
panded the rights of subjects and limited those of the king (and later served as
the inspiration for a large part of the United States Bill of Rights). Thus,
William III and Mary II became co-monarchs, with all the authority of the
throne resting with William. Mary unreservedly acquiesced to this arrange-
ment, stating that women "should not meddle in government."

The deposition of James II and the invitation of his Protestant
daughter and son-in-law to rule as co-monarchs—with limited
powers—became known as the Glorious Revolution. But for
William and Mary, it all felt far more laborious than glorious.

William III bitterly resented the curbs on the Crown that had
been imposed upon his accession, as well as the constant battles
he had to fight with Parliament to obtain what he felt was necessary to rule effectively—primarily money. "The Commons
have treated me like a dog," he once blurted in exasperation.

The Dutch king never endeared himself to the English, who thought him cold and remote. "I see very well that this people is not made for me nor I for this people," William said. And he never took to England, either, especially London, where the pervasive, coal-fueled pollution sickened the asthmatic monarch.

Mary shared her husband's misery and, like him, longed to be back home in Holland—far from the fractious, scheming court she came to loathe. She had dreaded the prospect of becoming queen, knowing, she wrote, "my heart is not made for a kingdom and my inclination leads me to a retired quiet life." But perhaps worst of all, Mary was haunted by the specter of her deposed father in France.

She had been sharply rebuked upon her arrival in England for her apparent indifference to her father's fate. People thought her much too merry. "She came into Whitehall laughing and jolly, as to a wedding, so as to seem quite transported," John Evelyn wrote disapprovingly, while the Earl of Dartmouth reported that "she put on more airs of gaiety upon that occasion than became her, or seemed natural." Even Mary's admirer Gilbert Burnet was appalled. "I confess I was one of those who censured her in my thoughts," he recalled. "I thought, at least, she might have felt grave, or even passively sad, at so melancholy a reverse of fortune."

The new queen was nothing like her insensitive sister, Anne, however—far from it. People didn't know that Mary had been instructed by William to be cheerful lest anyone assume she was uneasy about the couple's taking James II's throne. Gilbert Burnet actually asked her "how it came that what she saw in so sad a revolution as to her father's person, made not a greater impression on her." Mary explained that the former king's unhappy fate did indeed weigh heavily on her, but that she dared not show it. She admitted to Burnet that she went too far in demonstrations of cheer, acting a part that did not come naturally to her. The queen shared her deepest thoughts with her cousin Sophia of Hanover (mother of the future King George I): "Many people have the fortune to be able to talk of things about which I have to be silent. You must not doubt the sincerity of my feelings when I say that I cannot forget my father, and I grieve for his misfortune."

The taint of usurpation clung to Mary throughout her six-year reign—sometimes in disconcerting ways. On one occasion, when she coolly greeted her father's mistress, Catherine Sedley, the woman tartly riposted: "Why so proud, Madam? For if I broke one Commandment with your father, you broke another in coming here." Surely the height of Mary's mortification came when she attended a performance of Dryden's *The Spanish Friar*, unaware of some of the play's all-too-relevant dialogue. "What title has this Queen but lawless force?" read one devastating line. "And force must pull her down." All poor Mary could do was shield her face behind her fan as such lines were delivered and the eyes turned from the stage and bore into her.

Mortification was often mingled with genuine danger, as when the deposed James sought to reverse his fortunes and reclaim his crown by first invading Ireland with a French force. William and Mary were told of the former king's landing the morning of their joint coronation,* which obviously put a bit of a damper on the ceremony, as did a letter Mary received from her father just before she left for Westminster Abbey. "Hitherto, I have been willing to overlook what has been done," James wrote, "and thought your obedience to your husband and

---

* The ceremony was unique in British history as the only time a king and queen were ever crowned together as co-monarchs. The procedures for anointing the sovereign were followed exactly for both of them, and a replica of the traditional coronation chair was made for Mary. It is now on display at the Westminster Abbey Museum, along with life-sized wax effigies of William and Mary.

compliance to the nation might have prevailed. But your being crowned is in your power; if you do it while I and the Prince of Wales are living, the curses of an angry father will fall on you, as well as those of a God who commands obedience to parents."

William sailed to Ireland in June 1690 to meet James's threat, while Mary suffered from "the cruel thought that my husband and my father would fight in person against each other, and if either should have perished in the action, how terrible it would have been to me."

The queen needn't have worried, at least about her father, who kept a safe distance from the clash known as the Battle of the Boyne, and quickly scurried back to Dublin as his forces were defeated by William's. (Arriving there, he made a critical remark to Frances, Lady Tyrconnel, about the Irish fighters who had scattered after the battle. "Madam," he said, "your countrymen have run away." To this she rejoined, "If they have, Sire, Your Majesty seems to have won the race.") The former king's hopes to recapture his kingdom militarily were now destroyed, while his decided lack of valor on the battlefield prompted the Irish to dub him Seamus a' chaca, James the shit.

Mary heard early reports that her father had been captured in the battle and implored her husband to ensure his well-being. "I know I need not beg you to let him be taken care of," she wrote, "for I am confident you will for your own sake. Yet add that to all your kindness, and, for my sake, let people know you would have no harm come to his person." Clearly the queen still had some tender feelings left for her father, but they were not to last.

After his defeat at the Battle of the Boyne and rather ignominious flight afterward, James was derided at the French court at Versailles. "He lives always surrounded by friars and talks of his misfortunes with indifference, as if he did not feel them or had never been a king," one observer wrote; "in this way he entirely lost the respect of the French." Yet the de-throned king still had some spit in him and, with his cousin and host, Louis XIV, planned an invasion of England set for the spring of 1692.

Foolishly, though, James issued a declaration in which he announced that, once restored to the throne, he would rule exactly as he had before. William was away at the time, and Mary, who ruled quite ably during his absences, seized on the propaganda value of her father's silly manifesto and had it printed and distributed. Her action had the desired effect of crippling the ex-king's cause in England, but an invasion by James and the French was nevertheless still imminent. And Mary's life was in danger. "I was told of dreadful designs against me [by James's supporters, known as Jacobites]," she wrote, "and had reason to believe if their success answered their expectations, my life was certainly at an end."

Fortunately for Mary, the French fleet was destroyed in a fierce naval battle and the plots against her came to nothing. Her father, however, was not quite finished, and directly involved himself in a plot to assassinate William. "I have been informed of the business," James wrote to the chief conspirator. "If you and your companions do me this service, you shall never want."

The would-be assassin was ultimately exposed, and Mary was urged to publish the details of his trial, in which James was implicated. The queen, however, was extremely reluctant to make public what she regarded as her shame—"that he who I dare no more name father was consenting to the barbarous murder of my husband."

Mary was indeed tortured by her father's actions. "I was ashamed to look at anybody in the face," she wrote. "I fancied I should be pointed at as the daughter of one who was capable of such things, and the people would believe I might by nature have as ill inclinations. I lamented his sin and his shame." Most of all, though, Mary worried what William would think—that somehow the plot against his life "might lessen my husband's kindness for me."

William was really all the queen had; she was childless, her relationship with her father had been destroyed, and a vicious feud with her sister, Anne (see Chapter 16), alienated her from the only immediate family remaining. Mary adored her wheezy, slightly hunchbacked husband, the cousin she had reluctantly married when she was just a girl of fifteen. Theirs was one of the rare arranged royal marriages that actually worked. Her feelings for him were perhaps best expressed in a scene between them, recounted in her journal, when William was preparing his invasion force to topple James II and encouraged Mary to remarry if anything should happen to him:

> I was so much astonished by this proposal that it was long before I was able to reply. He protested that it was solely the concern he had for religion which could make him speak as he did, I don't remember all that I said. The grief I felt made my answers confused, but I assured him that I had never loved anyone but him, and would not know how to love someone else. And apart from that, having been married so many years without its having pleased God to bless me with a child, I believed that sufficient to prevent me ever thinking of what he proposed. I told him, that I begged God not to let me survive him; if however I should do so, since it had not pleased God to give me a child by him, I would not wish to have one by an angel.

William loved Mary, too, though for much of their marriage he treated her more as an ornament than a true equal—a dynamic she seemed to encourage by her deference to him in all matters. He often preferred the company of his male friends and his mistress, Elizabeth Villiers, which wounded Mary deeply. In time, however, he came to appreciate his wife's political sense and admired the way she managed the kingdom during his frequent absences. Their shared isolation in England also drew the couple closer.

"There was a union of their thoughts, as well as of their persons," wrote Gilbert Burnet, who spent much time with the co-monarchs, "and a concurring in the same designs, as well as in the same interests. . . . He was to conquer enemies, and she was to gain friends. . . . While he had more business, and she more leisure, she prepared and suggested what he executed."

It was only when Mary contracted smallpox in 1694 that William's deepest feelings for her burst forth. "He cried out that there was no hope for the Queen," Burnet recalled, astonished by the usually undemonstrative king's great show of emotion, "and that from being the happiest, he was now going to be the miserablest creature upon earth." The king was even more expressive to his friend the prince of Vaudémont: "You know what it is to have a good wife. If I were so unhappy as to lose mine, I should have to retire from this world."

On December 28, 1694, Queen Mary II succumbed to smallpox at age thirty-two. William was inconsolable, fainting at his wife's deathbed and shutting himself away for weeks on end. He even gave up his mistress in her honor. "If I could believe any mortal man could be born without the contamination of sin," the king told his confessor, "I would believe it of the Queen."

The reaction in France to Mary's death was significantly more subdued. Her father forbade anyone at his court to mourn her, and requested that Louis XIV do the same. It was, James said, a mighty affliction for him to see "a child he loved so tenderly persevere to her death in such a signal state of disobedience and disloyalty."

16

Anne (1702–1714): A Feud Too Many

I desire nothing but that she would leave off teasing and tormenting me.

—QUEEN ANNE

Queen Anne succeeded her brother-in-law William III after his death in 1702. She had voluntarily given up her right to immediately succeed her sister, Mary II, who died in 1694, as this had been one of William's conditions when he took the crown during the Glorious Revolution. Anne's reign, during which England and Scotland were unified as one kingdom, lasted until her death in 1714.

Mary II and her sister, Anne, had each participated in the revolution against their father. But no sooner was James II removed from his throne than their own relationship disintegrated in the throes of a bitter feud. It was a clash nurtured by Anne's servant and close companion Sarah Jennings Churchill, a formidable woman who completely dominated her royal mistress—until their storied friendship itself imploded after Anne became queen.

Anne and Sarah met as young girls, when Sarah became a maid of honor to Anne's stepmother, Mary Beatrice of Modena. "We had used to play together when she was a child," Sarah wrote, "and she even then expressed a particular fondness for me." The shy, somewhat plodding Anne, just seven at the time and recently left motherless, was indeed attracted to the pert, supremely confident Sarah, five years her senior. What developed was a bit of a schoolgirl crush, albeit a one-sided one. For though Anne clearly adored her older friend, showering upon her devoted love letters and other marks of affection, Sarah seems to have sensed only opportunity. She became part of Anne's household but found her mistress painfully dull—"ignorant of everything but what the parsons had taught her when a child."

Sarah's unflattering portrait of Anne was written years after their friendship ended and is extremely self-serving in parts. Nevertheless, it offers an intimate glimpse into their relationship, as do the numerous letters Anne wrote to her. (Few of Sarah's letters to Anne survive, so the feelings she expressed at the time are unknown.)

It certainly emerges that Anne was extremely devoted to her servant, almost obsessively so. "I have been in expectation of you a long time but can stay no longer without desiring to know what you intend to do with me, for it is most certain I can't go to bed without seeing you," Anne wrote while Sarah was away from court. "If you knew in what a condition you have made me I am sure you would pity [me]."

Sarah, smothered by Anne's attentions and needs, was decidedly less enthusiastic about spending time together but claimed she did so out of duty. "Though it was extremely tedious to be so much where there could be no manner of conversation," she wrote, "I knew she loved me, and suffered by fearing I did wrong when I was not with her; for which reason I have gone a thousand times to her, when I had rather have been in a dungeon."

What Sarah lost in scintillating conversation, she gained in ascendency over Anne, who was completely enthralled by her and happily followed her lead in almost everything. "It is certain she at length distinguished me by as high, or perhaps a higher place in her favour than any person ever arrived at, with queen or princess," Sarah wrote; "and if from hence I may draw any glory, it is that I both obtained and held this place without the assistance of flattery."

And as far as Sarah was concerned, Anne was lucky to have her, especially considering the alternatives. "Her Highness's court was throughout so oddly composed," she wrote, "that I think it would be making myself no great compliment, if I should say, her choosing to spend more of her time with me, than with any of her other servants, did no discredit to her taste."

As a mark of Anne's favor, and of her insistence that they treat each other as equals, the women adopted cozy names for each other that they would employ for the remaining years of their friendship. Anne became Mrs. Morley, and Sarah was Mrs. Freeman. Eventually Sarah's overfamiliarity and sharp tongue would recoil against her, but for many years Anne basked in her friend's irreverence. Secure in her position as confidante and advisor, Sarah used her position to poison the relationship between Anne and her sister.

She was ambitious for her husband, John Churchill,* who she believed would be well rewarded for abandoning James II and supporting William of Orange in his invasion of the kingdom. William distrusted Churchill, however, calling him "a vile man," and told Gilbert Burnet that "though he [William] had himself profited by [Churchill's] treason, he abhorred the traitor." It quickly became apparent that the Churchills, aside from being granted the earldom of Marlborough, would have no friends in William and Mary, and that all their hopes for honor and advancement would have to be centered on the heir to the throne, Anne. Isolating her from the king and queen, in the guise of

* The famed general, ancestor of Winston Churchill, was also the lover of Charles II's mistress Barbara Palmer, Duchess of Cleveland, and was believed to have fathered the child King Charles refused to acknowledge as his own (see Chapter 13).

friendship, would serve their ends by increasing Anne's dependence on them and her gratitude for their service to her cause.

The seeds of estrangement were already there before the Churchills even made their first move. "It was indeed impossible [Anne and Mary] should be very agreeable companions to each other," Sarah wrote, "because Queen Mary grew weary of anybody who would not talk a great deal, and the Princess [Anne] was so silent that she rarely spoke more than was necessary to answer a question."

Furthermore, Anne had come to loathe her brother-in-law William, whom she lovingly referred to as "the Dutch abortion." She had already grudgingly ceded to William her place in the line of succession immediately after Mary, as he had insisted, but she really resented the king's treatment of her extremely dull husband, Prince George of Denmark.* William took as little notice of George "if he had been a page of the back stairs," Sarah noted, and even refused him a place in his coach on the way to the Battle of the Boyne. Anne, who loved her boring spouse, bristled at the slight.

In an act sure to stir up trouble between William and Mary and their heir, the Churchills helped arrange for a motion in Parliament that would give Anne an allowance far in excess of what she already received from the king and queen. Mary, stunned that Anne would go behind their backs in such an unprecedented way, confronted her sister. When Anne blithely informed her that she had some friends in the House of Commons who wished to see her income increased, Mary was incensed. "Pray," the queen replied imperiously, "what friends have you but the king and me?" With that, a feud was born.

William tried to reason with his stubborn sister-in-law by promising her an increased income if she would cease soliciting

---

* Charles II offered this assessment of his niece Anne's husband: "I have tried him drunk, and I have tried him sober; and there is nothing in him."

Parliament. But Sarah was right there to remind her that the king had broken promises to her before. Anne remained adamant, telling William's representative, Lord Shrewsbury, "The business is now gone so far that I think it reasonable to see what my friends can do for me." In the end, Anne won her parliamentary allowance, which both infuriated and frightened her sister the queen.

While William was away fighting her father in France, Mary was confronted by unrest at home among supporters of the deposed king, as well as threats from France. The last thing she needed was trouble from her sister, who should have been there to support her. The queen worried that her government was under siege by a Jacobite party that had formed around her father, a second party in favor of a republic, and, she wrote, "I have reason to believe that my sister forms a third."

Mary was placid by nature and wanted harmony with Anne but wrote that she "saw plainly that [Anne] was so absolutely governed by Lady Marlborough that it was to no purpose." Sarah, on the other hand, disingenuously claimed in her memoir that she in fact tried to be a peacemaker. "It was impossible for any body to labour more than I did to keep the two sisters in perfect unison and friendship," she wrote, "thinking it best for them not to quarrel when their true interest and safety were jointly concerned to support the revolution."

While Sarah claimed that she was encouraging Anne to support William and Mary's government, her disenchanted husband was at the same time making overtures of rapprochement to the exiled king he had betrayed, James II. Perhaps it was just a cynical maneuver on Marlborough's part to protect his interests should James or his son ever recover the crown, but to William and Mary it was unpardonable treason. Marlborough was relieved of all his offices in a sensational turn of events, made all the more so because William declined to publicly explain the reason. He told one member of Parliament only that "the Earl had treated him in such a manner that he would have asked him for satisfaction with the sword [in a duel] if he had not been king."

Marlborough's disgrace should have been his wife's as well. But just two weeks after the earl's dismissal, Anne came prancing into court with Sarah in tow. It was an astonishing breach of etiquette and a direct insult to the king and queen. Mary was livid. "I have all the reason imaginable to look upon your bringing her as the strangest thing that was ever done," she wrote to her sister. Not only should Anne have known better than to bring Sarah to court, the queen asserted, but it was wrong of Anne to even retain Sarah in her household. "I know what is due to me," Mary continued, "and I expect to have it from you. 'Tis upon that account I tell you plainly, Lady Marlborough must not continue with you, in the circumstances [in which] her lord is."

Anne had no intention of dismissing her friend, even if it meant disobeying her sovereign. In her reply to Mary, she expressed surprise that the queen had even made the demand, "for you must needs be sensible enough of the kindness I have for my Lady Marlborough, to know that a command from you to part from her must be the greatest mortification in the world to me, and, indeed, of such a nature, as I might well have hoped your kindness to me would have always prevented."

The honorable thing for Sarah would have been to resign, which is what some of her friends urged her to do. But Sarah wouldn't budge. There was too much to be gained from her relationship with Anne, and according to a report from the Dutch envoy, "she hopes to maintain herself in the Princess's favor for as long as possible." Besides, Anne would never have suffered her absence anyway. "Mrs. Freeman . . . must give me leave to tell her, if she should ever be so cruel to leave her faithful Mrs. Morley, she will rob her of all the joy and quiet of her life; for if that day should come, I could never enjoy a happy minute, and I swear to you I would shut myself up and never see a creature." Thus, Sarah remained in Anne's service and presided over a dramatic escalation of the feud between the royal sisters.

In a rather dramatic gesture of defiance, Anne abandoned "the Cockpit," as her apartments at Whitehall Palace were known, and absented herself from court, writing to her sister sarcastically that she was "too much indisposed to give Your Majesty any further trouble at this time." Mary retaliated by removing Anne's guards and decreeing that anyone who visited her sister would not be welcome at court. In a final insult, William's Dutch guards refused to salute Anne's husband, Prince George, as he departed Whitehall. "I cannot believe it was their Dutch breeding alone without Dutch orders that made them do it because they never omitted it before," Anne told Sarah, adding, "These things are so far from vexing either the Prince or me that they really please us extremely."

Mary did come to see her sister in the spring of 1692, after Anne gave birth to yet another child who died almost immediately.* As Sarah reported, the queen "never asked how she did, nor expressed the least concern for her condition, nor so much as took her by the hand." She did, however, reissue a by now familiar order: "I have made the first step in coming to you," she said, "and now expect you should make the next by removing my Lady Marlborough."

"I have never disobeyed you but in that one particular," Anne replied, "which I hope will some time or other appear as unreasonable to you as it does to me."

Of course it would never seem unreasonable to Mary that the wife of a disloyal subject be removed from her sister's service. As the breach with Anne widened, the queen despaired that the

---

* Anne endured eighteen pregnancies, but only one of her children, William, Duke of Gloucester, survived infancy. His death at age eleven opened the way for the Hanoverian succession.

conflict might be the natural consequence of what she and her sister had done to their father. "In all this I see the hand of God," she wrote, "and look upon our disagreeing as a punishment upon us for the irregularity by us committed upon the revolution."

The sisters never were reconciled. It was only when Mary was on her deathbed that Anne rushed to be with her. But by then it was too late. Tireless in her troublemaking, Sarah later asserted that Anne had been deliberately kept away during her sister's illness so as "to leave room for continuing the quarrel, in case the Queen should chance to recover. . . . How this conduct to a sister could suit with the character of a devout Queen, I am at a loss to know."

With Mary dead, and William to follow seven years later, Sarah turned on her friend Anne with a ferocity that left poor Mrs. Morley shattered.

On April 23, 1702, Anne was crowned queen to near universal acclaim. The reign of the dour Dutchman William III was over, and no one seemed to miss him. The new monarch, while warmly welcomed, hardly presented a regal figure. Eighteen pregnancies had ruined her health, and gout left her so crippled that she had to be carried to her coronation in a chair. Still, she aimed to be a moderate ruler in an era of venomous party politics, which would be a triumph in itself. But it ruined her relationship with Sarah.

The new queen had showered her favorite with the highest honors upon her accession, and soon created the dukedom of Marlborough for her husband in recognition of his valor in fighting the French. But Sarah wanted something more: She wanted to be *obeyed*. Anne had always been willingly led by her domineering friend, but now she was the sovereign and a shift in the relationship was inevitable. Sarah refused to accept that. It was bad enough that the queen bored her, but for Anne to ignore her increasingly strident exhortations on behalf of the Whig Party was simply intolerable.

The queen had a more natural affinity for the Tory Party, traditional supporters of the monarchy and of Anne's beloved Anglican Church. She found Sarah's aggressive Whig affiliation bewildering, particularly her wild assertion that all Tories were secret Jacobites conspiring to restore James II. "I own that I can not have that good opinion of some sort of people that you have," the queen wrote to Sarah, "nor that ill one of others, and let the Whigs brag never so much of their great services to the country [in the Glorious Revolution] and of their numbers, I believe the revolution had never been, nor the Succession settled as it is now, if the Church party [Tories] had not joined with them, and why those people that agreed with them in these two things should all now be branded with the name Jacobite I can't imagine."

Anne's refusal to complacently accept direction, combined with the fact that she found court life stultifying, caused Sarah to stay away for extended periods. Yet her absences also made her paranoid that she was being supplanted in the queen's affection by her own relative Abigail Hill, a bedchamber woman who Sarah believed was poisoning Anne's mind against her.

Sarah's fears did not prompt her return to court. Instead, she bombarded the queen with shrill letters that essentially said Anne was too stupid, or stubborn, to see reason. In one particularly outrageous missive, fired off over Queen Anne's persistent refusal to appoint Sarah's son-in-law as secretary of state, she wrote: "I desire you would reflect whether you have never heard that the greatest misfortunes that ever happened to any of your family [the Stuarts] has not been occasioned by having ill advises and an obstinancy in their tempers that is very unaccountable."

This kind of audacious attack clearly indicated that something in Sarah had snapped. She had "grown into a shrew," P. F. William Ryan wrote colorfully in his early-twentieth-century study of Queen Anne's court, "a virago, afraid of nothing, in love with nothing, a mad woman when crossed, so disastrously had the natural tyranny of her disposition been pampered by the compliance of those who had learned to dread her tongue." No wonder the ailing queen was beginning to prefer the quiet company of her servant Abigail Hill.

Anne was actually growing frightened of her once beloved Mrs. Freeman, though she wasn't quite prepared to part with her. "I agree that all Lady Marlborough's unkindness proceeds from [the] real concern she has for my good," the queen wrote to her minister Sidney Godolphin, "but I can't hope as you do, that she will ever be easy with me again. I quite despair of it now, which is no small mortification to me, however I will ever be the same, and ready on all occasions to do her all the service that lies in my poor power."

As it turned out, Sarah's abuse of the queen had barely even begun. She raged at the influence she believed Abigail had on Anne, and went so far as to assert that they were lesbians. "I remember you said . . . of all things in this world, you valued most your reputation," Sarah wrote spitefully, "which I confess surprised me very much, that Your Majesty should so soon mention that word after having discovered so great a passion for such a woman, for sure there can be no great reputation in a thing so strange and unaccountable, to say no more of it, nor can I think the having no inclination for any but of one's own sex is enough to maintain such a character as I wish may still be yours."

Several weeks later, on the way to a thanksgiving service for the Duke of Marlborough's victory over the French at Oudenaarde, Sarah berated the queen for not wearing the heavy jewels she had laid out for her. Anne was responding as their coach arrived at St. Paul's Cathedral, when the duchess snarled, "Be quiet!" This was truly no way to treat a queen, but Sarah was unrepentant. In fact, she added to the grievous insult by sending Anne a nasty note chastising her for what had transpired: "Your Majesty chose a very wrong day to mortify me, when you were just going to return thanks for a victory obtained by Lord Marlborough."

The already precarious relationship between Mrs. Morley and Mrs. Freeman was further fractured after the death of Anne's beloved husband in 1708. Perhaps there was no time in the queen's life when she needed a true friend more. Alas, all she found was Sarah.

The duchess swooped into Kensington Palace and found Anne at Prince George's deathbed, weeping and kissing him tenderly. She decided the queen should leave the scene, but Anne silently demurred, pointing to her watch to indicate that she needed more time. After indulging this, reluctantly, Sarah gripped Anne's arm firmly to lead her away. Then the dreaded Abigail crossed their path. Sarah was outraged by the acknowledgment the queen accorded her loyal servant, writing that "at the sight of that charming lady, as her [Anne's] arm was upon mine, which she had leaned upon, I found she had strength to bend down towards [Abigail] like a sail, and in passing by, went some steps more than was necessary, to be nearer her."

Such was the depth of Sarah's sympathy that she actually mocked the queen's sorrow by noting how she ate two hearty meals in the midst of it. She also decided to remove Prince George's portrait from Anne's bedroom because, she lamely explained, "I thought she loved him, and if she had been like other people 'tis terrible to see a picture while the affliction is just upon one." The queen thought otherwise, and was reduced to pleading with Sarah for the portrait's return: "I cannot end this without begging you once more for God sake to let the dear picture you have of mine, be put into my bedchamber for I cannot be without it any longer."

Having satisfied her duty to serve the newly widowed queen—her way—Sarah swept out of court and away from Anne, though she did continue to harass her. Now she wanted to expand the Marlboroughs' apartments at St. James's Palace, which Anne refused to allow. Sarah, "being resolved that I would vex her a little longer," insisted that the queen's denial be repeated publicly, certain it would be thought strange, she wrote, "that after the service Lord Marlborough had done her, she would not give him a miserable hole to make him a clean way to his lodgings."

The Duke of Marlborough made the mistake of entering Sarah's quarrel with the queen and taking his wife's side. He wrote to Anne, threatening to resign his services at the conclusion of the war with France, and "hoping that in time you will be sensible of the long and faithful services of Lady Marlborough and that God will bless you with the opening of your eyes."

This was too much for Anne, who, in her response to Marlborough, poured out all the hurt and anger that had accumulated within her. "You seem to be dissatisfied with my behaviour to the Duchess of Marlborough," she wrote.

> I do not love complaining, but it is impossible to help saying on this occasion, I believe nobody was ever so used by a friend as I have been by her since my coming to the Crown. I desire nothing but that she would leave off teasing and tormenting me and behave herself with the decency she ought, both to her friend and Queen, and this I hope you will make her do, and is what I am sure no unreasonable body can wonder I should desire of you, whatever her behaviour is to me, mine to her shall be always as becomes me.
>
> I shall end this letter as you did yours to me, wishing both your eyes and the Duchess of Marlborough's may be opened and that you may ever be happy.

Sarah launched a fierce tirade against the queen in a series of long missives. She not only threatened to publish Anne's gushing letters but once again essentially accused her of having a homosexual affair with Abigail. The friendship was now finally and irretrievably dead. Still, Sarah sought to vindicate herself and asked for a personal interview with the queen. Anne would not agree, however, and commanded the duchess to put her thoughts in writing. Of course Sarah didn't listen.

Several days later she again wrote to Anne and insisted she speak to the queen: "If this afternoon be not convenient, I will come every day, and wait till you please to allow me to speak with you. And one thing more I assure Your Majesty which is, *that what I have to say will have no consequence either in obliging you to answer* or to see me oftener hereafter than will be easy to you."

The two women did meet for the last time that afternoon at Kensington Palace. Queen Anne was as cold and hardened as her statue in front of St. Paul's Cathedral. "There is nothing you can have to say but you may write it," she kept repeating after every point Sarah tried to make. Then, in response to the duchess's direct questions, Anne was equally noncommunicative: "I shall make no answer to anything you say."

Furious at the queen's intransigence, and desperate about the power and influence she saw slipping away, Sarah was reduced to threats and blackmail. "Such things are in my power," she declared, "that if known by a man, that would apprehend and was a right politician, might lose a Crown."

After being dismissed from the queen's service, Sarah vindictively trashed her apartments at St. James's Palace, ripping out everything—right down to the doorknobs. In retaliation, Anne ordered a temporary halt to construction of the Marlboroughs' magnificent new home, Blenheim Palace, stating angrily "that she would not build the Duke a house when the Duchess was pulling hers to pieces."

The Duke and Duchess of Marlborough left England in disgrace in 1713, not to return until the day after Queen Anne died less than two years later. By then it had been ages since Mrs. Morley had been able to write confidently, "I really believe one kind word from dear Mrs. Freeman would save me if I was gasping."

PART III

House of Hanover

GEORGE I
(reigned 1714–1727)

GEORGE II
(r. 1727–1760)

GEORGE III
(r. 1760–1820)

GEORGE IV
(r. 1820–1830)

WILLIAM IV
(r. 1830–1837)

VICTORIA
(r. 1837–1901)

House of Hanover

GEORGE I
r. 1714–1727
m. Sophia Dorothea of Celle

GEORGE II
r. 1727–1760
m. Caroline of Anspach

Frederick,
Prince of Wales
m. Augusta of Saxe-Gotha

William,
Duke of Cumberland
(defeated Charles Edward Stuart
"The Young Pretender" at Culloden)

Augusta
m. Charles William Ferdinand,
Duke of Brunswick

GEORGE III
r. 1760–1820
m. Charlotte of Mecklenburg-Strelitz

Others

Caroline of   m.   **GEORGE IV**
Brunswick   r. 1820–1830

Frederick,
Duke of York

WILLIAM IV
r. 1830–1837
m. Adelaide of
Saxe-Meninger

Charlotte
m. Leopold of Saxe-
Coburg-Saalfeld
(later King Leopold I
of Belgium)

Louisa   Others
m. Frederick V of Denmark

Caroline Matilda ------ m. ------ Christian VII of Denmark

Edward,   Ernest,   Others
Duke of Kent   Duke of Cumberland and
m. Victoria of Saxe-Coburg-Saalfeld   King of Hanover

VICTORIA
r. 1837–1901
m. Albert of Saxe-Coburg and Gotha

EDWARD VII
(House of Saxe-Coburg-
Gotha to Windsor)

17

George I (1714–1727): His Heart
Was in Hanover

In private life he would have been called an honest
blockhead.

—LADY MARY WORTLEY MONTAGU

*Following the death of Queen Anne in 1714, her Protestant cousin George,
sovereign of the German duchy of Hanover, succeeded her as King George I.
Although the late queen had closer relatives, including her exiled father,
James II, and his son, James Edward Stuart, the Act of Settlement of 1701
barred these Catholic Stuarts from inheriting the throne. Instead, the law
decreed that the crown would pass to the Protestant descendants of James I's
daughter, Elizabeth (see Stuart family tree, pages 70–71). Thus, Elizabeth's
grandson came to Britain from Germany and established the royal House of
Hanover. George I would rule until his death in 1727.*

George I was accompanied by a rather eccentric retinue when
he came from Hanover to claim the British throne in 1714.
Among them were the king's stalk-thin mistress, Melusine von
der Schulenburg, whom the English immediately dubbed the
Maypole, and his enormous half-sister, Sophia von Kiel-
mansegg (also rumored to have been his mistress), who came to

be known as the Elephant and Castle.* Then there were George's Turkish servants, Mehomet and Mustafa, and his dwarf, Christian Ulrich Jorry. The only person missing from this odd mélange was the new king's wife, Sophia Dorothea of Celle. She was stuck back in Germany—imprisoned in a castle for cheating on the husband she hated.

The marriage had not been a good one—arranged, like so many royal unions, for reasons of state. Sophia Dorothea was horrified when she learned she was to be wed to her boorish cousin from the neighboring duchy of Hanover. And with good reason. Her intended was, according to his own mother, "the most pigheaded, stubborn boy who ever lived, and who has round his brains such a thick crust that I defy any man or woman ever to discover what is in there."

George wasn't overly enthused about the arrangement, either. But Sophia Dorothea's fat dowry had its compensations. "He does not care for the match itself," his mother reported, "but one hundred thousand thalers a year have tempted him as they would have anybody else."

The woefully mismatched couple were wed on November 22, 1682. "There were priests and prayers and benedictions," wrote historian William Henry Wilkins, "all the pomp and heraldry and the pageantry of Courts; yet when all was stripped away this marriage was nothing but a shameless bargain, and a young girl's life [she was sixteen] was sold to a man steeped in

* The essayist Horace Walpole, son of King George's minister Horace, left a particularly vivid description of this oversized matron, who apparently terrified him as a child: "Two fierce black eyes, large and rolling beneath two lofty arched eyebrows, two acres of cheeks spread with crimson, an ocean of neck that overflowed and was not distinguished from the lower part of her body, and no part restrained by a stay . . . no wonder that a child dreaded such an ogress, and that the mob of London were highly diverted at the importation of so uncommon a seraglio!"

selfishness and profligacy and who did not even make a pretext of loving her."

Almost as soon as he said "I do," George abandoned his bride and took up with his emaciated mistress, Melusine, by whom he had three daughters. Sophia Dorothea was left alone and isolated in the scheming court at Hanover. Her harridan of a mother-in-law hated her, while her father-in-law's grasping mistress, Countess Clara von Platen, actively conspired against her. "I believe all my troubles will come through her," Sophia Dorothea wrote of Clara. And she was right.

Living in this lonely, oppressive atmosphere made Sophia Dorothea more than receptive to the attentions of a dashing Swedish officer named Philip Christoph von Königsmarck. The relationship began innocently enough, with Königsmarck's flattering flirtations, but quickly evolved into a passionate affair that proved disastrous.

Both lovers unwittingly prophesied their doom in the letters they exchanged. "I am ready to cast at your feet my life, my honour, my future, my fortune," Königsmarck wrote in one slightly overwrought missive. In another letter, Sophia Dorothea declared that life without him would be intolerable, "and imprisonment within four walls pleasanter than to go on living in the world." As it turned out, his life would be sacrificed and she would find herself locked away.

The lovers were dangerously indiscreet, and their plans to run away together revealed them to be hopelessly naïve as well. This was a matter of state, the powers of which would be activated against them should they ever attempt to flee.

It has been said that Clara von Platen, furious over Königsmarck's rejection of her advances, informed George and his father, the elector of Hanover (who was also her lover), about the affair. She also allegedly arranged for the ambush of Königsmarck outside Sophia Dorothea's apartments on the night of July 1, 1694. Though this is just one of several theories about what happened that night, what remains certain is that Königsmarck was never seen again. One widely circulated story held that George ordered the body of his wife's lover hacked to pieces and buried beneath the floorboards of his palace. His treatment of Sophia Dorothea was arguably even crueler. She was shut up in a castle prison, deprived of her children, for the rest of her life.

Such was the situation when Queen Anne, Britain's final Stuart monarch, breathed her last and George, as her nearest *Protestant* relative, was proclaimed king. Almost immediately upon his arrival, he became the object of ridicule. There was just something vaguely absurd about the dull, remote German who couldn't even speak the language of his new subjects. "The King's character may be comprised in very few words," wrote Lady Mary Wortley Montagu. "In private life he would have been called an honest blockhead."

King George was horribly out of his element in his new kingdom, with its vicious party politics and the gross irreverence shown the sovereign. The statesman Philip Stanhope, Lord Chesterfield, was one wickedly precise commentator on the king's peccadillos. "The standard of His Majesty's taste," he wrote, "as exemplified in his mistresses, makes all ladies who aspire to his favour . . . strain and swell themselves, like the frogs in the fable, to rival the bulk and dignity of the ox. Some succeed, and others . . . burst."

George I ruled Britain for just under thirteen years, an effective but uninspiring monarch who never warmed to his people nor they to him. "His heart was in Hanover," William Makepeace Thackeray wrote of the king. "He was more than fifty-four years of age when he came amongst us: we took him because we wanted him, because he served our turn; we laughed at his uncouth German ways, and sneered at him."

Then they forgot him.

18

George II (1727–1760): A Boorish,
Oversexed Bully

I lost my eldest son, but was glad of it.

—King George II

Like his father, George I, whom he succeeded in 1727, George II was born in Hanover, and was thus Britain's last foreign-born monarch. His reign was marked by the Seven Years' War—from which Britain emerged as Europe's dominant colonial power—and even more savage domestic battles with his son and heir, Prince Frederick.

George I introduced to Britain not only a new royal dynasty but a virulent tradition among the Hanoverian monarchs of hatred toward their heirs. The first George so loathed his son, the future George II, that after one particularly nasty spat he had the prince arrested, snatched away his children, then booted him out of St. James's Palace. But that behavior was positively tender compared with the way George II treated his own son Frederick, of whom he once lovingly said, "Our first-born is the greatest ass, the greatest liar, the greatest canaille and the greatest beast in the whole world and we heartily wish he was out of it."*

---

* Those sweet sentiments have also been attributed to Frederick's mother, Queen Caroline of Ansbach.

It is not exactly clear what Frederick might have done to earn his father's unceasing animosity, other than exist. Sure, he was a little on the lecherous side, but so was George II, and George I before him. As a matter of fact, all three generations availed themselves at various times of the same mistress, Madame d'Elitz, who was rather ancient by the time she deflowered Frederick when he was sixteen. (When someone once observed that there was nothing new under the sun when it came to Madame d'Elitz's promiscuity, the English politician and wit George Selwyn is said to have retorted, "Or under the grandson.")

Frederick was abandoned in Hanover as a little boy of seven when his parents and siblings left the German duchy to join George I as he claimed the British crown in 1714. There the child languished, essentially orphaned, for the next fourteen years. His parents hoped it would be longer. They actively schemed to keep Frederick out of England, not even inviting him to his father's coronation after the death of George I in 1727. "Poor Fred," as he came to be called, had no idea that his mom and dad were conspiring against him. "My only consolation in this sad affliction [grief over the death of his grandfather King George] is the knowledge of my dear parents' goodness," he wrote to his sister. "I flatter myself that I shall always conduct myself in a manner deserving of their esteem and friendship for me."

It was only when Frederick tried to marry his cousin Princess Wilhelmina of Prussia—in essence, conducting his own foreign policy*—that he was allowed to come to England, where he might be more carefully controlled. The welcome was not exactly warm. Frederick barely knew his mother and father and would soon find out how horrible they really were.

---

* George II had this to say about nixing the proposed match: "I did not think that ingrafting my half-witted coxcomb upon a mad woman would improve the breed."

George II was a boorish, oversexed bully who, Lady Mary Wortley Montagu wrote, "looks on all men and women he sees as creatures he might kiss or kick for his diversion." Queen Caroline of Ansbach, who shared her husband's hatred for their eldest son, was a brilliant politician but grasping and manipulative. "Her predominant passion was pride," Lord Hervey wrote, "and the darling pleasure of her soul was power." Caroline indulged the king's lusty forays outside the marriage, even discussing with him in vivid detail the relative merits of his unattractive mistresses,* all the while pursuing her own political agenda with Prime Minister Robert Walpole. A popular verse of the time satirized the royal power structure:

> *You may strut, dapper George, but 'twill all be in vain,*
> *We all know 'tis Queen Caroline, not you, that reign.*

George and Caroline had once been outcasts from the court of George I, establishing their own alternative court at their London residence, Leicester House, where they made fun of the oafish king and nurtured opposition to his government. But the glitter and excitement that surrounded them as Prince and Princess of Wales all but disappeared once George II came to the throne. The king established a stultifying routine in which nearly every activity was militaristically timed—down to when he would sleep with his mistress. "No mill horse ever went on a more constant track or a more unchanging circle," Lord Hervey wrote.

Prince Frederick, by contrast, brought a refreshing lack of pretense with him from Hanover, as well as spontaneity, generosity, and charm. "I am extremely pleased that I can tell you without flattery or partiality that our young prince has all the

---

* "No woman comes amiss of him if she were but very willing and very fat," was one devastating commentary on the king's tastes.

accomplishments that 'tis possible to have at his age," Lady Montagu wrote to a friend, "with an air of sprightliness and understanding, and something so very engaging and easy in his behaviour, that he needs not the advantage of his rank to appear charming." All of London seemed enamored with the affable, sometimes outrageous prince, which distressed his parents no end. "My God!" Queen Caroline exclaimed. "Popularity always makes me sick, but Fretz's popularity makes me vomit."

The hostility of the king and queen toward their son was reflected in his allowance, which was about half of what George II enjoyed when he was Prince of Wales. Frederick was also kept far away from any matters of state, which left him plenty of time for mischief. His debts were enormous and his dalliances indiscriminate. Indeed at one point he managed to impregnate not only his mistress, Anne Vane, but her chambermaid as well. Furthermore, like his own father in the previous reign, the prince was beginning to attract opponents of the king's policies. A mighty rift was growing, one that nearly destroyed the great composer George Frideric Handel when he was dragged into it.

When it came to culture, George II was a Philistine.* Nevertheless he loved Handel, who composed the music for his coronation. The king and queen, along with their daughter Princess Anne, faithfully attended his operas at the King's Theatre, where the socially ambitious gathered to bask in the royal presence. Handel came to represent the very essence of refinement. Recognizing this, Frederick set out to wound his father by ruining his favorite composer. The prince and his supporters established a rival opera company at the Lincoln's Inn Fields Theatre, run first by the Italian composer Giovanni Battista

---

* So was his father. "I hate all boets and bainters," George I famously remarked.

Bononcini, then by another Italian, Nicola Porpora. Talent was lured away from Handel's theater, as well as patronage by the younger nobility, among whom Frederick was far more popular than his father. On many nights the King's Theatre was nearly empty, forcing Handel to spend more and more money in an effort to keep competitive and stay afloat. His nerves, to say nothing of his wallet, took a severe beating. And though the opera wars eventually ended peacefully, the clash between King George and Prince Frederick only grew in ferocity.

Frederick married sixteen-year-old Augusta of Saxe-Gotha in 1736 and wanted an income for his new wife. He also wanted an increase in his own paltry allowance, which could be reduced at the whim of his father. So, he appealed to Parliament. The king and queen trembled with rage when they learned that their son had maneuvered around them; it would be a tremendous blow to their prestige if he prevailed. Lord Hervey recorded Queen Caroline's reaction as she watched Frederick walking across a palace courtyard:

"Look there he goes—that wretch! That villain! I wish the ground would open up and sink the monster to the lowest hole in hell. You stare at me, but I can assure you if my wishes and prayers had any effect, and that the maledictions of a mother signified anything, his days would not be very happy or very many."

Anxious as the king and queen were about the political consequences if Frederick succeeded in Parliament, they couldn't bring themselves to simply pay the prince what the king himself received when he was in the same position. Thus, the matter did go before both the Commons and the House of Lords, and thanks in part to some well-placed bribes by the king, Frederick lost. His parents were thrilled. They wanted to toss him out of St. James's Palace as punishment for his insolence but were dissuaded only by Walpole's suggestion that the popular prince on the loose—made a martyr by his mother and father—might become too potent a political force. Still, they were determined to make their son's life as miserable as possible.

When Frederick announced that his young wife was pregnant, the couple was ordered to Hampton Court so that the king and queen could keep a closer eye on them and also avoid any popular acclamation of the birth in London. Of course the atmosphere was toxic, and as Augusta prepared to deliver, Frederick was determined to whisk her away from his noxious parents. The couple escaped under cover of darkness and made their way back to St. James's Palace by coach. By the time they arrived, Princess Augusta was in labor.

Meanwhile, back at Hampton Court, the king and queen were awakened with the news that Frederick and Augusta had escaped. Queen Caroline had suggested that her son was impotent and was therefore determined to be present at the birth to assure that a changeling wasn't proffered as legitimate royal issue. "At her labour I positively will be," she declared, "let her lie-in be where she will." Caroline, her daughters, and the rest of the royal retinue raced off to London, where they were amiably greeted by Frederick and told that the child, a baby girl, had already been delivered. After seeing the little princess, Queen Caroline pronounced herself satisfied that the baby was indeed Frederick's.

"I owe . . . I had my doubts upon the road that there would be some juggle," she said afterward. "And if, instead of this poor, little, ugly she-mouse, there had been a brave, large, fat, jolly boy, I should not have been cured of my suspicions. Nay, I believe that they would have been so much increased, or rather, that I should have been confirmed in my opinion, that I should have gone about this house like a mad woman, played the devil, and insisted on knowing what chairman's brat he [Frederick] had bought."

Running away with one's wife in labor was not as bad as, say, abandoning one's seven-year-old son in another country. But for King George and Queen Caroline it was an act of unforgivable defiance. "I hope in God that I shall never see the monster's face again," ranted the queen, while the king gleefully plotted his revenge—even as he appointed himself godfather to the new baby. "This extravagant and undutiful behaviour in so essential a point as the birth of an heir to my crown is such an evidence of your premeditated defiance of me," the king wrote, "and such a contempt of my authority and of the natural right belonging to your parents, as cannot be excused by the pretended innocence of your intentions, nor palliated or disguised by specious words only."

The prince and his little family were banished from all the royal palaces. Notice was then given to all foreign diplomats and members of the nobility that anyone who paid their respects to the Prince and Princess of Wales would no longer be welcome in the king's presence. "Thank God tomorrow night the puppy will be sent out of my house," King George rejoiced on the eve of his son's removal.

It was a precipitous decision, reminiscent of the king's own banishment by George I, and it rebounded badly. The opposition rallied around Frederick, just as it had around George II when he was Prince of Wales. Furthermore, it was utterly ineffective in its intent to harm the prince. On the contrary, Frederick reveled in the freedom he found far away from his father and his suffocating court. Worst of all, his popularity soared.

Queen Caroline expressed her desire never to see her son again. And in the end she got her wish. Two months after Frederick's banishment, she lay dying. The prince asked that he might visit his mother and comfort her in her illness, but King George wouldn't hear of it. "He wants to come and insult his poor dying mother," the indignant monarch roared. "But she shall not see him. I could never let that villain come near her. And whilst she has her senses she would never desire it. No. No! He shall not come and act any of his silly plays here, false, lying, cowardly, nauseous puppy."

Caroline's deathbed scene was touching as she bade farewell to the children she liked and urged her husband to remarry. ("No," the king sobbed. "I shall have mistresses.") As for Frederick, the queen was unmoved, stating that "at least I shall have one comfort in having my eyes eternally closed: I shall never see that monster again."

After siring eight more children,* including the future King George III, Prince Frederick died in 1751 at the relatively young age of forty-four. "This has been a fatal year to my family," George II wrote several months later. "I lost my eldest son, but was glad of it."

* Frederick was, by all accounts, a much kinder father than his own father had been. "He played the father and husband well," a contemporary observed, "always most happy in the bosom of his family, left them with regret and met them again with smiles, kisses and tears."

19

George II (1727–1760):

Bonnie Prince Charlie

I have taken a firm resolution to conquer or to die.

—CHARLES EDWARD STUART,

AKA BONNIE PRINCE CHARLIE

The first two Hanoverian kings of Britain faced regular threats from the Catholic heirs of the previous Stuart dynasty, who had been barred from the throne by the Act of Settlement in 1701. The most dangerous of these periodic uprisings was the one led by Charles Edward Stuart in 1745.

George II had a far greater cause for concern than his despised son, Frederick, when, in 1745, a dashing remnant of the old Stuart royal dynasty—popularly known as Bonnie Prince Charlie—rose up and came dangerously close to capturing his kingdom. Though the enterprise ultimately ended in a bloody massacre (overseen by the one son King George actually did like), it was filled with enough daring and adventure to make the charismatic Stuart claimant a legend.

Charles Edward Stuart, the would-be conqueror, also

known as the Young Pretender,* was the grandson of James II, the Catholic king with autocratic tendencies, and the son of James Edward Stuart, or the Old Pretender, whose birth in 1688 helped precipitate the Glorious Revolution that swept King James off his throne (see Chapter 14).

The exiled Stuarts had made numerous attempts to reclaim the crown since James II's ignominious flight from England in 1688, all of which had been spectacular failures. This left the Old Pretender—or King James III, as he called himself after the death of his father in 1701—utterly dejected and in a near constant state of melancholy as he tried to maintain the pretense of majesty in his shadow court. "For me," the Old Pretender groaned to his officers after one of his many failed attempts to capture the crown, "it is no new thing to be unfortunate, since my whole life from my cradle has been a constant series of misfortunes." It was an honest assessment, but hardly an inspiring one.

In contrast to his brooding, morose father, Charles Edward Stuart practically pulsated with vigor and was driven to take up the cause the demoralized Old Pretender had all but abandoned. The Young Pretender's infectious spirit and bold ambition rallied people around him and left them in awe of his princely qualities. "There is . . . such an unspeakable majesty diffused through his whole mien as it is impossible to have any idea without seeing," one young Scot enthused after meeting Charles in Rome. "He appears to be born and endowed for something extraordinary."

Another of the Young Pretender's supporters, Arthur Elphinstone, Lord Balmerino, praised him effusively, even as he faced the executioner's axe for having supported the Stuart cause: "I am not a fit hand to draw his character. I shall leave

---

* A pretender is a claimant to either an abolished throne or, as in the case of Charles Edward Stuart and his father, a throne occupied by someone else.

that to others. But I must beg leave to tell you the incomparable sweetness of his nature, his affability, his compassion, his justice, his temperance, his patience, and his courage are virtues seldom to be found in the person. In short he wants [lacks] no qualifications requisite to make a great man."

Greatness was the Young Pretender's most ardent desire, because he believed it was his birthright as a Stuart prince. But the chances of achieving it looked dismal in 1744, when Charles, aged twenty-three, began his quest to capture King George II's throne for his father. Early that January he had slipped away from a hunting party outside Rome, where "James III" had his court-in-exile, and secretly made his way to France, all the while evading agents of King George who would be eager to capture or kill him. The French were to be his allies in the effort to restore the Stuart monarchy, but just as preparations for the invasion of England neared completion, wicked storms destroyed much of the French fleet and prompted King Louis XV to withdraw his support.

Charles was stuck in France, "imprisoned," as he put it, without money or prospects—and saddled with a fractious group of supporters. "You may well imagine how out of humour I am," the Young Pretender wrote to his father in Rome, "when for comfort I am plagued out of my life with *tracasseries* [petty bickering] from our own people, who as it would seem would rather sacrifice me and my affairs than fail in any private view." It was a rare display of pique for the normally exuberant youth.

Rather than endure enforced idleness in France, and all its attendant miseries, Charles decided to invade on his own, declaring that he was "determined to come the following summer to Scotland, though with a single footman." It was an audacious plan for the penniless Pretender, the kind of "rash or ill-conceived project," his father warned, that "would end in your ruin and that of all those who would join with you in it." Charles, however, would not be deterred.

"I have, above six months ago, been invited by our friends to go to Scotland," the Young Pretender wrote to the Old, "and to carry what money and arms I could conveniently get; this being, they are persuaded, the only way of restoring you to the crown, and them to their liberties." The challenge would be daunting, Charles conceded, but the time had come for action lest their Stuart supporters, or Jacobites, lose faith in his ability to lead. "If a horse which is to be sold if spurred does not skip, nobody would care to have him, even for nothing," Charles argued; "just so my friends would care very little to have me, if after such usage as all the world is sensible of, I should not show that I have life in me."

With some covert help from the French government, the Young Pretender was able to amass arms, several hundred men, and two ships, and, on July 16, 1745, the tiny invasion force set out for Scotland. "Let what will happen," Charles boldly declared to his father. "The stroke is struck, and I have taken a firm resolution to conquer or to die, and stand my ground as long as I shall have a man remaining with me."

That stout resolution would serve Charles well when, en route to Scotland, an English warship attacked and left him without the French gunship that carried most of the men, arms, and provisions he had planned to use in his quest to conquer Britain. The ragtag remnants of his invasion party would hardly be enough now to rally much support in Scotland. Indeed, soon after landing in the midst of what was described as "a very wet dirty night," without shelter, Charles learned that the promised assistance of several clan chiefs from the Highlands would not be forthcoming.

Undaunted by this sorry state of affairs, Charles dismissed suggestions that he return to France until such a time as his prospects improved. "I am come home, sir," he said to one skeptical Scot, "and I will entertain no notion at all of returning to that place from whence I came, for that I am persuaded my faithful Highlanders will stand by me."

His faith was gradually vindicated as some Highlanders came to recognize his unshakable determination and gathered in ever increasing numbers under his banner. Charles seemed to understand the soul of the Scots, especially of the fierce clansmen of the north, and spoke to it. He appealed to their native pride, which had been severely battered by the hated Hanoverians since the union of Scotland with England in 1707. He presented himself as *their* prince; the heir of an ancient line of Scots kings, who had come, despite all odds, to fight that bulgy-eyed foreign usurper, George II.

For this, Bonnie Prince Charlie was rewarded with astonishing loyalty, even though many Scots were still not prepared to follow him. Clan chiefs pledged never to abandon him, while soldiers became so devoted that, according to one contemporary, "there was scarce a man among them that would not have readily run on certain death if his [Charles's] cause might have received any advantage."

The growing support the Young Pretender amassed behind him was entirely unexpected, and the British government was woefully unprepared for it. War on the Continent diverted many troops, but there had also been a casual indifference to the potential threat the exiled Stuarts posed.* In fact, George II was enjoying one of his extended sojourns in his Hanoverian homeland, frolicking with his mistress, when Charles Stuart arrived in Scotland.

The Young Pretender's path was largely cleared for him, and within the first month of landing in Scotland, he was able to capture the capital of Edinburgh with little resistance. Then, in

---

* Only Robert Walpole seemed to understand the danger, and frequently raised the alarm during his twenty-one years as prime minister under George I and George II. "I am not at all ashamed to say I am in fear of the Pretender," he once said. "It is a danger I shall never be ashamed to say I am afraid of, because it is a danger we shall always be more or less exposed to."

what he described to his father as "one of the most surprising actions that ever was," Charles's army smashed the ill-prepared government force that finally gathered to challenge them at Prestonpans, outside of Edinburgh. "The field of battle presented a spectacle of horror," one British officer reported, "being covered with heads, legs, arms and mutilated bodies, for the killed all fell by the sword."

With such rapid success, the fall of London no longer seemed like a remote possibility. "I leave for England in eight days," Charles announced confidently to France's special envoy, Alexandre Jean Baptiste de Boyer, Marquis d'Éguilles. "England will be ours in two months." Such bravado was necessary to spur needed support from Louis XV, who was still noncommittal, but it also reflected the Young Pretender's unwavering belief in his destiny. "As matters stand," he wrote to his father, "I must either conquer or perish in a little while."

Early in November 1745, the Jacobite army of about five thousand foot soldiers—many of them teenaged boys—and five hundred cavalry crossed the border into England and assembled outside the city of Carlisle. Charles delivered a message to the mayor: "Being come to recover the King our Father's just right, for which we arrived with all his authority, we are sorry to find that you should prepare to obstruct our passage. We, therefore, to avoid the effusion of blood, hereby require you to open your gates, and let us enter."

The mayor was unwilling to concede quite so easily, though, and so began the siege of Carlisle. A week later the city surrendered.* The Young Pretender's army next received a rousing

---

* George II's despised son, Frederick, seemed to celebrate the threat to his father's throne when he ordered his pastry chef to prepare a replica of the citadel of Carlisle in sugar for a banquet he was giving. The prince and his guests then amused themselves by pelting the fortress with sugarplums, as if to siege it.

welcome in Manchester, before blowing through Leek, then Ashbourne, and finally to Derby—all without encountering a single government troop. "We are now within a hundred miles of London," one Jacobite soldier wrote home from Derby, "without seeing the face of one enemy, so that in a short time I hope to write to you from London, where if we get safe, the whole of our story and even what has happened already must appear to posterity more like a romance than anything of truth."

Panic erupted in London as news of the Young Pretender's unlikely successes spread. "There was never so melancholy a town," wrote Robert Walpole. "Nobody but has some fear for themselves, for their money, or for their friends in the army." Rumors were rife about the size of the invading army, and of its savagery. The city was all but shut down in anticipation of a massive invasion. Catholics and Jacobites were put under strict surveillance, priests were seized, and antigovernment literature and speech were ruthlessly suppressed. In *The True Patriot*, playwright Henry Fielding warned of a menacing swarm of terrorists, who would, if the Catholic Stuarts prevailed, persecute Protestants "with all the fury which rape, zeal, lust and wanton fierceness could inspire into the bloody hearts of Popish priests, bigots, and barbarians."

What the frightened Londoners did not know was that Bonnie Prince Charlie had already reached the pinnacle of his success, and that his fortunes were soon to take a terrible turn.

While Charles Stuart's forces were celebrating their triumph in Derby, King George II's favored son, the porcine-faced William, Duke of Cumberland, was thirty miles away in the town of Stone—at the head of a ten-thousand-strong government force. A clash was coming, the Pretender's men believed, and they were eager for it. "They were to be seen," one officer wrote, "during the whole day [December 5], in crowds before the shops of the cutlers, quarreling about who should be the first to sharpen and give a proper edge to his sword." But, as it turned out, there would be no encounter the next day.

Charles had received news in Derby that eight hundred Irish and Scots troops fighting in the French army had arrived in Scotland to supplement his forces, and two thousand more Scots had been recruited as well. Plus, he was told, King Louis was sending an even larger French force that was to embark in two or three weeks. This kind of encouragement should have been the spur forward; instead, it actually destroyed the Young Pretender's momentum.

The various leaders and clan chiefs within Charles's army determined that it would be wiser to retreat back to Scotland and join with the reinforcements there before confronting Cumberland. This was the better way, they argued, and they were united in their opposition to pushing forward to London. It was a stunning blow to Charles, who believed the crown was within his grasp. His men were with him—now—and turning back on the cusp of victory would utterly deflate them. It made no sense—indeed, it was an outrage—but there was nothing he could do in the face of such resistance. "You ruin, abandon, and betray me if you do not march on," he raged, ineffectively, before reluctantly ordering the retreat.

"In future," he said sullenly, "I shall summon no more councils, since I am accountable to nobody for my actions but to God and my father and therefore I shall no longer either ask or accept advice."

The next morning Charles's men rose with the full expectation that they were about to fight King George's son William. When they learned otherwise, their good cheer turned to "expressions of rage and lamentation," as one officer reported, adding that even if they had been beaten in battle, "the grief could not have been greater."

The Young Pretender's prospects were bleak when he and his demoralized men recrossed the Scottish border on December 20. The Jacobites controlled only a few pockets of Scotland; much of the rest was either loyal to the Hanoverian regime or under its control. And though Charles was unaware of it at the time, the French fleet he expected—poorly provisioned and plagued by the attacks of British privateers—would never sail.

Confronted with the dismal situation in Scotland, Charles decided to lay siege to Stirling—the fortified town and castle on a bluff above the plains northwest of Edinburgh, where James VI and I spent his unhappy childhood (see Chapter 7). There he hoped to base his operations for the total conquest of Scotland. But by the middle of January, little progress had been made.

It was then that the new Hanoverian commander in Edinburgh, Lieutenant General Henry Hawley, decided to march on the Jacobites assembled at Stirling. Though Hawley fully expected the "rascals" would run when confronted by his cavalry, Charles's forces instead gathered at Falkirk Muir and entrenched themselves, muskets held at the ready. It was nearly dark, in the midst of strong winds and a heavy downpour, when Hawley sent three cavalry regiments to confront them. When the horsemen were just ten feet away, the order was given to fire. Scores of horses and men, including the cavalry commander, fell in this lethal volley. The remainder spurred their horses to trample the rebel infantry.

"The most singular and extraordinary combat immediately followed," James Johnstone recalled. "The Highlanders, stretched on the ground, thrust their dirks into the bellies of the horses. Some seized the riders by their clothes, dragged them down, and stabbed them with their dirks; several again used their pistols; but few of them had sufficient space to handle their swords."

It was a magnificent rout, yet another in a long series of triumphs for Charles Stuart. It would also be his last. Rather than take advantage of the victory and pursue Hawley's forces,

Charles decided to refocus on the siege of Stirling. That came to nothing, however, and by the end of January he was persuaded that the best course of action would be to retreat north to the town of Inverness and wait out the winter. His men were "struck with amazement," according to Lord Elcho, "for everybody expected a battle and it appeared very strange to run away from the very army that had been beat only a fortnight before."

It was a miserable trek north. Not only had victory been snatched from them, but they were weary and bitterly cold. "Men were covered with icicles hanging on their eyebrows and beards," wrote one member of Charles's army, "and an entire coldness seized all their limbs, a severe contrary wind driving snow and little cutting hail down upon our faces, in such a manner that it was impossible to see ten yards before us."

The situation was little improved in Inverness. Charles became dangerously ill with pneumonia, and though he did recover, the gathering of supplies had been neglected. So had the maintenance of discipline among the fighting men, many of whom returned to their homes for the rest of the winter. Such was the dismal state of affairs when, on April 13, the Young Pretender learned that his nemesis, the Duke of Cumberland, son of George II, was marching toward them.

Charles rallied what remained of his army, about forty-five hundred men, and marched the ill-equipped, underfed band to Culloden Moor, a flat, featureless plain about four miles north of Inverness. It was not an ideal spot—far better suited to Cumberland's mighty artillery—but it was the place Charles had chosen to confront his enemy at last. He was not going to be dissuaded. What followed was one of the bloodiest battles ever fought on British soil.

The Jacobite army slept fitfully after arriving at Culloden, fully expecting to fight Cumberland the next day. But the duke never arrived. He was celebrating his birthday at Nairn, the Hanoverian encampment some twelve miles away. While

Cumberland's men were swilling brandy distributed among them for the occasion, Charles's were scrounging for food—that day's ration having been one biscuit. With supplies so low, the clash would have to come immediately or be abandoned.

With no sign of Cumberland, it was decided to ambush him late that night at Nairn. The twelve-mile march began at eight in the evening, but it was nearly paralyzed due to the darkness of the night and the unfamiliar terrain. This, one officer recalled, "did not allow us to follow any track" and was "accompanied with confusion and disorder." Dawn began to break after eight miles, and the element of surprise would be lost entirely once they arrived at Nairn. The only solution was to turn around and march back to Culloden. "'Tis no matter then," Charles was heard to say. "We shall meet them and behave like brave fellows."

But the futile endeavor depleted what little strength remained among the Stuart army. Some men simply lay down in the bushes to snatch whatever sleep they could that cold, wet morning; others straggled away to find food. Even the ever resilient Bonnie Prince Charlie collapsed in exhaustion. Then, suddenly, came word that the Hanoverian army was a mere four miles away.

Officers struggled to form their men into battle lines in preparation for the coming onslaught, but the once fierce warriors had been driven way past the point of endurance, and the fight had simply left many of them. One officer recalled the "visible damp and dejection" he saw in his men, while another noted that "they were not the clans that had fought with such verve and vigor at Prestonpans and Falkirk."

The Marquis d'Éguilles, Louis XV's special envoy, observed the terrible disarray and lack of spirit in the Stuart army and tried desperately to persuade Charles to avoid the clash, which he feared would become a massacre. His pleas were entirely unsuccessful. "The Prince," he reported to King Louis, "who believed himself invincible because he had not yet been beaten, defied by enemies whom he thoroughly despised, seeing at their head the son of the rival of his father; proud and haughty as he was, badly advised, perhaps betrayed, forgetting at this moment every other object, could not bring himself to decline battle even for a single day."

The Hanoverian line emerged at Culloden—a mighty force of nine thousand men, dressed in scarlet, marching in order, bayonets as fixed as their determined expressions. "The enemy being by this time in full view, we began to huzza and bravado them in their march upon us," recalled one Jacobite. "But, notwithstanding all our repeated shouts, we could not induce them to return one: on the contrary, they continued proceeding, like a deep sullen river; while the Prince's army might be compared to a streamlet running among stones, whose noise sufficiently showed its shallowness."

As Cumberland's army pressed menacingly forward, Charles did his best to rally his men. "Here they are coming, my laddies! We'll soon be with them. They don't forget Gladsmuir, nor Falkirk, and you have the same arms and swords—let me see yours! I'll answer this will cut off some heads and arms today." But, as one of his officers noted, there was something missing from the Young Pretender's normal vigor and assurance. He saw Cumberland's great scarlet horde and "had no great hopes."

Indeed there was no hope. After an initial Jacobite volley, Hanoverian guns and cannonade began ripping through the Young Pretender's ranks. Legs, arms, and heads were torn away in the lethal barrage, as the men waited in vain for the order to charge. One government officer wrote that he could see they "fluctuated extremely and could not remain long in the position they were in without running away or coming down upon us." It was in fact a hideous situation for the Jacobites, especially as the Hanoverians began to literally shred them with grapeshot.

Some ran, or fell to the ground for cover. The rest ran screaming toward the wall of red coats. "They came up very boldly and fast all in a cloud together," wrote one government soldier. Then they were slaughtered.

"The Highlanders fought like furies," reported one of Cumberland's soldiers. "It was dreadful to see [their] swords circling in the air as they were raised from the strokes. And no less to see the officers of the army, some cutting with their swords, others pushing with their spontoons, the sergeants running their halberds into the throats of the opponents, the men ramming their fixed bayonets up to the sockets."

It was all over in less than an hour. Thousands of Jacobites lay dead or dying. Those who managed to escape the massacre were hunted down mercilessly by the government troops whose bloodlust had barely been sated in battle. And Bonnie Prince Charlie began a five-month odyssey as a fugitive as he tried to make his way back to France. It was a storied adventure, filled with peril, extreme deprivation, and even an episode when he escaped detection disguised as a woman. Charles was eventually picked up by two heavily armed French ships on Scotland's west coast, near the spot where he had first arrived a year earlier. He was safe at last, but the rescue also marked the end of a dream. There would never be a grand Stuart restoration, and the Young Pretender would spend the rest of his life as an embittered paper prince.

20

George III (1760–1820): Caroline
Matilda: Something Rotten in
the State of Denmark

It is worse than dying.

—ELIZABETH CARTER

George II was preceded in death by his despised son, Prince Frederick, so when the king died in 1760, he was succeeded by Frederick's oldest son, who became George III. Frederick's youngest daughter, Caroline Matilda, married King Christian VII of Denmark. It was a disastrous union.

Life for an English princess was very rarely pleasant. Exalted rank aside, she was really little more than a commodity, a diplomatic tool sent off to a foreign land and wedded to a stranger as a matter of statecraft. Few of these arranged marriages were fairy tale. Most, in fact, were utter misery. And so it was for Caroline Matilda, the youngest sister of King George III, sent away at age fifteen to marry Denmark's mad monarch, Christian VII. The union was a disaster, but Caroline Matilda, unlike so many other princesses before her, refused to accept her unhappy state. Her determination to liberate herself in the name of love unleashed forces that very nearly destroyed her.

Marriage to the Danish king, her first cousin,* meant that

Caroline Matilda would have to leave everything she loved in England forever. And the prospect of being queen in her new country was small comfort, especially since she would not be allowed even one English companion. The severance of all ties to home was to be brutally efficient.

"It is worse than dying," wrote the princess's contemporary Elizabeth Carter; "for die she must to all she has ever seen or known; but then it is only dying out of one bad world into another just like it, and where she is to have cares and fears, and dangers and sorrows, that will all yet be new to her." Prophetic words indeed, if a bit understated.

Before she was sent away to Denmark, Caroline Matilda was married at St. James's Palace. The bridegroom was not present, however, a common enough occurrence in arranged royal unions. Instead, the princess's older brother stood in for King Christian.[†] The teenaged girl had been calm in the months leading up to the wedding, but as the actual date approached she became increasingly agitated, and by the time she arrived for the ceremony on October 1, 1766, she was a complete mess. The Duchess of Northumberland reported that "before she set out on the procession," Caroline Matilda "cried so much that she was near falling into fits," and that her brother William, who escorted her, "was so shocked at seeing her in such a situation, that he looked as pale as death, and as if he was ready to faint away."

All that weeping and wailing, and Caroline Matilda had not yet even met her crazy cousin across the North Sea. King Christian had come to the Danish throne the previous January,

---

* Caroline's father, Prince Frederick (see Chapter 18), was the older brother of Christian's mother, Princess Louise. (See Hanover family tree, pages 164–65.)

† There would be a more formal ceremony, with Christian actually present, when Caroline Matilda arrived in Denmark.

just before he turned seventeen. His favorite pastimes were picking up prostitutes, masturbating excessively, and breaking things. He also loved to be punished, especially being tied to a chair and whipped like a common criminal.

One thing Christian VII most certainly did not like was being king. The fearful and delusional young man found his royal role repressive and sought any means of escape. Sometimes he would disguise himself and pick fights with people on the streets of Copenhagen or, after a night of whoring, smash windows and break furniture. Mostly though, Christian lost himself in his disordered, racing mind.

"I have to talk to him all through the night, or read to him," the king's valet reported. "Such an extraordinary imagination and so much wit are given to few people. He notices everything that happens around him and afterwards points out all the things that annoy him, as well as the oddest and most ridiculous. In this way words stream out of him the whole night through, and I sweat with fear and try to hide my reserve and fatigue with trivial answers. Often things happen that I can in no way understand."

It was with this exceedingly unbalanced person that Caroline Matilda—or the Danish Mathilde, as she would henceforth be known—would be forced to spend her life. The day after her proxy wedding, weeping bitterly, she set off for Denmark. "May the most cordial affection ever subsist between you and the King of Denmark," wrote her brother King George III, "may you be happy in your children and may you always look on those private blessings as the sole objects worth your concern." Alas, not one of the king's banal blessings would ever come to be.

Almost as soon as the new queen of Denmark arrived in Copenhagen, she was abandoned by her husband, who had planned a special vacation for himself. "I fear that I shall not go with the King this spring to Holstein," Caroline Mathilde wrote to her brother King George. "He seems to think there is no occasion to be troubled with me. He told it to me when I had not been here longer than a week. I wish it was in my power to write more openly to you but you know it is not my fault."

Despite being saddled with a lunatic husband who cared nothing for her, the young queen was determined to forge her way in her adopted country and make it her own. Within a few months of arriving, "she took great pains to learn the Danish language and in a short time she spoke it with a fluency that greatly flattered her subjects," reported the courtier Otto von Falkenskjold. Still, she was isolated at court, only politely tolerated by her in-laws, and unable to communicate effectively with her own family, as her letters were often intercepted or heavily edited.

King Christian was reluctantly coaxed into his wife's bed, and by May 1767, Caroline Mathilde was pregnant. Having done his duty, the king took off again, this time into the arms of his mistress, a courtesan known as Catherine of the Bootees because of her dainty feet. Not content with a discreet affair, Christian flaunted his adulterous relationship by bringing his mistress to Christiansborg Palace and showing her off. Because he was an absolute monarch who ruled without a governing body, such as Parliament, to curb his powers, no one could stop him from demeaning his wife with this outrageous insult. Louise von Plessen, head of the queen's household and her close confidante, reported to the king's chief minister, Count Bernstorff, the effect Christian's behavior had on Caroline Mathilde: "Her mind is too good and fine not to be deeply hurt by the lack of tenderness and politeness with which she is being treated."

Hurt was eclipsed by anger when the king arbitrarily dismissed Madame von Plessen. Then, after the birth of their son, Crown Prince Frederick, Christian announced he was leaving—without his wife—on an extended journey, including a visit to her homeland. Caroline Mathilde was not happy; her brother King George, even less so. "You know very well that the whole of it *is very disagreeable to me*," the English king wrote emphatically to one of his ministers. Christian went anyway, made a complete nuisance of himself, then capped his unwelcome stay with a thorough trashing of St. James's Palace. Left alone in Denmark, meanwhile, Caroline Mathilde remained quietly dutiful. Soon enough, though, her passions would explode.

Among King Christian's retinue of physicians was Johann Friedrich Struensee, a charismatic young German steeped in Enlightenment principles and brimming with ambition, who quickly gained the king's complete trust. He had, the British ambassador reported ruefully, "the most alarming ascendency over His Majesty." Before long, the queen was smitten as well. And in defiance of all danger, not to mention propriety, she and the handsome physician started sleeping together.

"Their intimacy showed that they loved each other, searched for each other and were happy when they found one another," Struensee's friend Enevold Brandt later said, adding, "their love showed in a way that can be noticed but not described."

The affair was indeed noticed. The cramped Danish court left little room for secrecy, and the couple made little effort to hide the affair anyway. As if to symbolize their forbidden love, Struensee bought the queen a pair of red embroidered silk stockings, which she took to wearing every day. They were, she said, her "ties of feeling."

Immersed as he was in his own world of delusion, King Christian either didn't know about the affair or didn't care. He was just happy to abdicate his responsibilities, ceding increasing amounts of government control to his physician and friend.

Thus, with the queen by his side, Struensee emerged as Denmark's de facto monarch, a prime minister with absolute powers and an ambitious agenda: to reshape Danish society into a better reflection of his Enlightenment values.

The first order of business was to grant complete freedom of the press in September 1770, which, historian Stella Tillyard wrote, "created at a single stroke the most liberal climate for opinion anywhere in Europe." More drastic reforms soon followed. "In not much more than a year," Tillyard continued, "the thirty-three-year-old doctor from Halle had grown from being the king's physician and friend into the lover and confidant of the queen and then the unchallenged ruler of a country where all decrees issued by the king had the immediate force of law. . . . [I]n its swiftness and completeness, his was a rise to power unparalleled anywhere in Europe. The malady of the king and the love of the queen had placed a nation in his hands."

Struensee's rapid rise to power coincided with a notable change in Caroline Mathilde. The once sad, neglected wife now asserted herself boldly as a lover. Struensee's power was hers as well, and it was reflected in a large portrait of the queen commissioned in 1770. Dressed in the uniform of the Royal Danish Lifeguards, Caroline Mathilde looks positively masculine with sword, boots, and spurs—a declaration of sorts that *she* was now the font of royal authority, not the king.

Yet despite the domineering statement being made in the portrait (which apparently turned on the masochistic King Christian), Caroline Mathilde was also happy to simply be Struensee's wife in all but name. She lived with him in quiet domesticity at the country palace of Hirschholm, bearing him a daughter there, while Christian literally smashed things elsewhere. It was an odd arrangement, which Struensee and Caroline Mathilde marked by commissioning a trio of matching oval portraits—one of each of them and a third of the king.

"This court has not the most distant relationship to any other under the sun," reported one British observer. But the idyll at Hirschholm was not destined to last.

Struensee rattled many among the establishment who felt his reforms were far too radical and undermined the very pillars of Danish society. "A malignant leveler," the British ambassador called him, echoing the sentiments of a growing opposition. A plot soon emerged among the disgruntled to destroy Struensee, gain control of the king, then rule through him as *they* saw fit. Christian's stepmother, the dowager queen Juliane Marie, as well as his half brother Frederick, were recruited by the plotters to give their cause a degree of royal authority.

"The Almighty has chosen [you] to be the instrument by which your brother the king . . . [may] be fortified on his throne," Juliane Marie wrote to her son, Prince Frederick. "Be not horrified at the danger you should meet with."

In the early-morning hours of January 17, 1772, the conspirators crept through Christiansborg Palace and into the king's bedchamber. Startled out of his sleep, the paranoid monarch began to scream in terror. "My son, Your Majesty," Juliane Marie said soothingly, "we are not here as enemies, but as your true friends." After some time, Christian was coaxed into signing two orders: one ceding control of the kingdom to the dowager queen and her son Frederick; the other ordering the arrests of Struensee and Caroline Mathilde. "My God," the king said in a moment of lucidity, "this will cost streams of blood."

Struensee, asleep in his chamber, was arrested first, along with his friend and confidant Enevold Brandt. Both men were hustled out of the palace and taken by carriage to a fortress prison at the edge of Copenhagen. There they were shackled and chained, bound hand to foot and then to the wall of their respective cells. Unfathomable horrors awaited them.

Caroline Mathilde was taken next. "Madame," Christian

had written in a prepared note, "I have found it necessary to send you to Kronborg, your conduct obliges me to it. I am very sorry. I am not the cause, and I hope you will sincerely repent." It was actually Juliane Marie who had insisted that the queen be taken to the remote fortress-castle of Kronborg,* where she would be far away from the king and thus unable to influence him in any way—especially back under Struensee's spell. That, the queen dowager recognized, would have doomed them all.

Caroline Mathilde's thoughts immediately turned to Struensee when they came for her that freezing cold January morning. She leapt out of bed and ran into the hallway. "Where's the count?" she cried, hoping he would hear her. "Where's the count?" The queen was then handed the note King Christian had written and, now fully aware of what was in store for her, fought ferociously against her captors. Foreign minister Adolph Sigfried von der Osten, who had switched sides and joined the new regime, managed to persuade the furious queen that resistance was futile and that she had no choice but to follow the king's command. Caroline Mathilde reluctantly agreed, but only if her children could accompany her. There was no way the leaders of the revolt would ever give her Crown Prince Frederick, but the baby Princess Louise they allowed to go. It was commonly believed that the child was Struensee's, not the king's, so the girl mattered little to the new regime. She would mean everything to the captive queen.

As Caroline languished with her daughter at Kronborg, George III received the news of his sister's fate. The new government in Denmark had every reason to fear the king's reaction, as Britain could crush them militarily. Nevertheless, the Danish leaders were determined to proceed against the queen

---

* Kronborg Castle is known by many also as Elsinore, the setting of Shakespeare's great tragedy *Hamlet*. Elsinore is actually the town in which Kronborg is situated.

and remove her from her high station by divorcing her from Christian. "God, goodness, and the justice of our cause" were on their side, Osten assured Juliane Marie. And the king was in their pocket. They had him write to Caroline Mathilde's mother, rather than King George, in an attempt to emphasize that the queen's arrest was a family matter, not a matter of state. The British king played along with the pretense, while he secretly prepared for war.

Meanwhile, just over a month after his arrest, Struensee was unchained and taken before a group of commissioners, who questioned him relentlessly about all manner of his dealings. The once all-powerful regent (in all but name) remained steadfast throughout the inquisition and conceded nothing—until the end—when he was asked directly about his relationship with the queen. Then he broke, admitting that things "had gone as far as they could between people of two sexes." The next day he provided all the explicit details of the affair. It was a remarkable confession—not only damning but bewildering as well.

"His courage, I am assured, forsook him upon hearing from the Commission that the queen was no longer at Copenhagen which he did not know before," wrote the British diplomat Ralph Woodford. "Yet I cannot believe him wretch enough to have done a thing infamously aggravating his own guilt."

What made Struensee confess so readily? Had he been tortured, as many suspected? Or did he have another motive? The answer remains elusive. What is certain is that Caroline Mathilde, confronted with her lover's signed admission, and the promise of leniency for both of them if she, too, acknowledged the adulterous relationship, signed a confession as well—and immediately regretted it.

The new regime was triumphant and wrote to King George in King Christian's name: "Your Majesty will see that the Queen, far from contradicting Struensee, has confirmed his confession by her own admission and by her signature. After having replied in the affirmative to the questions, she has agreed to a divorce and to a dissolution of our marriage."

The queen, however, was not quite as compliant as the letter sent to King George suggested. Indeed, she retracted her confession within a few days of signing it and stubbornly declared her innocence. She also questioned the validity of Struensee's confession, insisting that he had been tricked—or worse. "They also caught me unawares," she told Peter Udall, the lawyer assigned to her, "then I signed everything they wanted."

Despite the queen's protests, divorce was now inevitable. And King George would have little choice but to accept it. The king's minister Lord Suffolk wrote to the British ambassador in Denmark conceding as much after receiving Caroline Mathilde's confession: "I must frankly tell you that His Majesty's justice cannot be so warped, even by his fraternal affection, as to deny that, supposing this to be a true state of the case, the King of Denmark has a right to sue for the dissolution of the marriage."

What the British king would not tolerate was the planned removal of his sister to the Danish city of Aalborg, where, he feared, she might be conveniently killed. He wanted her out of Denmark entirely, and was prepared to force the issue militarily. In the end it was agreed that Caroline Mathilde would be sent to the German town of Celle, within King George's Hanoverian domains. Though she would be deprived of both of her children, it was a fate far more agreeable than what awaited Struensee.

Having committed what the court of commissioners called "a certain atrocious crime, at the bare recital of which human nature shudders, and which the faltering tongue seems unwilling to repeat," the queen's lover was condemned to a barbaric death, one far more representative of savage medieval justice than of eighteenth-century Enlightenment. The sentence declared that Struensee "has forfeited his honour, his life and his estates;

that he shall be degraded from his dignity as Count, and all other dignities conferred upon him; that his Coat of Arms which he has as Count, shall be broken by the executioner; that his right hand, and afterward his head shall be cut off while alive; and that his body shall be quartered and laid upon the wheel, but his head and hand shall be stuck upon a pole."*

On April 28, 1772, upon a scaffold erected for the occasion outside Copenhagen's eastern gate, the ghastly sentence was carried out. And not without a hitch: Part of Struensee's chin was left on the block when the executioner botched the decapitation. The corpse were then chopped into quarters, while the offending genitalia were hacked off and tacked up beside the other dismembered pieces—the sharpest, most symbolic penalty possible for one who had dared sleep with the queen.

Within a week of Struensee's execution, Caroline Mathilde was on her way to Germany aboard the British ship *Southampton*. But the twenty-year-old woman who had given up everything to become Denmark's queen was not about to accept her circumstances gently. "She went into exile with anger in her arms and only hatred for company," wrote Stella Tillyard. "Her heart was in Denmark, and she must return."

In the meantime, though, she was at the mercy of her brother King George, who insisted that she live a quiet, retired life in Celle, with a moated castle as her home. Denmark, he told her, would be best banished from her mind. Stuck in such circumstances, Caroline Mathilde may have felt some connection to her ill-fated great-grandmother, Sophia Dorothea (see Chapter 17), who, after years of imprisonment in a castle, deprived of her children, now lay buried in Celle.

---

* Struensee's friend Enevold Brandt was sentenced to the same fate, and suffered on the same scaffold just moments before Struensee did.

The fallen queen was determined not to endure a similar fate. Though she seemed to be making the best of her new situation—gaily greeting visitors and, in the absence of her own children, even adopting a young girl—Caroline Mathilde burned with the ambition to be restored to her former glory, and to exact revenge on those who had snatched it away from her.

"Her countenance is not entirely free," observed one visitor, "and in her eyes, especially as soon as she stops smiling, glares something defiant and very fiery. Her complexion is healthy, though more pale than red, and her face is certainly not what one could describe as beautiful. One can see there, in my opinion, the courage and resolution which she certainly displayed at her arrest."

Caroline Mathilde's secret maneuverings to regain power in Denmark were usually thwarted when her letters were intercepted or her activities reported by spies. However, there was one plot that did show promise. It involved an English adventurer named Nathaniel William Wraxall, who, with a group of disaffected Danish exiles, colluded to topple the current government in Denmark and restore the deposed queen to her throne. Even the ever cautious George III indicated that he would not stand in the way of the plotters and would recognize the new regime if the coup was successful.

But Caroline Mathilde would never see Denmark again, for on May 11, 1775, at the age of twenty-three, she succumbed suddenly to scarlet fever. The supporters who had rallied to her cause were shocked by her sudden death, while those who had dethroned her in Denmark were relieved. "Alas, it is not until now that I feel that my head is safe," one of them remarked.

Despite her untimely demise, Caroline Mathilde did leave a pronounced legacy in Denmark. Her son became regent for his mad father in 1784 and immediately removed the government that had dethroned his mother, the memory of whom he always revered. He became King Frederick VI in 1808. Caroline Mathilde's daughter, Louise, went on to have her own daughter, Caroline Amelia, who was the wife of King Christian VIII.* Thus, in one of history's great ironies, Struensee's granddaughter wore Caroline Mathilde's crown as queen of Denmark.

* Christian VIII succeeded his cousin Frederick VI as king of Denmark in 1839. (He was the grandson of dowager queen Juliane Marie, the royal figurehead of the coup against Struensee and Caroline Mathilde.)

21

George III (1760–1820):

The Reign Insane

I wish to God I may die, for I am going to be mad.
—KING GEORGE III

Five years after losing the American colonies in 1783, George III began to lose his mind. It was a frightening decline for the once restrained and dutiful monarch, marked by strange hallucinations, inappropriate behavior, and incessant babbling. Most historians now attribute the king's unsettled state of mind to a particularly virulent form of the metabolic disorder known as porphyria.

Early one August morning in 1788, the pages at Windsor Castle were shocked to see the king's wife, Queen Charlotte, run out of the royal apartments "in great alarm, in her *shift*, or with very little clothes." The men turned their backs to save the queen the embarrassment of being seen in such a state, but she came right up to them and told one to go immediately and fetch a doctor in Richmond. King George III was in a terrible state, suffering through the early stages of what would soon become a nightmare of madness.

The fifty-year-old monarch was seized by violent stomach pains that left him hunched over in agony. These were accompanied by painful cramps in his legs and a rash on his arms that his daughter Elizabeth described as vivid red "and in great weal, as if it had been scourged with cords."

The doctors were bewildered by the symptoms. Some said it was gout; Sir George Baker concluded that the king's illness was caused by his having "walked on the grass several hours; and, without having changed his stockings (which were very wet) went to St. James's; and that at night he ate four large pears for supper," having had no dinner. Soon enough, though, worrisome signs of mental distress began manifesting as well.

Fanny Burney, a member of Queen Charlotte's household, reported in late October that the normally composed king spoke in "a manner so uncommon, that a high fever alone could not account for it; a rapidity, a hoarseness of voice, a volubility, an earnestness—a vehemence, rather—it startled me inexpressibly. . . . The Queen," she added, "grows more and more uneasy."

Poor Charlotte was actually growing frightened of her husband, with whom she had shared a loving relationship. "Their behaviour to each other speaks the most cordial confidence and happiness," one of the queen's attendants had observed several years earlier. "The King seems to admire as much as he enjoys her conversation. . . . The Queen appears to feel the most grateful regard for him." Now Charlotte couldn't keep far enough away, even as George became ever more dependent on her in his disordered state. "How nervous I am!" the queen exclaimed to Fanny Burney. "I'm quite a fool. Don't you think so?"

The queen was worried about what she called King George's "great hurry of spirits and incessant loquacity." One day at chapel, he suddenly jumped up during the sermon, threw his arms around Charlotte and his daughters, and exclaimed, "You know what it is to be nervous. But, was you ever as bad as this?" On another occasion, Sir George Baker found him at a concert recital at Windsor, repeatedly rising and sitting throughout, "not seeming to attend to the music," and talking continuously, "making frequent and sudden transitions from one subject to another."

The king was aware of his incessant babbling and endeavored unsuccessfully to control it. He had his attendants read aloud to him in the hope that that would keep him quiet, but he just spoke right over them. He even suggested that he be taken to General Sir George Howard's home in Buckinghamshire, where, he said, the general would give an account of the campaigns he made in Germany, "and that will keep me from talking."

Sadly, King George still had enough presence of mind to realizing he was losing his. "They would make me believe I have the gout," he said, kicking one foot against the other; "but if it was gout how could I kick the part without any pain?" In despair, the king sobbed on the shoulder of his favorite son, the Duke of York. "I wish to God I may die," he cried, "for I am going to be mad."

That seemed certain on the evening of November 5, when the king's heir, George, Prince of Wales, dropped by Windsor for dinner. Father and son had always had an uneasy relationship (see Chapter 23), but something snapped that evening that sent King George into a blind frenzy. He suddenly rose from the table, grabbed his son by the collar, pulled him out of his chair, and slammed him against the wall. It was a devastating scene that left Queen Charlotte in hysterics and the weeping Prince of Wales on the verge of fainting. Sir George Baker concluded afterward that the king was now "under an entire alienation of mind and much more agitated than he had ever been."

King George was a frightening sight the next day. Charlotte told Lady Harcourt that his eyes were like "black currant jelly, the veins in his face were swelled, the sound of his voice was dreadful. He often spoke till he was exhausted, and, the moment he could recover his breath, began again, while the foam ran out of his mouth."

"I am nervous," King George insisted. "I am not ill, but I am nervous. If you would know what is the matter with me, I am nervous."

With the king in such a state, it was decided that he should be moved out of the queen's bedroom under the pretext that she was ill. Unsettled by her absence, George got up in the middle of the night and stole into Charlotte's room. For a half hour he hovered over her, candle in hand. The next night the queen moved to apartments farther away. Finding her door locked, the king burst into tears. "We've been married twenty-eight years," he said to the queen, "and never separated a day until now; and now you abandon me in my misfortunes."

As George's condition worsened, he became increasingly violent and uncontrollable. His incessant chatter, which one day went on "for nineteen hours without scarce intermission," was now sprinkled with obscenities that would have once mortified the normally pious monarch. Then there were the delusions. The king gave orders to dead people, or to individuals who never even existed. On one occasion be became convinced that London was flooded and ordered his yacht there. Looking through a telescope, he insisted that he could see his ancestral homeland of Hanover. He composed letters to foreign courts filled with fanciful tales, and lavished honors on all who approached him—even the lowliest servant.

A succession of doctors was brought in to treat the king, but each was baffled by his condition. They prescribed wildly divergent courses of treatment, most of them barbaric, none successful. Dr. Richard Warren, for example, ordered that the king's shaved head be blistered to draw out the bad humors from his brain. Leeches were attached to his forehead. He was administered strong purges and emetics, followed by sedatives, and his room was kept freezing cold. Little wonder there was no improvement.

Then, on December 5, Francis Willis took on the task of

curing the king, assisted by his son John. It was not a good match. "I hate all the physicians," railed the ailing monarch, "but most the Willises; they beat me like a madman." The king's distaste for Francis Willis was evident from the beginning, when Willis acknowledged that he had been a clergyman before becoming a doctor.

"I am sorry for it," George said with mounting agitation. "You have quitted a profession I have always loved, and you have embraced one I most heartily detest."

"Sir," Willis protested, "Our Savior Himself went about healing the sick."

"Yes, yes," the king answered irritably, "but He had not 700 pounds a year for it, hey!"

The treatment that followed this testy introduction was nothing short of torture. Willis was determined to tame his wild patient. If the king spoke out of turn, became too restless, or refused to eat, he would be confined in a straightjacket. Willis also had a chair specially made to confine the king until he complied with the doctor's demands. With bitter irony, George called the horrible contraption his "coronation chair." Once Willis kept him strapped in the chair, gagged, while he lectured the king on the impropriety of his lewd ranting about a certain lady of the court.

Brutal as Willis's methods were, they did seem to cow the king and keep him grudgingly compliant. "Dr. Willis remained firm and reproved him in determined language," Colonel Robert Fulke Greville reported. "He conducted himself with wonderful management and force. As the King's voice rose, attempting mastery, Willis raised his and its tone was stronger and decided. As the King softened his, that of Dr. Willis dropped to softening unison. . . . The King found stronger powers in Dr. Willis, gave way and returned to somewhat of composure."

Gradually King George began to improve, and by April

1789 he was considered cured. A service of Thanksgiving was held at St. Paul's Cathedral, and all of London seemed to celebrate. The only one who regretted the king's recovery was his eldest son, George. The Prince of Wales hoped his father would remain mad, a state that would propel the heir to the regency and all the attendant powers of the sovereign. Alas, he would have to wait two more decades for that, drowning in debt all the while.

George III suffered through two more brief episodes of his strange disorder—first in 1801 and again in 1804. Then in 1810, when he was a little over seventy years old, permanent insanity came upon him. For the next decade Britain's sovereign, beyond all reason and nearly blind, was confined to a set of apartments at Windsor Castle, shambling around with a long white beard. The only indication of the king's former greatness was the badge of the Star of the Order of the Garter pinned to his chest. George finally found peace in 1820, when he died at age eighty-one.

Sometime after midnight on May 31, 1810, the duke claimed to have been awakened in his bedchamber at St. James's Palace by a blow to the head. At first he thought a bat had flown into the room and hit him, but, he later testified, he was then struck several more times with his own sword by an assailant he couldn't see. Dazed and bloody, he tried to make his way to his valet, Cornelius Neale, who was sleeping in the next room. "Neale!" he shouted. "I am murdered!" After a final thrust, according to the duke, the unknown attacker slipped out of the room and escaped.

It was during a subsequent search of the royal apartments that another of the duke's valets, a Sardinian named Joseph Sellis, was discovered lying on his bed, his throat slit from ear to ear, with a bloody razor resting nearby. An inquest determined that it was Sellis who had entered the duke's chamber and attacked him. Then, ruing what he had done, or fearing arrest, he went back to his own room and nearly beheaded himself.

Sellis's corpse was unceremoniously buried beneath Charing Cross, with a stake reportedly driven through the heart as a symbol of the suicide's eternal damnation. Meanwhile, tickets were issued to the curious who wished to view the death scene. Sarah Spencer (an ancestor of Princess Diana's) was appalled: "Can you imagine . . . that the finest, most delicate ladies in town went in parties to look at those nasty rooms as a morning lounge, and to examine the slops of blood which covered the bed, the floor, and even the walls and pictures, of the scene of this horrible murder and suicide? It was a spectacle which I should think the stoutest heart would hardly bear to look at, and yet these soft beings were able to stand it, out of mere curiosity."

In the same letter, Sarah also noted the duke's quick recovery from his wounds and remarked blithely, "Thank Heaven, we shall have no court mourning to keep us in black gowns all the summer."

22

George III (1760–1820):
A Royal Murder Mystery

Sellis was not his own executioner.

—THE INDEPENDENT WHIG

George III and Queen Charlotte had thirteen children who lived to be adults, among them seven sons, including Ernest, Duke of Cumberland. As the fifth son, Ernest was too far down in the line of succession to rule Britain. Nevertheless, he did inherit the throne of Hanover—his family's German kingdom— in 1837 (after the deaths of his four older brothers), and ruled there until his own death in 1851. Before assuming the Hanoverian crown, though, the duke was deeply involved in a murder mystery that remains unsolved.

While most historians believe that it was a hereditary disorder known as porphyria that plunged George III into babbling fits of insanity, the behavior of his large brood of debauched sons no doubt contributed mightily to the king's unsettled state of mind. The royal dukes were a troublesome lot indeed—"the damnedest millstones about the neck of any government that can be imagined," the Duke of Wellington said of them. Ernest, Duke of Cumberland, was a particularly loathsome fellow—a tyrannical military officer known to torture his men, and a lecher who reportedly seduced his own sister. He was "at the bottom of all evil," wrote his niece Princess Charlotte. But was he a murderer? Many of his contemporaries believed so.

Ernest's convalescence was indeed brief, which may be explained by the superficial nature of his wounds. The royal physician Sir Henry Halford treated them the night Sellis died and immediately reported to King George: "One upon the side of the head above the right ear, which bled profusely but is not dangerous—another on the back of the right hand—a third upon the left—and two or three others of less importance upon various parts of the body. . . . There is no danger to the Duke of Cumberland's life." It was "a most providential escape," the doctor concluded; a bit *too* providential, others said.

The conclusions of the inquiry into Sellis's death—that he had killed himself after attacking the duke—did little to end the speculation surrounding the case. Too many questions were left unanswered, one of the most significant being motive. *The News* said it could not discover anything "to induce a man to imbue his hands in the blood of his benefactor and also ruin his own family." It was strange that a man who had loyally served the duke for over a decade, and even named his son after him (Ernest served as godfather at the child's christening four months earlier), would suddenly attack him so ferociously.

Sellis's wife said that her husband had "frequently complained of a giddiness in the head," and it was the opinion of Colonel Henry Norton Willis, the well-informed comptroller for Princess Charlotte's household, that Sellis, disturbed in the mind, had been goaded into a fury by Ernest, who, "in his violent, coarse manner," taunted him.

Cornelius Neale, the duke's other valet, offered another possible motive at the inquiry. He testified that Sellis was of "a very malicious disposition" and hated Neale. "My opinion is . . . Sellis meant to murder the duke, thinking that the blame should be put on me. . . . I have no more doubt he did it to cause me to be suspected than I have of my own existence."

There was evidence produced at the inquiry that Sellis did indeed have issues with Neale. A letter he wrote to one of the duke's bedchamber grooms, Captain Benjamin Stephenson, was read aloud at the hearing. In it, Sellis asked Stephenson to tell the duke "of the roguery of this man." He then continued, "I have been told, sir, that Mr. Neale cheats His Royal Highness in everything he buys. . . . This man is as great a villain as ever existed." This bit of evidence was far from compelling, however, as it forced the conclusion that after documenting his accusations against Neale, Sellis then tried to kill Ernest to prove what a monster Neale was, only to cut his own throat when he was about to be caught.

"Sellis was not his own executioner," *The Independent Whig* declared, echoing a belief widely shared by many. Rumors about what really happened that fateful night were rampant and dogged the duke for years. Some concluded that Sellis had caught Ernest in a compromising position with Neale and had to be silenced; others said that the valet had rejected the duke's advances and was killed as a result. And, they posited, Ernest's wounds were self-inflicted to cover the crime.

Given the duke's nasty reputation, people were prepared to believe the worst. Nearly twenty years after Sellis's death, Charles Greville wrote in his journal of "the universal and deep execration" in which Ernest was held, noting, "Sellis's affair was never cleared up. . . . Everybody believes there is some mystery of an atrocious character in which he is deeply and criminally implicated."

Ernest successfully prosecuted several publishers for criminal libel after they alluded to his guilt, but that did little to enhance his standing. Rather, it only "induced multitudes of people to believe the calumnies," as the foreman of the original inquiry noted in a letter to the duke's attorney.

A libel trial in 1833 was notable for Ernest's testimony. He told the jury that he had seventeen wounds, not the five or six the royal physician had reported to King George. He also stated that the wounds were so severe that "I was in a state of agony, I suppose, from six weeks to two months. . . . It was not,

I believe, till the beginning of August that I was able to leave the house." Actually, historian John Wardroper has noted, he was out of bed in three days and made his first public appearance less than two weeks later.

At the same trial, the duke's lawyer addressed for the first time the suspicions that surrounded his client. He denied that Ernest "endeavoured, by inflicting wounds upon himself, to induce the belief that the deceased valet had attempted to assassinate the duke." That, he declared, would have been "worthy not only of a Machiavel, but of the most wicked of the human race." Perhaps the lawyer never stopped to consider that that was exactly how many people—including members of his own family—perceived Ernest.

The questions surrounding Sellis's death remained unresolved long after the duke (who eventually became king of Hanover) died in 1851. Then, in 1899, a significant document, written more than seven decades earlier, was donated to the Royal Library at Windsor. It was the memoir of Ernest's private secretary, Captain Charles Jones, and it contained some startling revelations. The duke, Jones claimed, actually confessed to killing Sellis.

It was Christmas Eve, 1815, five years after the valet's death. The Duke of Cumberland was "in a gloomy phrenzy," Jones wrote, and said that "he believed he had not one sincere friend in the whole world." After some hours in this agitated state, he supposedly told Jones that he had much on his mind—"more than I can bear. I want to unbosom myself but know not whom to trust."

Jones tried to calm the duke, writing "that I would freely sacrifice my existence on the spot if it could procure for him the slightest of his wishes, & indeed I felt most perfectly ready & willing to do so, for the state in which I saw H.R.H. [His Royal Highness] gave me the greatest of pain." But, he added, "had I known what was to follow, no power on earth could have induced me to have heard the dreadful confession."

After swearing his secretary to secrecy, Ernest at last spoke of the fatal night five years before. "You know how I am treated & you can feel for me more than I deserve," Jones reported him saying. "You know that miserable business of Sellis's, that wretch, I was forced to destroy him in self defense, the villain threatened to propagate a report & I had no alternative." The duke had more to say, but, Jones wrote, "thunderstruck & breathless I could scarcely hear the remaining statement & will therefore not set it down."

The confession, according to Jones, seemed to have eased Ernest's conscience. "H.R.H. ever afterwards appeared to me more cheerful," he wrote, "and to have lost a certain weight which appeared to be hanging on his mind." But for Jones, the burden of hearing it was shattering. "I have never known peace of mind since," he reported. "In fact H.R.H. had thrown the black secret of his guilt from his own into my breast. From this time I became gloomy, lost all spirit & energy, was unwilling to meet the duke and invented all sorts of excuses to be absent from his table."

Despite what he claimed were serious reservations, Jones remained in his master's service for another five years. Then, when he believed he was dying in 1827, he made out his will and wrote his memoir. "He has laid on me a weight that is pressing me by degrees to the grave," Jones stated on the opening page. "I find it impossible to quit this life with the secret of a murder upon my conscience. . . . A thousand contending reflections place me upon the rack. I must destroy the little reputation which remains to a man whom I had devoted my very existence."

Compelling though it may be, Jones's memoir does not offer definitive proof of the duke's culpability in Sellis's death. Indeed, some historians have dismissed it as a possible misunderstanding of what Cumberland actually said. Therefore, unless more evidence is uncovered, this royal murder mystery remains unsolved.

23

George IV (1820–1830):

A Wife on the Side

Too much every lady's man to be the man of any
lady.

—RICHARD SHERIDAN

George III's eldest son, the future King George IV, ruled for his father as regent beginning in 1810 and succeeded him ten years later.

Next to his wicked brother Ernest, George, Prince of Wales, was, well, a prince. Nevertheless, it was he—above all his misbehaving brothers—who offended George III the most with his antics, and the one for whom the rigidly moralistic monarch reserved most of his ire.

King George had doted on the prince as a baby, but as the boy grew older, his father turned on him ferociously—as Hanoverian monarchs were wont to do. Discipline was harsh and unrelenting. One of the prince's sisters later recalled seeing young George and his brother Frederick "held by their tutors to be flogged like dogs with a long whip." And the concept of gentle encouragement to bring forth a child's good qualities was entirely lost on the king. Instead, he found fault in almost everything the boy did. "He hates me," the younger George later lamented; "he always did, from seven years old."

Some children of disapproving parents will do anything to gain their approbation. The Prince of Wales, on the other hand, grew up to exceed even his father's worst fears. Though he could be charming, witty, and gracious, with a sophisticated eye for art and architecture, he was also a drunken fop who staggered his way through London society, bedding indiscriminately a long succession of mistresses, and generally making a grand spectacle of himself. His excessive drinking was exceeded only by his extravagance. The obscene amounts he spent on his homes and his person resulted in staggering debts that became a public scandal and left his father sputtering with indignation.

"It is now almost certain that some unpleasant mention of you is daily to be found in the papers," the king wrote to his wayward son. Indeed, the prince was a fixture in the broadsheets. *The Times* of London, for example, condemned him as a hard-drinking, swearing, whoring man "who at all times would prefer a girl and a bottle to politics and a sermon," and whose only states of happiness were "gluttony, drunkenness, and gambling."

The king despaired of his son's undignified behavior and regularly reproached him for it, to little effect. "The Prince of Wales on the smallest reflection must feel that I have little reason to approve of any part of his conduct for the last three years," the king wrote as his heir approached his twenty-first birthday, "that his neglect of every religious duty is notorious; his want of common civility to the Queen and me, not less so; besides his total disobedience of every injunction I had given and which he . . . declared himself contented with. I must hope he will now think it behooves him to take up a fresh line of conduct worthy of his station."

Far from reforming, though, the prince, who not only offended his father with his various dissipations but openly flirted with the king's political opposition party, performed the ultimate act of defiance in 1785 when he entered into a secret—and very illegal—marriage with a twice widowed Roman Catholic named Maria Fitzherbert.

———

The Prince of Wales had a rather loose definition of love in that his fervent declarations of eternal devotion to a woman would quickly evaporate when the next buxom lady caught his eye. Playwright Richard Sheridan, author of *The School for Scandal* and one of the prince's drinking buddies, observed wryly that George was "too much every lady's man to be the man of any lady."

But the prince's feelings for Maria Fitzherbert, six years his senior, were different—perhaps because he couldn't have her. She was too moral to be his mistress, and two laws made it impossible for her to be his wife. The Act of Settlement decreed that anyone married to a Catholic could not inherit the throne, and the Royal Marriages Act of 1772* required that all members of the royal family obtain the sovereign's permission to wed. And there was no way King George would ever allow his heir to marry a Catholic commoner.

Desire drove George into a total emotional frenzy. He swooned and sobbed, took to his bed, and declared hysterically that he would kill himself if he couldn't have the woman he loved. Finally he determined to marry Mrs. Fitzherbert, damn the consequences. Yet Maria wasn't so sure. Overwhelmed by his ardor, knowing of his inconstancy with other women, and all too aware of the dangers such an arrangement would entail,

* George III pushed this act through Parliament after his brother Prince Henry, Duke of Cumberland, married Lady Anne Horton, a woman with a reputation for being rather loose and one whom the king found entirely unsuitable. Horace Walpole, referring to her reputedly generous favors, wickedly noted that she was "the Duke of Grafton's Mrs. Horton, the Duke of Dorset's Mrs. Horton, everyone's Mrs. Horton."

the widow resisted. She planned to go abroad to escape the prince's attentions, which, upon hearing of it, propelled George to an act of utter desperation.

Four of the prince's associates arrived at Mrs. Fitzherbert's home and informed her that he had stabbed himself, was near death, and that only her immediate intervention could save him. Maria was reluctant to attend the prince, however, fearful that her arrival at his home unaccompanied would be seen as scandalous. It was only when a female chaperone was provided for her that she agreed to go. What she found was horrifying. The Prince of Wales was in his bed, pale and lethargic, his sheets soaked in blood. The sight nearly made Maria faint, and in this state—with the prince's plea that "nothing in the world would induce him to live unless she promised to become his wife"—she consented to marry him.

It is uncertain whether the future king had actually stabbed himself or had simply ripped off the bandages from an earlier medical bleeding.* But after the shock of seeing George in such condition wore off, Mrs. Fitzherbert regretted her promise to become his wife. Her emotions had been manipulated, she insisted, and though she blamed not the prince but rather his associates, she signed a deposition stating that "promises obtain'd in such a manner are entirely void." The next day she sailed for France.

Now George was more frantic than ever. He bombarded Maria with lovesick letters begging her to reconsider and be his wife. Otherwise, he swore, he would die. "Come then," he pleaded. "Oh! Come, dearest of wives, best and most adored of women, come and forever crown with bliss him who will through life endeavour to convince you by his love and atten-

---

* Bleeding was a common medical procedure of the day to restore balance among the four "humours," or bodily fluids, that were believed to control a person's disposition.

tion of his wishes to be the best of Husbands and who will ever remain until the last moments of his existence, *unalterably thine.*"

When the prince wasn't spewing out melodramatic missives, "he cried by the hour," one member of his household reported, and "testified the sincerity and violence of his passion and his despair by the most extravagant expressions and actions, rolling on the floor, striking his forehead, tearing his hair, falling into hystericks, and swearing that he would abandon the country, forego the crown, sell his jewels and plate, and scrape together a competence to fly with the object of his affections to America." And, of course, he drank himself stupid.

After a year in France agonizing over what to do, Maria Fitzherbert finally decided to return home. "I have told him I will be his," she wrote to Lady Anne Lindsay. "I know I injure him and perhaps destroy forever my own tranquility." What had changed her mind remains a mystery. Did she really love the prince? Or had she simply been worn down by his incessant pursuit? Whatever the case, George was ecstatic.

"I hardly know, *my dearest and only beloved Maria,* how I am to begin this letter to you," the prince wrote at the beginning of a forty-two-page letter. "Such a train of extraordinary and wonderful events have happened lately, which at first created apprehensions and alarms in my bosom, and since have tended to the facilitating and entire arrangement of our plan, so that nothing now is wanting but the arrival of my adored Wife in this country to make me the happiest of men."

Sensing that an illicit union was in the making, the prince's friend and political ally, Charles James Fox, tried to deter him from the "very desperate step" he was about to take. It would destroy his chances of ever becoming king, Fox warned, and, he continued, were he Mrs. Fitzherbert's father or brother, he "would advise her not by any means to agree to [a marriage], and to prefer any other species of connection . . . to one leading to such misery and mischief." George earnestly assured his friend that there was no marriage planned.

Meanwhile, the search for a minister to perform the secret ceremony was under way. Given that the Royal Marriages Act made it a felony to officiate over an unsanctioned union, finding a willing priest was no easy feat. Several wisely declined before John Burt, a disreputable clergyman languishing in debtors' prison, finally agreed once the prince promised to pay off his debts and make him a bishop when George became king.

On the evening of December 15, 1785, the Prince of Wales and Maria Fitzherbert were illegally wed at her London home, with her brother and uncle serving as the only witnesses besides Burt. Clandestine as the wedding was, however, it was hardly a secret. Rumors and reports of the union spread, as Horace Walpole wrote, "even from London to Rome."

Despite all the chatter, the couple maintained appearances by living separately and denying that they were married. The prince called reports of the union "pooh," and when the matter came up in Parliament (in connection with debates over George's enormous debts) he persuaded Charles James Fox to rebut the allegations. Fox was so vigorous in his speech—calling reports of the marriage a "low malicious falsehood"—that he earned Maria Fitzherbert's unyielding enmity. He had in effect unwittingly proclaimed her to be the prince's mistress, and, she complained, "rolled her in the kennel like a street-walker."

Maria was miffed at George as well, having concluded that he was more interested in resolving his money problems than he was in protecting her honor. Relative harmony was eventually restored, but the marriage was ultimately doomed. Infidelity was one factor. Mrs. Fitzherbert had managed to tame the prince, at least for a time, but soon enough he was eager to seek fresh conquests—and there was quite a succession.

None of these affairs was too serious, until George fell in love with Frances Villiers, Countess of Jersey, a "clever, unprincipled" woman, as one contemporary described her, "but beautiful and fascinating." The countess urged her lover to inform his wife that he had found happiness elsewhere, which he did, and soon came to regret it. He wanted *both* women.

The Countess of Jersey certainly undermined the prince's marriage, but his staggering debts finally destroyed it. George realized it would be impossible for him even to begin to extricate himself from his enormous financial burden unless he wed a princess of his father's choosing. Only then would he be allotted more income. So Maria Fitzherbert was sent away. A divorce was unnecessary because, under English law, the couple was never married (although Pope Pius VII did decree the union valid).

Alas, the king's choice of a bride for his son—George's first cousin Caroline of Brunswick—was most unfortunate (see Chapter 24) and resulted in one of the most miserable royal marriages in the history of the kingdom, which was no easy feat.

As the prince embarked on an odious marriage with a woman he came to loathe—the "infamous wretch," as he called Caroline—his first wife preoccupied him. On the way to the wedding ceremony, he turned to his brother the Duke of Clarence and said sadly, "William, tell Mrs. Fitzherbert she is the only woman I shall ever love."

The following year, when he believed he was dying, George wrote a rambling will and bequeathed all his "worldly property . . . to *my Maria Fitzherbert, my wife, the wife of my heart & soul,* and though by the laws of the country she *could not avail herself publicly of that name, still such she is in the eyes of Heaven, was, is, and ever will be such in mine.*" The prince declared that he wished to be buried with "the picture of my beloved wife, my Maria Fitzherbert . . . suspended round my neck by a ribbon as

I used to wear it when I lived *and placed right upon my heart*." (As for his despised wife, she "who is called the Princess of Wales, I leave one shilling.")

As his corrosive marriage to Caroline ground on, the prince managed to woo back Mrs. Fitzherbert, employing the same hysterics he had when first courting her. "He is so much improved," Maria wrote to Lady Anne Lindsay after the reconciliation, "all that was boyish and troublesome before is now become respectful and considerate." Or so she thought. The Prince of Wales was, and would always remain, a rake, utterly incapable of monogamy. And though Mrs. Fitzherbert tolerated his succession of passing trysts, his passion for Isabella Ingram-Seymour-Conway, Marchioness of Hertford, was hard to overlook. That flaunted affair, Maria wrote, "has quite destroyed the entire comfort and happiness of both our lives; it has so completely destroyed mine, that neither my health nor my spirits can bear it any longer." And so the couple—man and wife, except by law—finally parted, this time for good.

Two decades later, as King George IV lay dying in 1830, he begged the Duke of Wellington to ensure that he would be buried "with whatever ornaments [that] might be upon his person at the time of his death." The duke agreed, and after George died, he realized the reason for the king's request. Peering into the coffin, Wellington observed a black ribbon around the late king's neck. Curious, he drew aside the collar to see what was hanging from the ribbon. What he found was a diamond locket with a miniature portrait of Mrs. Fitzherbert inside. Maria said nothing when she was told, but it was seen "that some large tears fell from her eyes."

24

George IV (1820–1830):
Hello, I Loathe You

Nature has not made us suitable to each other.
—GEORGE, PRINCE OF WALES (LATER KING GEORGE IV)

The future King George IV was still Prince of Wales when he was forced into a second marriage, with his first cousin Caroline of Brunswick in 1795. The couple were, as shall be seen, horribly mismatched, though they did manage to produce an heir, Princess Charlotte, in 1796.

The Prince of Wales called his first wife his "dearest and only belov'd Maria." The words he chose for his second were slightly less effusive. She was, he said, "the vilest wretch this world ever was cursed with, who I cannot feel more disgust for her personal nastiness than I do from her entire want of all principle. She is a very monster of iniquity."

The calamitous union of the future king George IV with his cousin Caroline of Brunswick was doomed before it ever began. The prince was a selfish, overindulged libertine, thoroughly loathed by the British people, who only agreed to marry as a means of abating his colossal debts. And Princess Caroline came with her own set of deficits, not the least of which was her reputation for being, as Lord Holland reported, "exceedingly loose." She also smelled, bathing infrequently and rarely changing her underwear. And she lacked all tact.

Sir James Harris, Earl of Malmesbury, was given the task of asking for Caroline's hand and escorting her to England. He thought her not unattractive, even if she was short and stocky, with "a head always too large for her body, and her neck too short." And though at first he found the princess's exuberance appealing, he soon discovered "that her heart is very, *very* light, unsusceptible of strong or lasting feelings." The more Caroline spoke, the more Malmesbury urged her to keep quiet when she met her betrothed; otherwise he was sure the Prince of Wales would be repelled by this gauche creature. She had "no judgment," he observed; "caught by the first impression, led by the first impulse . . . loving to talk, and prone to confide and make missish friendships that last twenty-four hours. Some natural, but no acquired morality, and no strong innate notions of its value and necessity."

Few saw any chance of a happy marriage, particularly Queen Charlotte, who had heard horrifying tales about Princess Caroline's out-of-control behavior and reported them to her brother: "They say that her passions are so strong that the Duke [of Brunswick, Caroline's father] himself said that she was not to be allowed even to go from one room to another without her Governess, and that when she dances, this lady is obliged to follow her for the whole of the dance to prevent her from making an exhibition of herself by indecent conversations with men."

King George was one of the few who were enthusiastic about the bride he had selected, his niece, "whose amiable qualities will, I flatter myself, so fully engage your attention that they will divert it from objects not so pleasing to the nation." Lady Jersey, the prince's mistress, also approved. Lord Holland reported that, according to the Duke of Wellington, her support of her lover's marriage to a woman of supposedly "indelicate manners, indifferent character, and not very inviting appearance" arose "from the hope that disgust for the wife would secure constancy to the mistress."

It was Lady Jersey, not the prince, who was there to greet Caroline upon her arrival in England, and she immediately set to work trying to make the already dumpy princess look worse. She insisted on a less flattering gown for Caroline and over-applied rouge to her cheeks. The mistress needn't have worried, however, as the prince was instantly repelled when he met his bride-to-be on April 5, 1795. Lord Malmesbury recorded the scene at St. James's Palace: "He raised her (gracefully enough), and embraced her, said barely one word, turned around, retired to a distant part of the apartment, and calling me to him, said, 'Harris, I am not well; pray get me a glass of brandy.'"

George then stormed out of the room, leaving the bewildered princess alone with Malmesbury. "My God," she cried, "is the Prince always like that?" Then, seemingly aware of what sent the prince scurrying away, she remarked, almost in retaliation, "I find him very fat, and nothing like as handsome as his portrait."

Princess Caroline may have been flighty and impulsive, but she wasn't stupid. She not only recognized that she was not pleasing to the prince, but she understood Lady Jersey's agenda—and she resented it, especially since the mistress was to be a member of her household. That night at dinner she tried to make light of what was turning out to be an untenable situation. Her attempt failed—utterly. She was, according to Malmesbury, "flippant, rattling, affecting raillery and wit, and throwing out coarse vulgar hints about Lady Jersey, who was present." The Prince of Wales was, he added, "evidently disgusted."

Three days after their first, disastrous meeting, the prince and the cousin he was coming to despise were married in the Chapel Royal at St. James's Palace. George was so bombed on brandy that the Duke of Bedford had to keep him propped up, while Lord Melbourne noted that he "was like a man doing a thing in desperation; it was like Macheath going to his execution."

After the wedding ceremony, the Prince of Wales conducted his new bride to a reception in the queen's apartments. They barely spoke a word. Lady Maria Stuart said he looked "like Death and full of confusion, as if he wished to hide himself from the looks of the whole world. . . . I think he is much to be pitied. The bride, on the contrary, appeared in the highest spirits, when she passed by us first, smiling and nodding to every one. . . . What an odd Wedding!"

That evening the prince passed out in the fireplace, where he stayed all night. The next morning he consummated the union. "It required no small [effort] to conquer my aversion and overcome the disgust of her person," he wrote. Sex hardly improved George's disposition toward his wife, but at least she got pregnant and bore the next heir to the throne, Princess Charlotte. With that accomplished, the prince left her bed for good. He wanted nothing more to do with his wife. "I had rather see toads and vipers crawling over my victuals than sit at the same table with her," he declared.

Caroline was all but abandoned by George, who preferred dallying with his mistress, Lady Jersey, and racking up more debts. While he was away, he made sure his wife's movements were severely restricted. "She drives always alone," the lawyer Charles Abbot noted in his journal, "sees no company but old people put on her list. . . . She goes nowhere but airings in Hyde Park. The Prince uses her unpardonably."

Except for the king, who always took her part, Caroline had no support within the royal family. "I don't know how I shall be able to bear the loneliness," she wrote to a friend in Germany. "The Queen seldom visits me, and my sisters-in-law show me the same sympathy. . . . The Countess [of Jersey] is still here. I hate her and I know she feels the same towards me. My husband is wholly given up to her, so you can easily imagine the rest."

Although Lady Jersey's influence over the prince was beginning to wane, she was still a formidable adversary, a monster, really, who, having "no happiness without a rival to trouble and torment," as one contemporary said of her, relished humiliating the Princess of Wales at every opportunity. "It cannot have been difficult," wrote author Thea Holme. "Caroline was gauche, unversed in etiquette, stumbling in her English and apt when nervous to blurt out tactless comments and opinions, or to make coarse jokes, all of which were noted by Lady Jersey and relayed to the Prince." No wonder Caroline loathed her, or bristled over the fact that her husband's mistress had been foisted upon her as a member of *her* household.

When Caroline wrote to George requesting Lady Jersey's removal, she received a curt response, and a dismissal of sorts. "Nature has not made us suitable to each other," the prince wrote. "Tranquil and comfortable society is, however, in our power; let our intercourse therefore be restricted to that."

By this time, George's hatred of his wife had grown virulent. The marriage had not served its one purpose: to resolve his money problems. In fact, they had become even worse. Infinitely more galling, though, was Caroline's popularity with the people—especially as he was so reviled. "Poor woman," the novelist Jane Austen later wrote. "I shall support her as long as I can, because she is a Woman and because I hate her Husband." *True Briton* lavished praise upon "the amiable and accomplished personage [Caroline], who had been the object of so much unmerited ill treatment."

Caroline's mass appeal as the wronged wife was vividly demonstrated one evening when she attended the opera. "The house," *The Times* reported, "seemed as if electrified by her presence, and before she could take her seat, every hand was lifted to greet her with the loudest of plaudits. The gentlemen jumped on the benches and waved their hats, crying out '*Huzza!* '. . . . If the Princess will only afford the public a few more opportunities of testifying their respect for suffering virtue, we think it will bring more than one person to a proper reflection." Her sense of humor intact, the princess told the Duke of Leeds that "she supposed she could be guillotined . . . for what had passed this evening."

George was desperate to be rid of the "infamous wench," but his father, George III, absolutely forbade a formal separation. "You seem to look on your disunion with the princess as merely of a private nature," the king wrote to his son, "and totally put out of sight that as Heir Apparent of the Crown your marriage is a public act, wherein the Kingdom is concerned; that therefore a separation cannot be brought forward by the mere interference of relations."

Caroline did eventually establish her own residence near Blackheath. Before leaving her husband's home, she blasted him for his abominable behavior toward her: "Since I have been in this house you have treated me neither as your wife, nor as the mother of your child, nor as the Princess of Wales: and I tell you that from this moment I shall have nothing more to say and that I regard myself as being no longer subject to your orders—or to your rules."

Free from the tyranny of the prince, who had reunited with Mrs. Fitzherbert, Caroline really let loose—on an epic scale. "The poor Princess is going headlong to her ruin," wrote Lady Charlotte Campbell. "Every day she becomes more imprudent in her conduct, more heedless of society. . . . The society she is now surrounded by is disgraceful." Lady Hester Stanhope called Caroline "an impudent woman . . . a downright whore . . . she danced about, exposing herself like an opera girl . . . she was so low, so vulgar." Most scandalous of all, Lady Douglas alleged the princess had gotten pregnant and that the little boy whom she more or less adopted—William Austin, or Willikin, as Caroline called him—was actually her child.

An inquiry into this allegation, known as the Delicate Investigation, produced some extremely lurid testimony—like the statement from Roberts, the princess's footman, who said she was "very fond of fucking." Ultimately, though, there was no proof that Caroline had committed adultery, which would have been a treasonable offense and, George had hoped, grounds for the dissolution of their miserable marriage. (The princess later remarked that she had only committed adultery once, "with the husband of Mrs. Fitzherbert!")

Although Princess Caroline was exonerated after the Delicate Investigation, her reputation was in ruins. Even the king, her most stalwart supporter, was forced to concede that she was guilty of great "levity and profligacy" and declared that "no nearer intercourse" with the royal family could be "admitted in future than outward marks of civility."

The unrelenting hostility between the Prince and Princess of Wales, as well as their own selfish pursuits, left little room for parenting. Their daughter, Princess Charlotte, was sometimes used as a public relations prop in their escalating marital war, "dandled by each parent in turn for extra dramatic effect," as Thea Holme wrote. Mostly, though, she was ignored. George appeared particularly indifferent to his daughter, even if he did occasionally dote on the little girl. Charlotte felt his absence keenly.

"Oh how I wish I could see more of you!" the princess wrote to her father. "But I hope I shall in time. I am sensible how irksome it must be to you to see me, feeling I can be no companion to you to amuse you when in health; and am too young to soothe you when in affliction. Believe me that I am always truly happy when I do see you."

Part of the prince's lack of regard for his daughter sprang from the unsettling characteristics she shared with her mother, his detested wife. Charlotte was a vibrant, engaging, and essentially good-hearted girl, but at times a bit wild.

"One of her fancies was to ape the manner of a man," recalled Charlotte's childhood friend George Keppel. "On these occasions she would double her fists, and assume an attitude of defence that would have done credit to a professed pugilist. What I disliked in her, when in this mood, was her fondness for exercising her hands upon me in their clenched form."

There was indeed something of the rough-and-tumble tomboy in the princess, a high-spiritedness some of her contemporaries deemed distinctly unladylike. She "goes swaggering about," reported Lady Albina Cumberland, "and twangs hands with all the men, is in awe of no one and glories in her independent way of thinking." Lord Glenbervie recorded in his diary that the princess's conversation was "forward and dogmatical on all subjects, buckish about horses, and full of expressions very like swearing." Few of these characteristics were likely to endear the boisterous princess to her dad.

When King George III finally succumbed to permanent madness late in 1810, the Prince of Wales became regent. He planned an extravagant party to celebrate. "I have not been invited, nor do I know if I shall or not," fifteen-year-old Charlotte wrote to her governess. "If I should not, it will make a great noise in the world, as the friends I have seen have repeated over and over again it is my duty to go there; it is proper that I should. Really I do think it will be very hard if I am not asked." She wasn't.

If Charlotte craved affection from her father, she was more ambivalent about her mother. Caroline's maternal instincts—like so much else about her—were a little off-kilter. Certainly she never bothered to modify her outlandish behavior around her teenaged daughter, and thus Charlotte was exposed to a long line of Caroline's consorts. The young princess was understandably disturbed by her mother's antics and once said that "she could not think she was her daughter, as she showed such a want of character." Nevertheless, Charlotte did recognize how terribly mistreated her mother was. "I believe her to be both a *very unhappy* & a very *unfortunate* woman," she wrote, "who has had great *errors*, great *faults*, but is really oppressed and cruelly used."

The prince regent, as George was now known, ordered strict limitations on Caroline's visits with Charlotte, particularly after he learned that his estranged wife had been arranging liaisons in her home between their daughter and a womanizing officer by the name of Captain Charles Hesse.* Caroline's reaction to the restrictions was not really that of a broken-hearted mother deprived of her daughter; she didn't care all that much. Rather it was one of a vengeful wife who saw the opportunity to make trouble with George and his family—"teazing and worrying them," as she wrote.

When Queen Charlotte refused to intercede on Caroline's appeal for more time with Charlotte, the prince regent wrote to his mother to express himself gratified for the "very kind and considerate and well judged and most prudent method" she had adopted to "baffle this not only extraordinary . . . but most impudent fresh attempt on the part of this most mischievous and intriguing infernale" to affect a fondness for her daughter "which she never did feel and [was] totally incapable of feeling to create a discord or confusion in the family under the pretence of seeing her."

The prince regent's assessment of his wife's motives was fairly accurate, even if it was made in the midst of his blind hatred toward her. Caroline's concern for Princess Charlotte extended only so far as it suited her, as evidenced by her rash

---

* It remains unclear just how far the sexual relationship between Princess Charlotte and Captain Hesse went, but according to Charlotte's own account to her horrified father, Caroline left them alone in her room, locked the doors, and announced with a wink, *"A present je vous laisee, amusez vous!"* ("Now I leave you, have fun!")

decision to leave England for good in 1814. She had been warned that such a drastic step could jeopardize her daughter's position as heir apparent because George could divorce her while she was away, remarry, and sire a son. Plus, as shall be seen, Charlotte needed her at the time. Caroline didn't care.

"She decidedly deserts me," Princess Charlotte wrote in despair. "After all if a *mother* has not feeling for her child or children *are they to teach it to her* or can they *expect to be listened to with any hopes of success?*"

Caroline's desertion of her daughter occurred in the midst of a terrible situation Charlotte was enduring with her father. The prince regent was determined to exercise absolute control over his heir. In one instance he even told her governess that "Charlotte must lay aside the idle nonsense of thinking that she has a will of her own; while I live she must be subject to me as she is at present."

As part of the domination he maintained over his daughter, George herded her into an engagement with Prince William of Orange, even after assuring her that she would have a say in whom she wed. Such a marriage would entail living in Holland, at least for some part of the year, and sleeping with Prince William—neither of which appealed to the princess.

"As to going abroad," Charlotte wrote to her friend Priscilla Burghersh,

I believe and hope it to be quite out of the question, as I find by high and low that, naturally, it is a very unpopular measure in England, and as such of course (as my inclinations do not lead me either) I could not go against it, and besides which, I have now no manner of doubt that it is decidedly *an object and wish of more than one* to get rid of me if possible in that way. . . . You are far too sensible not to know that this [marriage] is only *de convenance,* and it is as much brought about by force as anything, and by deceit and hurry; though

I grant you that, were such a thing absolutely necessary, no one could be found so *unexceptionable* as he is. I am much more *triste* [sad] at it than I have ever chosen to write; can you be surprised?

Rather than proceed in an arrangement she found so odious, Charlotte took the bold step of breaking off the engagement. Her father was furious, and in his wrath he dismissed her servants and decreed that she would live, essentially, under house arrest. Desperate to escape such a fate, Charlotte ran away to her mother, only to find Caroline inflexible in her determination to leave England. The princess had no choice but to return and live in the isolated circumstances her father had ordered.

"Nothing can be so wretchedly uncertain and uncomfortable as my situation," she wrote to Priscilla Burghersh. "I am grown thin, sleep ill and eat but little. Bailly [Dr. Matthew Baillie] says my complaints are all nervous, and that bathing and sailing will brace me; but I say Oh no! no good can be done whilst the mind and the soul are on the rack constantly, and the spirits forced and screwed up to a certain pitch."

Harmony was eventually restored, and Princess Charlotte was allowed to marry the man of her choice, Prince Leopold of Saxe-Coburg-Saalfeld, in 1816. It was an ideal match; one of the rare royal marriages that actually worked. "We lead a very quiet and retired life here," Charlotte wrote from her country estate in Surrey, "but a very, *very* happy one." Alas, the sweet idyll would not last. The year after her wedding, Princess Charlotte died suddenly after giving birth to a stillborn baby son. She was only twenty-one, and the outpouring of grief that followed rivaled that for another Princess of Wales almost two centuries later.

As her daughter died, Princess Caroline was off gallivanting across Europe and making quite a spectacle of herself—as a stripper, essentially. At a ball in Naples, for example, she appeared "in the most indecent manner, her breast and her arms being entirely naked," and in Athens she had "dressed almost naked and danced with her servants." After seeing her at another ball, Lady Bessborough painted a particularly garish portrait of the princess in a letter to Granville Leveson-Gower: "I cannot tell you how sorry and ashamed I felt as an Englishwoman. In the room, [dancing], was a short, very fat elderly woman, with an extremely red face (owing I suppose to the heat) in a girl's white frock-looking dress, but with shoulder, back and neck quite low (disgustingly so) down to the middle of her stomach; very black hair [she was wearing a black wig] and eyebrows, which gave her a fierce look, and a wreath of light pink roses on her head."

Inappropriate dress aside, though, the most scandalous aspect of Princess Caroline's behavior was the flagrant affair she conducted with her strapping chamberlain, Bartolomeo Pergami, reports of which filtered back to Britain from all over Europe. There was the letter from Florence about her continuing "exceedingly prodigal behavior" and her "intimacy" with Pergami, which was "the subject of conversation everywhere." And from Hanover came news of Caroline's "very incongruous conduct," which "created general astonishment and justly merited indignation."

The couple simply seemed incapable of discretion, as a long list of servants and others attested. Caroline's coachman, Giuseppe Sacchi, for one, saw on several occasions Pergami slip into the princess's room, where he found them in the morning, "both asleep and having their respective hands upon one another. Her Royal Highness had her hand upon a particular part of Mr. Pergami, and Mr. Pergami had his own upon that of her Royal Highness. . . . Once . . . Pergami had his breeches loosened . . . and the Princess's hand was . . . upon that part."

Caroline had decided that she would never return to England, but that all changed early in 1820 when King George III died and her estranged husband became King George IV. The wayward princess now determined that she would take her place as queen. And there was nothing the government could do to stop her, despite the new king's most intensive efforts.

"It is impossible for me to paint the insolence, the violence and the precipitation of this woman's conduct," reported Lord Hutchinson, part of a deputation sent to France to urge Caroline's quiet retirement. "I never saw anything so outrageous, so undignified as a queen, or so unamiable as a woman. . . . She has really assumed a tone and hauteur which is quite insufferable, and which nothing but the most pure and unimpeached innocence could justify. . . . We have at length come to a final and ultimate issue with this outrageous woman. She has set the King's authority at defiance, and it is now time for her to feel his vengeance and his power. Patience, forbearance and moderation have had no effect on her. I must now implore His Majesty to exert all his firmness and resolution: retreat is impossible. The Queen has thrown down the gauntlet of defiance. The King must take it up."

Yet for all his huffing and puffing, King George IV was powerless against Caroline's onslaught. He was almost universally loathed, and she—personifying all opposition to the king and his government—was warmly embraced by the masses. "No Queen, no King!" the people shouted.

"This brave woman," as *The Times* called Caroline, was raucously received from the moment she arrived at Dover on June 5, 1820. The diarist Charles Greville rode out to watch the queen enter London and reported, "The road was thronged with an immense multitude the whole way from Westminster Bridge to Greenwich. Carriages, carts, and horsemen followed, preceded, and surrounded her coach the whole way. She was everywhere received with the greatest enthusiasm. Women waved pocket handkerchiefs, and men shouted wherever she passed."

George IV, faced with the nightmarish possibility of a revolution in support of his monstrous wife, had one weapon left to destroy her (or so he thought): Bartolomeo Pergami. A Bill of Pains and Penalties was introduced into the House of Lords accusing Caroline of having conducted herself toward Pergami with "indecent and offensive familiarity and freedom," and of having carried on "a licentious, disgraceful, and adulterous intercourse" with him. And for such behavior, the bill sought to "deprive her Majesty Caroline Amelia Elizabeth of the title, prerogatives, rights, privileges, and pretensions of Queen Consort of this realm, and to dissolve the marriage between his Majesty and the said Queen."

The inquiry that followed produced compelling evidence against Caroline, but the majority of people seemed not to care. "All the world is with her," declared Sir James Mackintosh. Roving mobs attacked anyone they believed was not on the queen's side, while cartoonists gleefully attacked the king. The nation was riveted by the case.

"No other subject is ever talked of," Charles Greville wrote. "If you meet a man in the street, he impatiently asks you, 'Have you heard anything new about the Queen?' All people express themselves bored with the subject, yet none talk or think of any other. . . . Since I have been in the world I never remember any question which so exclusively occupied everybody's attention, and so completely absorbed men's thoughts."

After a sensational trial in which all manner of lurid testimony was heard regarding Caroline's romps with Pergami, the Bill of Pains and Penalties narrowly passed in the House of Lords. But given the slim margin, as well as the widespread agitation in favor of the queen, the bill was withdrawn before it was sent for debate in the House of Commons. A massive three-day celebration erupted across the kingdom as a result. "There had never been such rejoicing since Waterloo," wrote historian Christopher Hibbert.

Though Caroline had won, she was still not going to be crowned. When she arrived at Westminster Abbey for George IV's coronation, the doors were slammed right in her face. Several weeks later she was dead, perhaps of stomach cancer, though some have suggested poison. The inscription on her coffin, which she wrote herself, read: DEPOSITED, CAROLINE OF BRUNSWICK, THE INJURED QUEEN OF ENGLAND.

George IV lived another nine years, reviled as ever.

25

William IV (1830–1837):

A Misbegotten Brood

Jordan's high and mighty squire
— John Wolcot, aka Peter Pindar

When George IV died in 1830, he was succeeded by his brother the Duke of Clarence, who became King William IV—the second (and last) of the sons of George III to reign in Britain.

The sons of George III were nothing if not prolific. Between the lot of them, they produced fifty-seven children before 1819—fifty-six of whom were illegitimate.* Most of these misbegotten offspring were secreted away and kept quiet by the princes who sired them. But the Duke of Clarence, who became King William IV, defied convention and lived openly— and quite happily—with his ten out-of-wedlock children and their mother, an actress named Dorothy Jordan. He even named his kids—the Fitzclarences, as they were called—after his own brothers and sisters.

Mrs. Jordan entered William's life at a fortuitous time in 1790. His naval career was in its decline and, thanks to his dis-

* Princess Charlotte was George III's only legitimate grandchild before 1819, when, as shall be seen later in this chapter, several more of the king's sons produced legitimate heirs after Charlotte's death in 1817.

approving father, he had few prospects for gainful employment. What he needed was a good companion. Having grown tired of the empty sexual encounters of his youth—"with a lady of the town against a wall or in the middle of a parade," as he wrote—the duke was seeking a woman to settle down with, or at least one who "would not clap or pox me every time I fucked."

A popular comedic actress, Mrs. Jordan had a gregarious good nature that blended well with the duke's own kindly—if sometimes crude—disposition. "Her face, her tones, her manner, were irresistible," wrote William Hazlitt in his *Dramatic Essays*. "Her smile had the effect of sunshine, and her laugh did one good to hear it." No wonder William was smitten. She was, he said, "one of the most perfect women in the world." And Dorothy's income as an actress had its own compensations as well, especially for a man with debts as heavy as the duke's. William's reliance on Mrs. Jordan's money prompted a few snickers, and John Wolcot's (aka Peter Pindar) sassy epigram:

> *As Jordan's high and mighty squire*
> *Her playhouse profits deigns to skim;*
> *Some folks audaciously enquire*
> *If he keeps her or she keeps him.*

Despite such occasional barbs, the couple's essential decency tended to mute most criticism of their unconventional domestic arrangement. "The truth of the matter was that it was extraordinarily difficult to denigrate any relationship so happy, domestic and virtuous," wrote biographer Philip Ziegler. "They were two likeable people, anxious to do no harm to anybody and devoted to each other. It would have been surprising if the public had not learned to look on them, at first with tolerance, in the end with affectionate approval."

Even the uptight king and queen grudgingly accepted Mrs. Jordan, though not—heaven forbid—at court. They even deigned to attend one of her performances. "The Duke of Clarence has managed so well that the King jokes with him about Mrs. Jordan," Lord Liverpool reported in 1797.

For twenty years the prince and his paramour lived in harmony with the children they both doted upon. She continued to act, even during her numerous pregnancies, while he devoted himself to farming. William thrived in the domestic idyll they had created. "We shall have a full and merry house at Christmas," Mrs. Jordan wrote to a friend. "'Tis what the duke delights in." Alas, the arrangement was not destined to last.

Money was the main problem; William never had enough. He knew, like his brother George before him, that a respectable marriage would increase his income. So in 1811, after two decades of domestic bliss, the duke abandoned his mistress and began the search for a wealthy wife. Poor Mrs. Jordan was crushed.

"Could you believe or the world believe that we never had for twenty years the *semblance of a quarrel*," she wrote to a friend. "But this is so well known in our domestic circle that the astonishment is greater. Money, money, my good friend, or the *want* of it, has, I am convinced made HIM at the moment the most wretched of men, but having done wrong he does not like to retract." Still, the scorned woman was surprisingly sympathetic: "But with all his excellent qualities, his domestic *virtues*, his love for his *lovely* children, what must he not at this moment suffer?"

The duke's suffering was not alleviated by his hunt for a rich woman to support him. Sadly, none of the ladies he pursued was willing to have him. "It was flattering to be courted by a prince of the blood," wrote Philip Ziegler, "but when the prince was forty-six and looked every year of it; portly, balding and uncouth with no small talk, a mountain of debts and ten illegitimate children; a romantic girl might be forgiven for finding that blood alone had only limited charm."

The need for a wife became more urgent in 1817 when Princess Charlotte, George III's only legitimate grandchild, died after childbirth. Now, after the king, only William's two older brothers stood between him and the throne. Charlotte's father, the Prince of Wales, was not likely to live long given his unhealthy lifestyle, and the wife of Frederick, Duke of York, was not expected to reproduce after twenty years of marriage. So, the race was on between the rest of the royal dukes to secure the succession. William saw an opportunity not only to do his duty by marrying, but to get paid for it as well.

"If the *Cabinet* consider the measure of *my* marrying one of consequence," he wrote to his mother, Queen Charlotte, "they *ought* to state to *me* what they *can* and *will* propose for my establishment: for *without previously* being acquainted with *their* intentions as to *money* matters I *cannot* and *will* not make any positive offer to any Princess. I have *ten* children *totally* and *entirely* dependent on *myself*: I owe *forty thousand* pounds of *funded* debt for which of course I pay interest, and I have a floating debt of *sixteen thousand pounds*."

A German bride, Princess Amelia Adelaide of Saxe-Coburg-Meiningen, was selected for the duke, and on July 13, 1818, they were married—just over a week after first meeting. It was a double ceremony with William's brother Edward, Duke of Kent (who ultimately won the reproductive race by fathering the future Queen Victoria the following year).* "She is doomed, poor dear innocent young creature, to be my wife," William wrote of Princess Adelaide before their wedding. "I cannot, will not, I must not ill use her."

---

* A younger brother, Prince Adolphus, Duke of Cambridge, also fathered a legitimate son earlier in 1819, but he was farther down in the line of succession. Thus, Victoria became queen.

The marriage was by all accounts a happy one. Adelaide was kind to William's ten children—some of whom lived at Windsor Castle—even as her own children were stillborn or died soon after delivery, and she seemed to tame the more uncouth side of the duke's disposition. "You would be surprised at the Duke of Clarence if you were to see him," Lord Colchester wrote; "for his wife, it is said, has entirely reformed him; and instead of that *polisson* [naughty] manner for which he used to be celebrated, he is now quiet and well-behaved."

Meanwhile, William's ill-used mistress, Mrs. Jordan, had fled to France in 1815 to escape her creditors. Largely ignored by her children, in increasingly bad health, and nearly destitute, she died alone in the summer of 1816. Although clearly not the most attentive of former lovers, William always revered the memory of Mrs. Jordan. He would snap up portraits of her whenever they came on the market and, after he became king in 1830, commissioned a bust of her that he tried to give to St. Paul's. The offer was politely refused, and thus Mrs. Jordan's sculpture stayed by the king's side—a persistent reminder of the past, indulged by the remarkably tolerant Queen Adelaide.

26

Victoria (1837–1901):
A Trip Down the Aisle

And you saw the want of rehearsal.

—BENJAMIN DISRAELI

William IV died in 1837 without a child of his own to succeed him, so the crown passed to his niece Victoria, daughter of George III's fourth son, Edward, Duke of Kent.

The accession of eighteen-year-old Queen Victoria in 1837 marked the beginning of a remarkable era—a second English Renaissance, as it has been called. But the coronation of the young monarch did not bode such a brilliant future—quite the opposite, in fact. The ceremony was an awkward affair—five hours filled with every manner of mishap, featuring participants who, Charles Greville noted, "were very imperfect in their parts."

The patina of magnificence was certainly present at the service, infused as it was with ancient tradition and the aura of royalty. Westminster Abbey was packed with richly adorned peers and peeresses, triumphant music filled the air, and the diminutive sovereign—standing at just five feet tall—dazzled in her rich regalia. Victoria was indeed the very image of majesty, and managed to maintain it, despite the blundering of almost everyone around her.

"The Queen looked very well, and performed her part with great grace and completeness, which cannot in general be said of the other performers," Benjamin Disraeli observed. "They were always in doubt as to what came next, and you saw the want of rehearsal."

The clergymen leading the ceremony seemed to be the most egregiously unprepared. Lord John Thynne, who officiated in place of the elderly and infirm dean of Westminster, admitted to Charles Greville "that nobody knew what was to be done . . . and consequently there was continual difficulty and embarrassment, and the Queen never knew what she was to do next."

Among the fumbling clergy was the "remarkably maladroit" bishop of Durham, who, Victoria wrote, "never could tell me what was to take place." The archbishop of Canterbury was also present, but he, too, was of little help. The queen recounted that at one point in the service he "came in and ought to have delivered the Orb to me, but I had already got it, and he (as usual) was so confused and puzzled and knew nothing, and went away." It was the archbishop who insisted upon cramming the coronation ring onto the queen's finger, even though it didn't fit, "and the consequence was that I had the greatest difficulty to take it off again, which I at last did with great pain."

Other participants rivaled the clergy in their clumsiness, including Prime Minister William Lamb, Viscount Melbourne. Loaded on laudanum and brandy, he "looked very awkward and uncouth," Disraeli wrote, "with his coronet cocked over his nose, his robes under his feet, and holding the great Sword of State like a butcher." Then there was the Duchess of Sutherland, "full of her situation," Disraeli noted, who "walked, or rather stalked up the Abbey like Juno."

Victoria's trainbearers certainly could have used some practice, for, as one of them acknowledged, "we carried the Queen's train very jerkily and badly, never keeping step properly, and it must have been very difficult for her to walk, as she did, evenly and steadily, and with much grace and dignity, the whole length of the Abbey."

While the trainbearers were tripping over themselves in the procession, the peers of the realm, members of the highest social order, were doing the same as they paid ritual homage to their new sovereign. "The Queen complained of a headache, from having her crown very unceremoniously *knocked* by most of the peers," recalled Lady Wilhelmina Stanhope—"one actually clutched hold of it, but she said she had guarded herself from any accident or misadventure by having it made to fit her head tightly."

One elderly peer, Lord Rolle, had an unfortunate accident as he tried to make it up the stairs to pay tribute to the queen. "It turned me very sick," recounted Harriet Martineau, who was observing from a balcony. "The large and infirm old man was held by two peers, and had nearly reached the footstool when he slipped through the hands of his supporters, and rolled over and over down the steps, lying at the bottom coiled up in his robes. He was instantly lifted up, and tried again and again, amidst shouts of admiration of his valour." Victoria managed to salvage the situation when she rose from the throne and walked down two or three steps to meet Lord Rolle as he continued his struggle up. The incident was recalled in a bit of verse by Richard Harris Barham:

> Then the trumpets braying, and the organ playing,
> And the sweet trombones, with their silver tones;
> But Lord Rolle was rolling;—'t was mighty consoling
> To think his Lordship did not break his bones!

Another aspect of Queen Victoria's coronation ceremony went wildly awry: the distribution of her coronation medals. "The noise and confusion were very great when the medals were thrown about by Lord Surrey, everybody scrambling with all their might and main to get them," Greville reported. Surrey was "nearly torn to pieces in the universal excitement," Lady Stanhope wrote, and "with his temper entirely gone," he "looked as red and voluble as a turkey-cock."

After nearly five hours, the bumbling service mercifully came to an end. Victoria returned to Buckingham Palace and immediately went to wash her dog. Though her coronation was inelegant at times, she recalled it with pride. "It was a memorable and glorious day for me," she wrote. "I likewise venture to add that people thought I did my part—very well."

27

Victoria (1837–1901):

The Queen's Prince Charming

I NEVER NEVER spent such an evening!!!

—QUEEN VICTORIA

Queen Victoria married her first cousin on her mother's side, Albert of Saxe-Coburg-Gotha, on February 10, 1840. The couple had nine children, many of whom married into the various ruling houses of Europe and produced, among others, Kaiser Wilhelm II of Germany, Queen Maud of Norway, Empress Alexandra of Russia, and Queen Marie of Romania.

Now that she was queen, the last thing Victoria wanted was a husband. She was young, powerful, and, for the first time in her life, independent. Having been dominated her entire life by her widowed mother, the Duchess of Kent, she found the prospect of ceding any of her newly found freedom odious indeed. "I said I dreaded the thought of marrying," the queen wrote, "that I was so accustomed to have my own way that I thought it was 10 to 1 that I shouldn't agree with anybody."

Yet despite the queen's most vigorous objections to the subject of marriage, no one expected she would remain, like her distant predecessor Elizabeth I, single forever. Even Victoria knew she would marry, just not right away. An early marriage, her prime minister, Lord Melbourne, assured her, was "*not* NECESSARY."

King Leopold I of Belgium, the queen's maternal uncle (and Princess Charlotte's widower), thought otherwise. He also had a definite idea who Victoria's consort should be: his nephew, Albert of Saxe-Coburg-Gotha. Leopold had been encouraging the match for years, but nothing had come of his efforts. In fact, there had been very few sparks when Victoria briefly met her cousin Albert in 1836, the year before she became queen. He was a tad too delicate for her tastes, even if he was handsome. "I am sorry to say," Victoria wrote to her uncle, "that we have an invalid in the house in the person of Albert."

Leopold was still pushing three years later when he suggested that Albert go to England again, as a prospective bridegroom. The queen was decidedly unenthused about the proposed visit, "which I am desirous should not transpire," and expressed her feelings to her uncle. "First of all," she wrote, "I wish to know if *Albert* is aware of the wish of his *Father* [Ernest, Duke of Saxe-Coburg-Gotha] and *you* relative to *me*? Secondly, if he knows that there is *no engagement* between us? I am anxious that you should acquaint Uncle Ernest, that if I should like Albert, that I can make *no final promise this year*, for, at the *very earliest*, any such event could not take place till *two or three years hence*. For, independent of my youth, and my *great* repugnance to change my present position, there is *no anxiety* evinced in *this country* for such an event, and it would be more prudent, in my opinion, to wait till some such demonstration is shown,—else if I were hurried it might produce discontent."

The queen was moody and irate in anticipation of Albert's visit, with her prime minister stoically bearing the brunt of her pique. But then suddenly everything switched. Albert arrived on October 10, 1839, and Victoria was almost immediately sent swooning. "It is with some emotion that I beheld Albert— who is *beautiful*," she wrote, beginning an avalanche of superlatives about Albert in her diary.

"Albert really is quite charming," she gushed in one entry,

"and so excessively handsome, such beautiful blue eyes, an exquisite nose, and such pretty mouth with delicate mustachios and slight but very slight whiskers; a beautiful figure, broad in the shoulders and a fine waist; my heart is quite *going*." Everything Albert did, he seemed to do "beautifully." "It is quite a pleasure to look at Albert when he gallops and valses, he does it so beautifully, holds himself so well with that beautiful figure of his . . . dearest Albert . . . dances so beautifully."

All the queen's objections about marriage vanished instantly, and just five days after Albert's arrival, she proposed to him. Both were trembling and uncertain before Victoria finally blurted out that it would make her "too happy" if he would consent to be her husband. She had barely finished before Albert took her hands in his and, while kissing and caressing them, whispered in German how pleased he would be to spend his life with her.

"We embraced each other over and over again," Victoria wrote in her journal, "and he was *so* kind, *so* affectionate; Oh! to *feel* I was, and am, loved by *such* an Angel was *too great a delight to describe*. He is *perfection*; perfection in every way—in beauty—in everything! . . . Oh! *how* I adore and love him, I cannot say!! *how* I will strive to make him feel as little as possible the great sacrifice he has made."

Albert was keenly aware of what the great sacrifice would entail. He would not only have to leave his homeland and loved ones for an alien kingdom, but he would have to sublimate his very identity to that of the British sovereign. "My future position will have its dark sides and the sky will not always be blue and unclouded," he confided to his brother Ernest. Nevertheless, he was prepared to do his duty and to love Victoria the best way he could. "How is it," he wrote to her, "that I have deserved so much love, so much affection? . . . I believe that Heaven has sent me an angel whose brightness shall illume my life."

The young cousins, both twenty years old, spent many hours

together after their engagement, kissing tenderly, reveling in each other's company, and planning their future. But it was soon time for Albert to return to Germany, briefly, before making the permanent move to Britain. "We kissed each other so often, and I leant on that dear soft cheek, fresh and pink as a rose," Victoria wrote the day Albert left. "It was ten o'clock and the time for his going . . . I gave Albert a last kiss, and saw him get into the carriage—and drive off. I cried so much, felt wretched, yet happy to think that we should meet again so soon. Oh! How I love him, how intensely, how devotedly, how ardently! I cried and felt so sad."

On November 23, 1839, just over a week after Albert's departure, Queen Victoria made her Declaration of Marriage before an assembly of privy councillors at Buckingham Palace. Her hands trembled terribly. "It was rather an awful moment," she wrote to her fiancé, "to be obliged to announce this to so many people, many of whom were quite strangers." Still, she admitted, the anxiety of publicly announcing that she had selected a mate for herself did not compare with the nervousness she had felt in anticipation of proposing to him.

Not everyone was as ecstatic as Victoria over her choice of a spouse. "The ultra-Tories are filled with prejudices against the Prince, in which I can clearly trace the influence of Ernest Augustus of Hanover," Baron Stockmar reported to King Leopold. "They give out that he is a Radical and an infidel, and say that George of Cambridge [Victoria's first cousin], or a Prince of Orange, ought to have been the Consort of the Queen."

It was indeed the queen's uncle, Ernest Augustus of Hanover*—the infamous Duke of Cumberland accused of

---

* All of the Hanoverian monarchs of Britain were kings of Hanover as well, except Victoria. Salic law prohibited a woman from occupying the throne, so upon the death of William IV in 1837, Ernest, Duke of Cumberland, became king.

killing his valet (see Chapter 22)—who worked most assidu-
ously against Victoria's wishes. She wanted Albert to take
precedence over all members of the royal family, but that "old
wretch," as the queen called her uncle Ernest, absolutely refused to yield to what he termed a "paper Royal Highness"
from an insignificant duchy. The matter was finally resolved
when it was determined that the queen could grant Albert
precedence by use of the royal prerogative, which was a constitutional right retained by the sovereign, a vestige of the vast
powers English kings once possessed.

Money was another matter, however. Only Parliament could
approve of the fifty-thousand-pound income for Albert that
the queen requested. And after years of funding the lavish
lifestyles of Victoria's debauched Hanoverian uncles, particularly George IV, the lawmakers were loath to indulge yet another royal parasite. Albert was given only a little more than
half of what had been expected.

"Everybody . . . thinks the allowance proposed for Prince
Albert very exorbitant," Charles Greville noted. "Fifty thousand a year given for pocket-money is quite monstrous, and it
would have been prudent to propose a more moderate grant for
the sake of his popularity." A bit of satirical verse reflected the
mood of some toward the penniless German prince Victoria
intended to import:

> He comes, the bridegroom of Victoria's choice,
> The nominee of Lehzen's* vulgar voice
> He comes to take "for better or for worse"
> England's fat Queen and England's fatter purse. . . .
> Saxe-Coburg sends him from its paltry race,
> With foreign phrases and mustachio'd face,

* Louise Lehzen had been Victoria's governess and wielded great influence
over her.

To win from Hymen, and a school-girl's love,
Treasures, his sire's whole revenue above. . . .
The hoyden Sovereign of this mighty isle
Welcomes her German with enraptured smile,
Telleth her "faithful Commons" to provide
Supplies, to make him worthy of his bride;
And thus transforms, by magic conjuring,
A lucky beggar to a puissant king.

The queen blamed the Tories for most of her troubles, including the "wicked old foolish" Duke of Wellington, who had voted down Albert's subsidy and even dared question whether he was Protestant. "Poor dear Albert, how cruelly they are using that dearest Angel! Monsters! You Tories shall be punished. Revenge! Revenge!"

Yet while the queen railed against all the indignities her beloved was made to suffer at the hands of those "abominable, infamous Tories," she was herself thwarting Albert in a number of ways, lording her sovereignty over him. When, for example, he declared his wish to have a bipartisan household to reflect his political impartiality, "chosen from both sides—the same number of Whigs as of Tories," as well as some German gentlemen, the queen sternly replied, "I must tell you quite honestly that it will not do."

Victoria's refusal seemed to startle the prince. "I am very sorry," he wrote to her from Coburg, "that you have not been able to grant my first request . . . for I know it was not an unfair one. . . . Think of my position, Dear Victoria, I am leaving home with all its associations, all my bosom friends, and going to a country in which everything is new and strange to me. . . . Except yourself I have no one to confide in. And it is not even to be conceded to me that the two or three persons who are to have the charge of my private affairs should be persons who already command my confidence."

The queen was not to be persuaded on the issue, and was similarly intransigent on the length of their honeymoon, which he hoped might last "at least a fortnight—or a week?" "My dear Albert," she replied imperiously, "you have not at all understood the matter. *You forget, my dearest Love, that I am the Sovereign, and that business can stop and wait for nothing.*"

Victoria adopted an entirely different tone as she rhapsodized about the honeymoon she had insisted upon keeping short: "When day dawned (for we did not sleep much) and I beheld that beautiful angelic face by my side, it was more than I can express! He does look so beautiful in his shirt only, with his beautiful throat seen."

It was a remarkably vivid account, particularly for a monarch whose name has become almost synonymous with rigid and repressed sexuality.* And it was just one journal entry. "I NEVER NEVER spent such an evening!!!" she gushed in another. "My DEAREST DEAREST DEAR Albert sat on a footstool by my side, & his excessive love & affection gave me feelings of heavenly love & happiness, I never could have *hoped* to have felt before! He clasped me in his arms, and we kissed each other again and again! His beauty, his sweetness and gentleness . . . really how can I ever be thankful enough for such a *Husband*!

---

* It was actually Albert who was the prude.

28

Victoria (1837–1901): Paradise Lost

Never do I enjoy myself more or more peacefully
than when I can be so much with my beloved
Albert—follow him everywhere.

— QUEEN VICTORIA

*The love Victoria had for Albert turned to worship as the queen grew entirely
dependent on her "beloved lord and master." As she later recalled, "I . . .
leant on him for all and everything." Without his approval "I did nothing,
moved not a finger, arranged not a print or photograph." Accordingly, the
retreat the couple purchased on the Isle of Wight was Albert's own kingdom,
where he held absolute dominion—even after death.*

The rains had been unrelenting that October day in 1844 as
Victoria and Albert sailed across the Solent toward the Isle of
Wight. There they hoped to purchase a private retreat for
themselves—a place far from the suffocating court life and unhealthy air of London—that they could call their very own.
There seemed to be no break in store from the abysmal weather
when the couple arrived on the island just off England's southern coast. But as they drove through the secluded Osborne estate on the outskirts of East Cowes, the sun managed to peek
through the stormy skies and shine upon a large three-story
home surrounded by stately trees, with grounds that sloped
gently toward the sea. The queen was enchanted.

"It is impossible to see a prettier place," she told Lord Melbourne, "with woods and valleys and *points de vue,* which would be beautiful anywhere, but all this near the sea . . . is quite perfection. We have a calming beach quite to ourselves. The sea is so blue and calm and the prince said it was like Naples. And then we can walk about anywhere by ourselves without fear of being followed and mobbed."

Victoria and Albert had found their Eden; their "dear and lovely little domaine," as the queen called Osborne. There they would spend some of their happiest days together, surrounded by their growing family, and completely at ease amid the estate's bountiful pleasures.

Albert immediately set about making improvements to the place where, he said, he could be "partly forester, partly builder, partly farmer and partly gardener." There was certainly plenty of work to be done on the neglected property, and the prince worked intently to create his personal paradise. "It does one's heart good to see how my beloved Albert enjoys it all, and is so full of the plans and improvements he means to carry out," Victoria wrote. "He is hardly to be kept at home."

One of the prince's first major projects was to replace the existing house on the estate, which he deemed too small, with a much larger structure in the style of an Italian Renaissance palazzo, complete with two belvedere towers that loomed over the landscape. Once completed, the new home was filled with Albert's personal touches—from the furniture he designed to fit his wife's tiny frame to the intertwined letters *V* and *A* over the doorways (except over the entry to the smoking room, where the letter *A* stands alone in deference to the queen's strong dislike of tobacco).

One of the most striking features of Osborne House (which is no longer a royal residence and is open to the public) is the number of nudes throughout—robust male and female nudes in paintings and sculpture that Victoria and Albert exchanged as gifts. This veritable celebration of naked human form is in vivid contrast to the popular image of a prudish queen who lent her name to an era of sexual repression. (Albert, who actually was a bit uptight about sex, did object to one sculpture that featured his bare legs and kept it hidden on a quiet cul-de-sac at the top of the house.)

With all of Albert's thoughtful touches, Osborne became a much loved escape for his family. The royal children were each given an individual plot to garden and even had a fully furnished Swiss-style chalet that was built just for them. They learned to cook in the cottage's miniature kitchen, with its full range of utensils, and kept their collections under glass cases in a mini-museum. "Yesterday there was a grand tea at the Swiss Cottage," Victoria reported—"and imagine good Affie [her second son, Alfred] by way of amusement exhibiting his air pump and steam engine (puffing and blowing all the time—in the tool house) . . . and pumping over himself and [third son] Arthur."

Victoria, too, delighted in Osborne. "Sat out under the trees, where it was really heavenly, and sketched," she wrote during the summer of 1855. "Every day, every year, this dear sweet spot seems more lovely and with its brilliant sunshine, deep blue sea and dazzling flowers, is a perfect paradise,—and all my beloved one's creation,—the result of his exquisite taste."

The queen took her first sea swim off the estate's private beach, but it could hardly be called a quick, spontaneous dip. First she stepped into a "bathing machine," a changing room on wheels where she slipped into her swimsuit. The bathing machine was then pulled by a horse to the very edge of the shore, after which Victoria emerged from the other side directly into the water. "I thought it delightful," she wrote, "till I put my head under water, when I thought I should be stifled."

Of all the joys Osborne had to offer the queen, nothing came close to simply being with her man—reading books together, taking walks, watching the ships sail by on the Solent, listening to the nightingales in the evening, or playing duets on the piano. "Never do I enjoy myself more or more peacefully than when I can be so much with my beloved Albert," she wrote—"follow him everywhere."

———

The relaxed and relatively carefree atmosphere at Osborne evaporated completely with Prince Albert's untimely death in 1861.* He was only forty-two, as was Queen Victoria, whose life all but ceased as well. For decades she lived in semi-seclusion, dressed in her widow's weeds, obsessively tending to her late husband's memory.

In her maudlin devotion to her mate, the queen ordered Osborne maintained exactly as Albert left it. During a visit in 1862, Lord Clarendon found it "difficult to believe" that the prince would not at any moment walk into his room because "everything was set out on his table and the pen and his blotting-book, his handkerchief on the sofa, his watch going, fresh flowers in the glass." Amid the gloom, Queen Victoria even dabbled in the occult, desperately trying to contact her prince. Alas, she had to content herself with his jacket, which she took to bed with her every night.

Writing from the estate during her first Christmas without her beloved, Victoria pronounced how she would conduct herself as queen now that Albert was gone. "I am . . . anxious to repeat *one* thing," she wrote, "and *that one* is my firm resolve, my *irrevocable decision* . . . that *his* wishes—*his* plans—about everything, *his* views about *every* thing are to be *my law*! And *no human power* will make me swerve from *what he* decided and wished. . . . I am *also determined* that *no one* person, may *he* be

* Typhoid was identified as the cause of Albert's death, although some historians have speculated that he may have had some other chronic disease, given how ill he was in the years preceding his death.

ever so good, ever so devoted among my servants—is to lead or guide or dictate *to me*. I know *how he* would disapprove it. And I live *on* with him, for him; in fact I am only *outwardly* separated from him, and only for a *time*."

Poor Princess Alice, Victoria and Albert's second daughter, had the misfortune of marrying Prince Louis of Hesse at Osborne less than seven months after her father's death. She had lovingly attended her grieving mother—even sleeping with her in her bedroom—and now the queen dreaded the day of Alice's "wretched marriage." Victoria described the ceremony as "more like a funeral than a wedding," which, thanks in large part to her, it was.

There were no joyous preparations before the ceremony. The queen made certain of that. "She [Alice] is dressing in her *Beloved Papa's* room, while *I* am having my widow's cap adjusted! I think it is a dreadful dream!" At least the bride was allowed to wear white for this special occasion, although her trousseau was the required black.

Only immediate family and a handful of relatives were invited to the service, which took place in the dining room of Osborne House—right under a family portrait dominated by Prince Albert. Victoria sat apart from everyone else, protectively flanked by her four eldest sons. "Fortunately for the bride and groom, who were much less the focus of attention than the huddled figure in black, the Archbishop of York kept the service short," wrote biographer Stanley Weintraub.

"It was *very solemn—very affecting, very sad*," the queen wrote after the ceremony. The archbishop, tears streaming down his face, "read the service . . . beautifully! But when it came to the words *till death us do part* I could not restrain my tears—tho' I struggled and I did command myself till all was over. Affie sobbed dreadfully all through."

Of course there was no reception. Immediately after the service the queen went to her room, where she ate lunch alone with the bride and groom. Alice and Louis were allowed a couple of days for their honeymoon, but Victoria expected her daughter back at Osborne to attend to her. A week later, Alice left for her new home in Hesse.

"I hardly miss her at all, or felt her going," the queen reported, "so *utterly* absorbed am I by that one dreadful loss."

After several decades of deep mourning the shroud lifted a little. Victoria was even bold enough to stray from Albert's original plan for Osborne and allowed an addition to be built. She enjoyed having her grandchildren and great-grandchildren visit her at the estate, where she provided entertainment for them and—occasionally—reveled in their company. Not all were enamored with Osborne, however.

"Even as a child I was struck by the ugliness of the house, which has been described as 'a family necropolis,'" wrote Victoria's great-grandson King Edward VIII. "The floors of the corridors and passages were inlaid with mosaic; set into the walls were numerous alcoves each displaying in life size a white marble statue of a dead or living member of 'Gangan's' large family."

Victoria spent her last Christmas at Osborne in 1900. It was not a joyous occasion for the queen, now eighty-one and in failing health. Looking up at the family Christmas tree (a holiday adornment Prince Albert had popularized in Britain), she could barely see the candles lighting it. "I feel so melancholy," she wrote, "as I see so very badly." Adding to her distress on Christmas Day was the news that her dear friend Lady Churchill had died the night before. "The loss to me is not to be told," she lamented, "and that it should happen here is too sad."

On January 22, 1901, at half past six in the evening, the long reign of Queen Victoria came to a close when she breathed her last in her bedroom at Osborne. Her coffin, stuffed by her order with mementos of Albert—including his dressing gown and a plaster cast of his hand—was taken down to the dining room. There the queen rested for a week before leaving the Isle of Wight for the last time.

PART IV

House of Saxe-Coburg-Gotha to Windsor

EDWARD VII

(reigned 1901–1910)

GEORGE V

(r. 1910–1936)

EDWARD VIII

(r. 1936)

GEORGE VI

(r. 1936–1952)

ELIZABETH II

(r. 1952–present)

House of Saxe-Coburg-Gotha to Windsor

EDWARD VII
r. 1901–1910
m. Alexandra of Denmark
(maternal aunt of Tsar Nicholas II)

GEORGE V
r. 1910–1935
m. Mary of Teck

EDWARD VIII
r. 1936
m. Wallis Warfield Simpson

GEORGE VI
r. 1936–1952
m. Lady Elizabeth Bowes-Lyon
(Queen Elizabeth, the Queen Mother)

ELIZABETH II
r. 1952–present
m. Prince Philip, Duke of Edinburgh

Charles, Prince of Wales
m. (1) Diana Spencer

Anne,
The Princess Royal

William   Harry

Others

Margaret Rose

Andrew,
Duke of York

Edward,
Earl of Wessex

29

Edward VII (1901–1910): Sex Ed

And to break your poor parents' hearts.

—Prince Albert

Upon the death of Queen Victoria in 1901, her eldest son succeeded her as Edward VII. He was fifty-nine. The name Saxe-Coburg-Gotha had come to the royal family in 1840, when Victoria married Prince Albert, and was thus adopted by the new king upon his accession. Although Edward's reign was relatively short, only nine years, he did lend his name to that era of aristocratic splendor that preceded the horrors of World War I.

They called him Edward the Peacemaker for his valiant attempts to keep Europe out of war at the dawn of the twentieth century. But when it came to the ladies, Edward the Maker might have been a more fitting sobriquet. A seemingly endless succession of mistresses—from actresses to aristocrats—shared the royal bed. "He was stimulated by their company," wrote Margot Asquith, "intrigued by their entanglements, flattered by their confidence, and valued their counsel."

Yet given the trauma surrounding his first encounter with the opposite sex, it's a wonder Edward VII wasn't celibate. Scarring doesn't begin to describe the experience.

From earliest childhood poor Edward* received very little

---

* He was christened Albert Edward.

approbation from his parents, Queen Victoria and Prince Albert. The boy's very appearance made his mother shudder. "Handsome I cannot think him," the queen sniffed, "with that painfully small and narrow head, those immense features and total want of a chin." But it was the prince's natural gregariousness that repelled his parents most.

Both Victoria and Albert were terrified of the genetic specter of her wicked Hanoverian uncles like George IV and Ernest, Duke of Cumberland (see previous chapters), and they were determined that the future king would be raised as a model of probity. What resulted was a rigidly proscribed education and deportment program that kept the boy in a cocoon, utterly deprived of joy or youthful companionship. The stringent rules and regulations that governed every aspect of the prince's life, Lord Redesdale wryly noted, might have been composed "for the use and guidance of a seminary for young ladies."

Queen Victoria essentially wanted her heir to be a clone of her beloved husband. "You will understand *how* fervent my prayers and I am sure everybody's must be, to see him resemble his angelic dearest Father in *every, every* respect, both in body and mind," she wrote to her uncle King Leopold I of Belgium.

Alas, the prince was nothing like his rigid and repressed father—a defect that irked his parents no end. He "takes no interest in anything but clothes and again clothes," Prince Albert wrote despairingly of his son. "Even when out shooting he is more occupied with his trousers than with the game!" Soon enough, the young man's sartorial interests would be the least of his father's worries.

Although Victoria and Albert were adamant that their son be isolated from the pernicious influences of his contemporaries, they did allow him a ten-week stint training with a battalion of the Grenadier Guards in Ireland. The prince received quite an education there, courtesy of an actress named Nellie Clifden.

Prince Albert was horrified when he heard about the affair. Ever the prude, he could not have reacted more vehemently had his son "butchered his brothers and sisters and scattered their remains in the lake at Buckingham Palace," wrote historian Giles St. Aubyn.

In a frenzied letter Albert informed his son that the affair had caused him "the greatest pain I have yet felt in this life," and warned him of the potentially devastating consequences. Nellie was already being called "the Princess of Wales," Albert wrote, and, if she became pregnant, she would claim the child was the prince's. "If you were to try to deny it, she can drag you into a Court of Law to force you to own it & there, with you in the witness box, she will be able to give before a greedy multitude disgusting details of your profligacy. . . . Oh horrible prospect, which this person has in her power, and any day to realize! and to break your poor parents' hearts."

Two months after composing this agonized screed, Prince Albert was dead. Queen Victoria blamed her son, refusing to acknowledge that typhoid had carried her adored husband away. The affair, she wrote to her daughter Vicky, was what made "beloved Papa so ill—for there must be no illusion about that—it was so; he was struck down—and I never can see [the prince]—without a shudder! Oh! that bitterness—oh! that cross!"

For the next forty years, until her own death in 1901, Victoria exacted her revenge. She was singularly determined to control every aspect of her heir's life, while at the same time depriving him of any real responsibility or training for his future role. Sir Lionel Cust, a servant of Edward's after he became king, wrote that "the great misfortune" of his life "was that his mother had lived too long . . . for the welfare of her son and successor."

The years immediately following Prince Albert's death were the worst. The very presence of the Prince of Wales seemed to revolt his mother, even as he tried to be solicitous toward her feelings. King Leopold of Belgium, Victoria's uncle and confidant, told the Earl of Clarendon "that the relations between the Queen and the Prince of Wales are as bad as ever, if not worse, and that his efforts to improve them had been fruitless—it seems to be an antipathy that is incurable but quite unjustifiable—it is entirely her fault as the poor boy asks nothing better than to devote himself to comforting his Mother and with that object would be delighted to give up his foreign expedition [planned before Prince Albert's death] but she would not hear of it and seems only to wish to get rid of him."

Despite the fact that his presence greatly disturbed her, the queen was nevertheless keen to interfere with his life—even after his marriage to Alexandra of Denmark in 1863, when the prince was twenty-one. Lord Stanley noted that year how all London was gossiping about the "extraordinary way" in which the queen insisted on directing "the Prince and Princess of Wales in every detail of their lives. They may not dine out, except with previous approval. . . . In addition, a daily and minute report of what passes at Marlborough House [their London residence] has to be sent to Windsor."

Victoria seemed convinced that her son was unworthy to succeed her. "What would happen if I were to die next winter!" she wrote to her daughter. "One shudders to think of it: it is too awful a contemplation. . . . The greatest improvement I fear will never make him fit for his position." On another occasion she declared, "I often pray he will never survive me, for I know not what would happen."

Even as she withdrew from many of her public duties as sovereign after Albert's death, the perpetually black-clad queen refused Edward the opportunity to fill the void she left. He was kept completely idle, which led Victoria to sharply criticize his lifestyle and, in a cruel twist, convinced her that he was too irresponsible to ably serve her.

"I am not of the slightest use to the Queen," the prince lamented. "Everything I say or suggest is pooh-poohed and my brothers and sisters are more listened to than I am."

Indeed, the queen put infinitely more faith in her son Leopold, twelve years the future king's junior. On one occasion Prince Leopold pulled a key from his pocket and told his companion: "It is the Queen's Cabinet key, which opens all the secret dispatch boxes. Dizzy [Prime Minister Benjamin Disraeli] gave it to me, but my brother the Prince of Wales is not allowed to have one."

Leopold's daughter Alice wrote in her memoirs of the impressive forbearance her uncle showed in the face of the queen's gross unfairness: "[He] was, of course, aware of the assistance which my father [Leopold] was giving to the Queen and knew that his younger brother had access to State papers which he, though Prince of Wales, was not allowed to see. He was understandably indignant at such treatment, and I cannot help being filled with admiration for his magnanimity, for he bore no grudge against my father and was always kindness itself to my mother and me. . . . I consider he showed real greatness of spirit in his attitude towards my family."

King Edward VII showed that same greatness of spirit toward Queen Victoria, despite all the indignities she heaped upon him. "It was evident from all he did and said that he greatly admired his mother," wrote Giles St. Aubyn, "and with that discriminating forgetfulness which is the measure of a generous mind he held her memory sacred."

30

George V (1910–1936): Georgie and
Nicky: A Fatal Friendship

Ever your devoted cousin and friend, Georgie
—KING GEORGE V

George V succeeded his father, Edward VII, in 1910. Four years later Britain was drawn into the bloody conflagration that became known as World War I. Unlike many other European monarchs in the aftermath of that war, King George managed to keep his crown—even in the midst of great social upheaval at home. He remained a well-regarded king, and was genuinely surprised and moved by the outpouring of affection he and his wife, Queen Mary, received during the celebration of his Silver Jubilee, which took place the year before his death in 1936. The king's cousin and friend, Tsar Nicholas II of Russia, on the other hand, never got to celebrate his Silver Jubilee—thanks in part to a momentous decision made by George V in the aftermath of the Russian Revolution.

They were first cousins who looked more like twin brothers, bonded since childhood in an enduring friendship. To their family, and each other, they were Georgie and Nicky. To the rest of the world they were King George V of Great Britain and Tsar Nicholas II of Russia. Though they saw each other only occasionally, the two monarchs were in constant correspondence, strengthening their ties through mutual support and encouragement—particularly as they faced their unstable and bellicose cousin Willy, better known as Kaiser Wilhelm II, in World War I. In the end, though, when Nicky needed Georgie most, friendship and family ties were not enough.

George V and Nicholas II were part of a vast network of interrelated European royals. Their mothers were Danish princesses: Alexandra, the elder sister, married the future king of England, Edward VII; the younger sister, Dagmar, married Russia's future emperor, Alexander III. The family gatherings that sometimes brought the two young princes together cemented their friendship. "Nicky has been kindness itself to me," George wrote to his grandmother Queen Victoria from Russia, where he attended Nicholas's wedding to another of Victoria's grandchildren, Alexandra of Hesse.* "He is the same dear boy he has always been and talks to me quite openly on every subject. . . . He does everything so quietly and naturally; everyone is struck by it and he is very popular already."

The uncanny resemblance of the two cousins often caused people to confuse them when they were together, as happened at George's wedding, when Nicholas was congratulated on his nuptials and George was asked about events in Russia. The confusion seemed to delight the normally dour Queen Victoria. There was "no end of funny mistakes," she remarked gaily, "the one being taken for the other!"

When they weren't with each other, Georgie and Nicky kept in constant contact. Nicholas, who inherited the Russian throne in 1894 after the death of Alexander III, wrote a touching letter to his cousin when George's father, Edward VII, died in 1910: "Just a few lines to tell you how deeply I feel for you the terrible loss you and England have sustained. I know alas! by experience what it costs one. There you are with your heart bleeding and aching, but at the same time duty imposes

---

* Alexandra was the daughter of Queen Victoria's daughter Alice, which made her George V's first cousin.

itself and people & affairs come up and tear you away from
your sorrow. It is difficult to realize that your beloved Father
has been taken away. The awful rapidity with which it all happened! How I would have liked to have come now & be near
you!"

The same letter also illustrated how closely intertwined
family relationships were with national interests. Georgie and
Nicky were now both sovereigns, after all.

> I beg you dearest Georgie to continue our old friendship
> and to show my country the same interest as your dear Fa-
> ther did from the day he came to the throne. No one did so
> much in trying to bring our two countries closer together
> than Him. The first steps have brought good results. Let us
> strive and work in the same direction. From our talks in
> days past & from your letters I remember your opinion was
> the same. I assure you that the sad death of your Father has
> provoked throughout the whole of Russia a feeling of sin-
> cere grief & of warmest sympathy toward your people. God
> bless you my dear old Georgie! My thoughts are always
> near you.
>
> >   With much love to you & dearest May,
> >   ever your devoted friend,
> >   Nicky.

King George and Tsar Nicholas were bonded even more
closely, politically and personally, as they faced their common
cousin Kaiser Wilhelm II in World War I. The German emperor had always been a troublemaker in the family, alienating
his English relatives by his monstrous treatment of his mother
(Queen Victoria's eldest daughter, Vicky) and unsettling them
with his belligerent saber-rattling. "Oh he is mad and a con-
ceited ass," Georgie's mother wrote to him about the kaiser—

"who also says that Papa [Edward VII] and Grandmama [Victoria] don't treat him with proper respect as the Emperor of old and mighty Germany. But my hope is that pride will have a fall some day and won't we rejoice then!"

Willy, as the emperor was known in the family, was jealous of the friendship between Georgie and Nicky, and came to believe that they were plotting against him. His paranoia was particularly apparent at the wedding of his daughter, Victoria Louise, in 1913. King George recalled that every time he and Nicholas tried to have a conversation, the kaiser was lurking about with his ear "glued to the keyhole." Wilhelm, for his part, believed that the king and tsar had planned the destruction of Germany at the wedding. His former chancellor Bernhard von Bülow recorded the Kaiser's rant: "History showed no greater perfidy. . . . God would punish them some day! . . . The Tsar's ingratitude was revolting: he had always been the Tsar's close friend. As for 'Georgie,' all the emperor had to say was that Queen Victoria, their grandmother, must have turned in her grave at the spectacle of her English grandson flinging down the gauntlet to the German."

The nuances of the British Constitution and the constraints on the monarch were clearly lost on the kaiser, who believed that his cousin actually had the power to declare war. Ultimately, none of the three monarchs, Georgie, Nicky, or Willy, would have much control over the great conflagration that would consume Europe and knock two of them off their thrones. As war approached, Tsar Nicholas wrote to King George: "We both have serious and grave times before us and my earnest prayer is that both our countries may meet them with calm and trust in Divine Providence, God bless and protect you, Georgie." The two cousins would remain closely united, at least for a time.

"My dear Nicky," King George wrote from Windsor Castle on August 8, 1915,

I feel most deeply for you in the very anxious days through which you are now passing, when your army has been compelled to retire on account of the lack of ammunition and rifles, in spite of the splendid and most gallant way [they] are fighting against our most powerful enemy. . . . I can assure you that in England we are now straining every nerve to produce the required ammunition and guns and also rifles and are sending the troops of our new armies to the front as fast as we possibly can. England has made up her mind to fight this awful war out to an end, whatever our sacrifices may be, our very existence is at stake. I am so glad to see by your letter that Russia also means to fight to the end and I know France is of the same opinion. God bless you my dear Nicky,

> Ever your devoted cousin and friend,
> Georgie.

Despite his protestations otherwise, Georgie's devotion had its limits, as Nicky was soon to learn. A succession of crushing losses and severe wartime deprivations contributed to a revolution in Russia that forced the tsar to abdicate in 1917. "Events of last week have deeply distressed me," King George telegraphed his cousin. "My thoughts are constantly with you and I shall always remain your true and devoted friend, as you know I have been in the past." The message never reached the fallen emperor, which was probably just as well, given how empty Georgie's sentiments proved to be.

The provisional government established in Russia in the wake of the revolution was eager to protect the ex-tsar and his family from the more radical Soviet faction, which was braying for Nicholas's blood. Sir George Buchanan, the British ambassador in Russia, reported to London that the provisional government was "most anxious to get the Emperor out of

Russia as soon as possible," and was seeking asylum for him in Britain. Buchanan was authorized to extend the invitation, which seemed to settle the matter—until King George stepped in.

The monarchy in Britain was in a precarious position during the war, and George V was particularly sensitive to the implications. It was in the midst of anti-German fervor, when his own patriotism was questioned, that he changed the royal family name from Saxe-Coburg-Gotha to the very English Windsor.* And with a rise in republicanism, he worried about his government's offer of sanctuary to Russia's royal family—"a gesture," wrote the king's biographer Kenneth Rose, "that would have identified him with Tsarist autocracy and imperiled his own repute as a constitutional monarch." Survival was the king's paramount concern in 1917, which may explain his vigorous campaign to revoke the offer of asylum to cousin Nicky.

"Every day, the King is becoming more concerned about the question of the Emperor and Empress coming to this country," wrote George's private secretary, Arthur Bigge, to Foreign Secretary Arthur Balfour.

His Majesty receives letters from people in all classes of life, known or unknown to him, saying how much the matter is being discussed, not only in clubs, but by working men, and that Labour members in the House of Commons are expressing adverse opinions to the proposal. As you know, from the first the King has thought the presence of the Imperial Family (especially of the Empress) in this country

* It was the king's private secretary, Arthur Bigge, Lord Stamfordham, who suggested the new name, after the castle and its unmistakable connections to the ancient English monarchy. On July 17, 1917, the Privy Council announced the change, along with the royal family's renunciation of all "German degrees, styles, dignitaries, titles, honours, and appellations."

would raise all sorts of difficulties, and I feel sure that you appreciate how awkward it will be for our Royal Family, who are closely connected both with the Emperor and the Empress. You probably also are aware that the subject has become more or less public property, and that people are either assuming that it has been initiated by the King, or deprecating the very unfair position in which His Majesty will be placed if the arrangement is carried out. The King desires me to ask you whether after consulting the Prime Minister, Sir George Buchanan should not be communicated with, with a view to approaching the Russian Government to make some other plan for the future residence of their Imperial Majesties.

Georgie eventually got his way, while Nicky and his family remained prisoners in Russia and were subsequently slaughtered by the Bolsheviks in 1918. "It was a foul murder," the king recorded in his diary. "I was devoted to Nicky, who was the kindest of men and a thorough gentleman: loved his country and people."

31

Edward VIII (1936):

An Abdication of Duty

He was not really interested in anything at all.
— ALAN "TOMMY" LASCELLES

Edward VIII came to the throne as a beloved prince in 1936, having suc-
ceeded his father, George V. Before the year was through, however, Edward
abdicated to marry the twice-divorced American Wallis Warfield Simpson—
a woman considered by the government to be thoroughly unsuitable as queen.
Edward was never crowned, and the throne passed to his younger brother,
who became King George VI.

He was Britain's fair-haired prince, heir to an empire and adored by the masses dazzled by his youth and charm. Yet beneath that brilliant exterior lurked the heart of a lightweight. "If only the British public knew what a weak, powerless misery their press-made national hero was," the future king Edward VIII said of himself, "they would have a nasty shock and be not only disappointed but damned angry too." After he ascended the throne in 1936, Edward's staggering self-absorption would nearly destroy the monarchy and lead to a life of utter vacuity. Still, some call his the love story of the twentieth century.

Duty was always an afterthought to Edward, something to be considered only when it didn't interfere with his personal desires and indulgences. A sense of responsibility requires a solid core, and that Edward always lacked. He was "like the child in the fairy story who was given everything in the world but they forgot his soul," said Alan "Tommy" Lascelles, who served as Edward's assistant private secretary when he was Prince of Wales. "He had no spiritual or aesthetic side at all. He did not know beauty when he saw it and even the beauty of women was only apparent to him when they were the sort of women who excited his particular passions. . . . He was not really interested in anything at all." Except, perhaps, sex.

"I can't raise much enthusiasm over . . . anything except women!!" the prince recorded in his diary. It was a perfectly normal preoccupation for a young man, but Edward's fixation had an unsavory twist. He was possessed by "the sexual perversion of self-abasement," according to Ulick Alexander, a courtier close to him. Freda Dudley Ward, one of Edward's married mistresses, agreed. "I could have dominated him if I had wanted to. I could have done *anything* with him! Love bewitched him. He made himself the slave of whomever he loved and became totally dependent on her. It was his nature; he was a masochist. He *liked* being humbled, degraded. He *begged* for it!"

Edward found the perfect dominatrix in Wallis Warfield Simpson, a grasping social climber and something of a shrew. "God, that woman's a bitch," exclaimed the prince's friend Edward "Fruity" Metcalfe. "She'll play hell with him before long." It was an inferno Edward entered gladly. Unfortunately, being abused and degraded by Mrs. Simpson left little room for his royal responsibilities, and people in the palace began to question if he was really fit to inherit the crown. Not the least of these was Edward's own father, George V. "After I am dead the boy will ruin himself in twelve months," the king reportedly said to his prime minister. It was a pronouncement that proved sadly prescient.

"My heart goes out to the Prince of Wales tonight as he will mind so terribly being King," wrote the diarist Henry "Chips"

Channon as King George V labored with his last breaths. "His loneliness, his seclusion, his isolation will be almost more than his highly strung and unimaginative nature can bear." Edward's solution was to simply ignore his duties as king and focus instead entirely on Mrs. Simpson. Yes, she was married, but her husband, awed by royalty, graciously stepped aside. It was a lucrative exchange for Wallis, dripping in the diamonds Edward lavished upon her. "For her, money and material possessions were of inestimable importance," wrote Edward's biographer Philip Ziegler; "she hungered for them and greeted every new acquisition as an incentive to grasp for more." And all she had to offer in return was the contempt and domination the king seemed to crave. His equerry John Aird noted Wallis's effect on Edward early in their relationship: He "has lost all confidence in himself and follows W around like a dog."

Like any good pet, the king immediately stopped whatever he was doing to respond to Wallis's call. "If he cancelled a dinner at the last moment the chances were that she had expressed a wish to see him," wrote Ziegler; "if he was two hours late for Lord Cromer it was almost certain he had been visiting her. Nothing mattered to him so much as the gratification of her wishes and the performance of her instructions." Naturally this all-consuming devotion to his mistress caused grave concerns among those closest to Edward. "I did not think the King was normal," recalled his private secretary, Clive Wigram, "and this view was shared by my colleagues at Buckingham Palace. He might any day develop into a George III, and it was imperative to pass the Regency Bill as soon as possible, so that if necessary he could be certified."

Disconcertment quickly gave way to horror when King Edward made it clear that he wanted to marry his mistress. *Queen Wallis!* It was an unthinkable prospect; the people would never stand for a twice-divorced American in such a role. Edward was insistent, however. His chronic unwillingness to sacrifice his personal desires for the public role he was born to fulfill now resulted in an unprecedented crisis for the monarchy. In the end, the king chose to abandon the crown rather than serve, as he put it in his abdication speech, "without the help and support of the woman I love."

It seemed so romantic on the surface—the gallant king sacrificing everything for his one true love. But Tommy Lascelles, who knew Edward all too well, dismissed such sentiment as "moonshine." The truth was that Edward never really wanted to be king and resented the many impositions of the role. Furthermore, Wallis was hardly the first woman with whom he fell madly in love. "There was always a *grande affaire* and, coincidentally, as I know to my cost, an unbroken series of *petites affaires*, contracted and consummated in whatever highways and byways of the Empire he was traversing at the moment," wrote Lascelles. "Mrs S. was no isolated phenomenon, but merely the current figure in an arithmetical progression that had been robustly maintained for nearly 20 years."

Far from a fairy-tale ending, the years following Edward's abdication were passed in a life of excessive indolence and frivolity, interrupted only by a series of embarrassing gaffes and petty squabbles with his family. King George VI, who succeeded his brother, once remarked in frustration that other British monarchs came to the throne after their predecessors were dead. "Mine is not only alive," he said, "but very much so!"

The abdication had caused extreme stress within the royal family, particularly for King George, a painfully shy man who had been forced to fill the void left by his brother (see Chapter 32). Edward, who was titled the Duke of Windsor after stepping down, was far too selfish to recognize the agony his actions had caused. He spent considerable energy harassing the new king about his finances and, even more fervently, about official recognition of his wife with the title "Her Royal Highness."

Edward had blatantly lied about his wealth, pleading near poverty during the negotiations that preceded his abdication, while he was really worth many millions. Now he insisted that his brother honor the terms of the settlement, in which the new king promised to pay him twenty-five thousand [pounds] a year. Wallis, after all, expected to live in grand style. "You were under great strain [at the time of the settlement] and I am not seeking to reproach you or anyone," George wrote after discovering that he had been duped. "But the fact remains that I was completely misled." Though Edward got his money in the end, the title for his wife was another matter indeed.

Wallis wanted "the extra chic," as she called it, of the HRH designation, and badgered Edward incessantly to fight for it. "I loathe being undignified," she complained, "and also of joining the countless titles that roam around Europe meaning nothing." When Wallis was unhappy, the duke was miserable. Thus the HRH issue became an obsession that drove a permanent wedge between him and his family. George VI was adamant on the issue, as was his mother, Queen Mary. It was a simple equation in their view. If Wallis was deemed unsuitable to be queen, prompting the abdication, then surely she was no more suited to be a member of the royal family. "Is she a fit and proper person to become a Royal Highness after what she had done in this country; and would the country understand it if she became one automatically on marriage?" the king asked. "I and my family and Queen Mary all feel that it would be a great mistake to acknowledge Mrs. Simpson as a suitable person to become Royal. The Monarchy has been degraded quite enough already."

It was for this reason that the family also refused to attend the wedding, or even to receive Wallis. To do so, they believed, would send the wrong message. "I simply hate having to tell you this," the king wrote his brother, explaining why no members of the family would be present at the wedding; "but you must realize that in spite of the affection which of course there still is towards you personally, the vast majority of people in this country are undoubtedly as strongly as ever opposed to a marriage which caused a King of England to renounce the throne. You know that none of us in the family liked it, and were any of them now, after a few months' interval, to come out and, so to speak, help you get married, I know that it would be regarded by everybody as condoning all that has happened; it would place us all in an impossibly false position and would be harmful to the Monarchy."

As far as Edward was concerned, however, it was an unforgivable snub. "I was bitterly hurt and disappointed that you virtually ignored the most important event of my life," he wrote to his mother, Queen Mary, after the wedding. "You must realize by this time, that as there is a limit to what one's feelings can endure, this most unjust and uncalled for treatment can have had but one important result; my complete estrangement from you all."

Estrangement, alas, did not mean silence. Edward continued to bombard his brother with demands that Wallis be accorded the dignities he felt she deserved, especially the HRH title, and that he be given a prominent place of honor on the world's stage.

While relieved to be rid of his duties as king, Edward wanted to retain the prestige—and the spotlight. An unsanctioned tour of Nazi Germany in 1937 seemed the perfect way to grab it. The duke had a ball, chatting up the führer at his Berchtesgaden lair and playing happily with a model railroad set Göring had assembled for his nephew. Best of all, he got to show off his duchess, and was gratified when the Nazi elite dignified her with the "Royal Highness" title his own relatives denied. Rudolf Hess's wife, Ilse, seemed to adore Wallis, describing her as "a lovely, charming, warm and clever woman with a heart of gold and an affection for her husband that she made not the slightest attempt to conceal." The abdication, Frau Hess concluded, had been brought about by Edward's "own sound attitudes on social issues and his pro-German inclinations." While not exactly treasonous, the tour did prove to be a tremendous propaganda vehicle for Hitler's regime, while causing great consternation to

King George. "The world is in a very troubled state," he said to his mother before the duke's tour, "and [Edward] seems to loom ever larger on the horizon."

The Duke and Duchess of Windsor were sunning themselves in the South of France when the news came that Britain had declared war on Germany after Hitler's invasion of Poland in 1939. "I'm afraid in the end this may open the way for world Communism," Edward lamented before diving into the swimming pool. King George graciously offered to send a plane to bring them back to England, but Edward was still smarting from his family's refusal to receive Wallis, and, as Walter Monckton reported in a government memo, he petulantly announced "that unless his brother was ready to have him and his wife to one of their houses they would not return to England." He still wanted the plane, however, to pick up his friend Fruity Metcalfe and his private secretary.

Metcalfe was appalled when the duke and duchess told him what they had done. "You have just behaved as two spoiled children," he told them. "You only think of yourselves. You don't realize that there is at this moment a war going on, that women and children are being bombed and killed while you talk of your PRIDE!"

The war was a wonderful opportunity for the duke to strut around in uniform, but when he started accepting royal salutes while visiting the front, the government insisted that such ostentatious behavior had to stop. Edward viewed the restriction as "being merely fresh evidence of my brother's continued efforts to humiliate me by every means in his and his courtiers' power." He complained loudly to Prime Minister Winston Churchill, whose response was withering: "Having voluntarily resigned the finest Throne in the world . . . it would be natural to treat all minor questions of ceremony and precedence as entirely beneath your interest and your dignity."

Eventually it was determined that the best place for Edward

to serve his country would be in the Bahamas, as royal governor. But that assignment proved a bit too taxing for the duke and duchess. They wanted to reclaim some of their servants from active duty in the war and bring them to the islands, because, Edward insisted, it would be a "serious handicap starting with a new valet." But Churchill thought not. "Such a step would be viewed with general disapprobation in times like these," he wrote with remarkable restraint, "and I should ill serve Your Royal Highness by countenancing it." Then there was the tropical weather. It was August and therefore quite hot when Edward and Wallis arrived at their new post, so the duke immediately put in for a leave. Once again, Churchill demurred. He was "very grieved to hear that you are entertaining such an idea," Walter Monckton wrote Edward. The prime minister hoped that, when the people of Britain were suffering so much, the duke "would be willing to put up with the discomfort and remain at your post until weather conditions made things less unpleasant."

A true patriot, Edward sucked it up and stayed. Still, he insisted that the royal accommodations were unacceptable in their current state. "We found Government House quite uninhabitable," the duke told his friend and predecessor as governor, Bede Clifford, "and fled from the place after a week's picnic and sand flies." While London endured the Blitz, Edward requested more money to bring the home up to Wallis's standards. "Comment is needless," Churchill jotted on the memo.

After the war ended in 1945 and the Windsors were free of their strenuous responsibilities in the Bahamas, they indulged themselves in a little leisure time. They managed to extend it for the next three decades, flitting between Paris, Palm Beach, and New York, always courting the wealthy and gorging on their hospitality.

Though he no longer wore the crown, Edward presided over a miniature kingdom of uniformed servants and pet pugs. Or rather Wallis did. The duke once made the grave mistake of issuing an order to the help during a dinner party the couple was hosting. Hearing this, the duchess raised her hands high in the air and slammed them down on the table with a terrible crash. "Never," she spat, "never again will you give orders in my house!" The guests sat stunned while the chastened duke muttered incoherent apologies.

With Wallis ruling the household, Edward was left with little to do but meekly obey her commands. In a moment of perhaps unintentional honesty, the man who had been born to rule an empire revealed the emptiness of his life to the wife of an American diplomat. "You know what my day was today?" he said. "I got up late, and then I went with the Duchess and watched her buy a hat, and then on the way home I had the car drop me in the Bois to watch some of your soldiers playing football, and then I planned to take a walk, but it was so cold that I could hardly bear it. . . . When I got home the Duchess was having her French lesson, so I had no one to talk to, so I got a lot of tin boxes down which my mother had sent me last week and looked through them. They were essays and so on that I had written when I was in France studying French before the Great War [World War I]. . . . You know, I'm not much of a reading man."

Busy as he was, Edward still managed to squeeze in some time to pressure his family into receiving Wallis and granting her the long-coveted title of "Her Royal Highness." "I cannot tell you how grieved I am at your brother being so tiresome about the HRH," Queen Mary wrote to her son the king. "Giving her this title would be fatal, and after all these years I fear lest people think that we condoned this dreadful marriage which has been such a blow to us in every way."

King George ultimately realized that his brother just didn't get it: "He has to consider others beside himself, and I doubt whether even now he realizes the irrevocable step he took nine years ago and the ghastly shock he gave this country."

32

George VI (1936–1952):
The Courage of a King

For Valour

—WINSTON CHURCHILL

The abdication of Edward VIII in 1936 was a tremendous blow to the pres-
tige of the monarchy, and it was up to the former king's brother, who suc-
ceeded him as George VI, to repair it. It was a task for which the new king
seemed woefully ill equipped, yet with the love and support of his wife, Queen
Elizabeth, George emerged as one of Britain's great monarchs.

"The British Crown is the greatest inheritance a man can have," Prime Minister William Gladstone once declared. King George VI disagreed. Unlike so many of his forebears who fought and killed for the crown, this painfully shy, ill-prepared monarch dreaded the heavy weight it represented. Yet duty propelled him, and in the end he wore it well—conquering his fears and restoring the monarchy's prestige after the ignoble abdication of his brother, then standing firm with his queen as potent symbols of British endurance during the darkest days of World War II.

"If the 'greatness' of a King can be measured by the extent to which his qualities correspond to the needs of a nation at a given moment in its history," wrote the French diplomat René

Massigli, "then George VI was a great King, and perhaps a very great King."

It was never supposed to be so. Albert, Duke of York, as King George was known before his accession (Bertie, to his family),* provided a rather drab contrast to his dashing, universally adored older brother, who was destined to become King Edward VIII. With his gaunt, almost sickly appearance (which belied his natural athleticism) and the persistent stammer with which he had been cursed since childhood, the duke was a singularly uninspiring figure. He was perfectly content to live a quiet, domestic life with his wife, Elizabeth, and two young daughters. Fate intervened, however, when in 1936 the brother he loved did the unthinkable and abdicated.

It was a monstrous blow for the reluctant heir, culminating months of tension during which the duke said he felt "like the proverbial sheep being led to the slaughter." When the inevitable end came he broke down and, by his own account, "sobbed like a child." But that naked display of emotion only briefly betrayed a stout heart.

The new king had struggled all his life with his shyness, stammer, and unrelenting stomach ailments, yet he never surrendered to them. Even his cold and critical father, King George V, recognized his second son's courage, especially compared with his other children. "Bertie has more guts than the rest of them put together," the king declared. Now at his accession—"that dreadful day," as he called it—Bertie's mettle would be tested as never before.

Though he proved to be a far better king than Edward VIII would have been, George VI was at first compared unfavorably to his charming older brother. Yet it was up to the new king to repair the damage Edward had done. "I hope that time

* The new king chose the name George when he took the throne to emphasize the continuity with the reign of his father, George V.

will be allowed me to make amends for what has happened," he wrote.

Many had their doubts, particularly as the coronation approached and George was due to address the nation. How could a stammering monarch ever hope to restore faith in the ancient institution? King George was determined to try. His biographer Sir John Wheeler-Bennett, who also suffered from a stammer, eloquently described the ordeal he faced: "Only those who have themselves suffered the tragedies of the stammer can appreciate to the full their depth and poignancy—the infuriating inhibitions and frustrations, the bitter humiliation and anguish of the spirit; the orgies of self-pity; and the utter exhaustion, mental and physical; perhaps, above all, the sense of being *different* from others and the shrinking from help prompted by pity."

After a number of rehearsals, which did not go particularly well, the newly anointed king sat down at the microphone to address millions of listeners on the evening of his coronation, which took place on May 12, 1937. It was a feat of extreme concentration and endurance, and it was a triumph. "It is with a very full heart I speak to you tonight," King George intoned in a voice *Time* magazine described as "warm and strong," without a stammer. "Never before has a newly crowned King been able to talk to all his peoples in their own homes on the day of his Coronation. . . . The Queen and I will always keep in our hearts the inspiration of this day. May we ever be worthy of the goodwill which I am proud to think surrounds us at the outset of my reign."

Robert Wood, a BBC engineer retained to help the king become a good broadcaster, recalled the effort in his memoir. "It was hard for the King," he wrote, "because you could see how he had suffered all his life because of his impediment and you could not help but feel sorry for him. . . . Little by little I helped him with tone formation and lip formation, and showed him how he could let the microphone do the work." It was an arduous process, but, Wood wrote, "the King struggled without let-up. I was full of admiration for his perseverance, his resolution." George VI eventually became a decent broadcaster, and it was his voice that would give comfort and reassurance to a nation staggered but unbowed in the midst of a ferocious Nazi onslaught.

War created an almost mystical bond between George VI and the British people. With his wife and children, he stood beside them throughout the conflict, unwavering, sharing many of the same dangers and deprivations they did. And in so doing he came to represent, with Churchill, the indomitable spirit of embattled Britain.

"The . . . King lived every minute of this struggle with a heart that never quavered and a spirit undaunted," Churchill said in a speech before the House of Commons in 1952. "But I, who saw him so often, knew how keenly, with all his full knowledge and understanding of what was happening, he felt personally the ups and down of this terrific struggle and how he longed to fight it, arms in hand, himself."

George VI did serve on the front lines during the German blitzkrieg that began in September 1940, because at that time London and other British cities *were* the front lines. Despite all danger, the king and queen were present at countless scenes of devastation to lend their support and encouragement to those whose lives had been ruined. "Never in British history," *Time* magazine declared, "has a monarch seen and talked to so many of his subjects or so fully shared their life."

The king's stalwart companion throughout the conflict was his beloved wife, Elizabeth (who would later become known as Queen Elizabeth, the Queen Mother, during the reign of her daughter, Elizabeth II). It was because of her brave spirit in boosting British morale that Hitler reportedly dubbed her "the most dangerous woman in Europe."

After one visit to London's East End, Queen Elizabeth wrote movingly about what she had witnessed: "All the houses evacuated and yet through the broken windows one saw all the poor little possessions, photographs, beds, just as they were left. . . . One could not imagine that life could become so terrible. We must win in the end."

The connection between monarch and people during these visits only deepened when Buckingham Palace was itself hit in an air strike. "I'm glad we've been bombed," Queen Elizabeth said. "I feel I can look the East End in the face." The king, who was nearly killed in the blast, also saw the advantage to his home being hit: "I feel that our tours of bombed areas in London are helping the people who have lost their relations & homes & we have both found a new bond with them as Buckingham Palace has been bombed as well as their homes, & nobody is immune."

In solidarity with the British people, as well as contributing to the war effort, King George instituted stringent conservation measures at Buckingham Palace and Windsor Castle. Rooms were kept frigid, with only one lightbulb allowed, and bathtubs were painted with a black or red line at the five-inch level as a reminder to save water. The food the royal family ate was, like everyone else's, horrible.

Eleanor Roosevelt stayed at Buckingham Palace during a visit in 1942 and was astonished to find the king and queen shivering in the bomb-shattered residence, enduring the same wartime deprivations as those in the humblest home. The first lady wrote about the experience in her autobiography:

> When we arrived at the palace they [the king and queen] took me to my rooms, explaining that I could have only a small fire in my sitting room and one in the outer waiting room, and saying that they hoped I would not be too cold. Through the windows they pointed out the shell holes. The windowpanes in my room had all been broken and replaced by wood and isinglas and one or two small panes of glass. Later the Queen showed me where a bomb had dropped

right through the King's rooms, destroying both his rooms and hers. They explained the various layers of curtains which had to be kept closed when the lights were on.

The conduct of King George and Queen Elizabeth during the war contrasted vividly with that of the former king, who was serving as royal governor of the Bahamas and complaining most vociferously about his accommodations there (see Chapter 31). Churchill, who had actually backed Edward VIII in the abdication crisis, certainly recognized how fortunate it was that George VI now wore the crown. "This war has drawn the Throne and the people more closely together than ever before recorded," the prime minister wrote to the king early in 1941, "and Yr Majesties are more beloved by classes and conditions than any of all princes of the past. I am indeed proud that it [should] have fallen to my lot and duty to stand at Yr Majesty's side as First Minister in such a climax of the British story."

King and prime minister worked closely together throughout the war, and their mutual respect and friendship flourished in the process. "I made certain he was kept informed of every secret matter," Churchill later said; "and the care and thoroughness with which he mastered the immense daily flow of State papers made a deep mark on my mind."

Though his powers as sovereign were limited, King George did exercise fully his constitutional rights to advise, encourage, and warn, which made him far more than a mere figurehead. Indeed he was, in his own way, a warrior-king, even if that role was defined differently than it had been for his ancient ancestors. He and Churchill stood side by side as wartime leaders, each with his own vital functions, and often with one sustaining the other. The exchange between the two men after the defeat of German forces at El Alamein well illustrates their relationship. Addressing his letter to "My dear Winston," King George wrote:

I must send you my warmest congratulations on the great Victory of the 8th Army in Egypt. I was overjoyed when I received the news and so was everybody else. In our many talks together over a long period I knew that the elimination of the Afrika Corps, the threat to Egypt, was your *one* aim, the most important of all the many other operations with which you have had to deal.

When I look back and think of all the many arduous hours of work you have put in, and the many miles you have travelled, to bring this battle to such a successful conclusion you have every right to rejoice; while the rest of our people will one day be very thankful to you for what you have done. I cannot say more.

Churchill graciously responded to his sovereign:

No minister in modern times, and I daresay in long days past, has received more help and comfort from the King, and this has brought us all thus far with broadening hopes and now I feel to brightening skies.

It is needless to assure Your Majesty of my devotion to Yourself and Family and to our ancient and cherished Monarchy—the true bulwark of British freedom against the tyrannies of every kind; but I trust I may have the pleasure of feeling a sense of personal friendship which is very keen and lively in my heart and has grown strong in these hard times of war.

Not content to merely observe events from home, George VI was always eager to join the fighting men whenever possible, boosting their morale as well as his own. "He liked the simple life of a soldier," Supreme Allied Commander General Dwight D. Eisenhower observed, "and was perfectly at home with all of us."

Though unable to carry a weapon into battle, the king did participate in an impressive bit of subterfuge that preceded the

Allied invasion of Europe. It was imperative that Hitler be mis-led as to where the Allies would be landing; otherwise he would amass all his forces there and smash the invaders. A massive feint was devised to fool the Nazis. As part of it, King George made a great show of "inspecting" a completely fabricated fuel-delivery complex, designed to make it appear that the Allies were planning to land at Calais rather than Normandy.

The king was eager to be a part of the actual invasion of Normandy in 1944, as was Churchill, which resulted in a rare clash of wills between the two leaders. George was ultimately persuaded that it would be foolish to have the monarch and the prime minister on the same ship in the midst of a massive in-vasion. The king reluctantly agreed to stay home but expected Churchill to do the same.

Writing to the prime minister, he suggested that "the right thing to do is what normally falls to those at the top on such occasions, namely to remain at home and wait. . . . I don't think I need emphasize what it would mean to me personally, and to the whole Allied cause if at this juncture a chance bomb, torpedo, or even a mine, should remove you from the scene." Similarly, he added, "a change of Sovereign at this moment would be a serious matter for the Country and Empire."

Churchill was not persuaded, even after being reminded by the king's private secretary that no prime minister could go abroad without the sovereign's consent. Although George was not prepared to stand on this right to refuse Churchill, and thus jeopardize their friendship, he was nevertheless vexed by the prime minister's obstinacy. "I am very worried of the PM's seemingly selfish way of looking at the matter," the king recorded in his diary. "He doesn't seem to care about the future, or how much depends on him."

The king tried once again to dissuade Churchill, arguing that it was a matter of fairness, as well as duty. "I want to make one more appeal to you not to go to sea on D Day," he wrote. "Please consider my own position. I am a younger man than you are, I am a sailor, & as King I am the head of all three Services. There is nothing I would like to do better than to go to sea but I have agreed to stay at home; is it fair that you should then do exactly what I should have liked to do myself? You said yesterday afternoon that it would be a fine thing for the King to lead his troops into battle, as in the old days; if the King cannot do this, it does not seem to me right that his Prime Minister should take his place."

Churchill eventually acquiesced to the king's entreaty—grudgingly—and harmony was restored. A little less than a year later both men stood on the balcony of Buckingham Palace before a massive crowd to celebrate the defeat of Germany.

"We congratulated each other on the end of the European War," the king wrote of his lunch with Churchill that day. "The day we have been longing for has arrived at last & we can look back with thankfulness to God that our tribulation is over. No more fear of being bombed at home & no more living in air-raid shelters. But there is still Japan to be defeated & the restoration of our country to be dealt with, which will give us many headaches & hard work in the coming years."

Churchill would not be by the king's side after the war; he was turned out of office by an apparently ungrateful nation in 1945. George would have to oversee the postwar challenges, particularly the dissolution of the British Empire, without his prime minister's stalwart presence. The king did stand impressively as the world dramatically shifted around him. But he was tired, and cancer was slowly destroying him.

On February 6, 1952, George VI died in his sleep of coronary thrombosis at age fifty-six. His wartime partner Churchill—who, after being reelected in 1951, would now serve as prime minister to the late king's daughter, Elizabeth II—left a wreath of white flowers as the king lay in state at Westminster Hall. With it was a simple two-word tribute, written in his own hand: "For Valour."

33

Elizabeth II (1952–present):
Good Queen Bess

God Save the Queen

—NATIONAL ANTHEM OF THE UNITED KINGDOM

Elizabeth II inherited a throne made more secure by the efforts of her father, George VI, and her mother, Queen Elizabeth (who, upon her daughter's accession in 1952, became known as the Queen Mother—or the Queen Mum, as she was affectionately called). Service has been the one constant of the queen's nearly six-decade reign, for, as Michael Mann, former dean of Windsor, wrote, "The one lesson that the abdication of Edward VIII burnt deep into the [souls] of the present Queen . . . was that you never, never abdicate your duty."

Is it good to be the queen? Well, maybe for a day. Sure, there are palaces and jewels and servants to attend your every need. But there are also tremendous, almost overwhelming responsibilities—the most important of which is to represent your country with dignity and honor. Imagine having to be on perpetual display, impeccably dressed and coiffed, without betraying so much as a burp. There are no spontaneous walks on the beach or nights at the movies. Almost every move is carefully choreographed, and the only opportunity to connect with other people is through stilted small talk at public events—

endless public events. Although she is head of state, the queen has very little power and is constitutionally forbidden from even offering a political opinion. Still, she is expected to embody all the mystique and glamour of the ancient monarchy while keeping the institution relevant in these modern times. No easy task.

Queen Elizabeth II has held the job for nearly six decades now, almost as long as her great-great-grandmother Queen Victoria, the longest-reigning monarch in British history. It is a position she did not seek but that was thrust upon her by the laws of heredity when her father, King George VI, died in 1952. She was just twenty-five. "I declare before you all that my whole life, whether it be long or short, shall be devoted to your service and the service of our great imperial family to which we all belong," Elizabeth had promised four years earlier, solemnizing the vow at her coronation. Most agree she has served exceedingly well.

Each of the queen's prime ministers, beginning with Winston Churchill, has marveled at her knowledge of the world, her astute political intuition, and her deeply ingrained sense of duty—a trait she inherited from both her parents. She is a monarch not afraid of hard work—from the stacks and stacks of state papers she reads every day to all the ceremonial investitures, court receptions, and state banquets she hosts. Then there is the travel. Elizabeth II has visited not only almost every corner of her own kingdom but nearly three-quarters of the world's nations as well, some many times over—all for the benefit of Britain.

Elizabeth's mother recognized how difficult her daughter's life as queen would be and, in a statement to the people after the death of George VI, commended to them "our dear daughter; give her your loyalty and devotion; in the great and lonely station to which she has been called she will need your protection and love."

There was scant evidence of that love and protection when Elizabeth II reached the nadir of her reign during the 1990s. The press gleefully reported every lurid detail of her children's failing marriages, then ferociously turned on the queen herself after the death of Diana, Princess of Wales, in 1997. SHOW US YOU CARE, MA'AM, screamed one headline, reflecting the popular sentiment that Elizabeth was an unfeeling monster. Her sin was not behaving the way they decreed she should in the midst of mass hysteria.

The British have always been an extremely fickle people when it comes to their monarchs. Even the greatest kings and queens, such as Elizabeth I, experienced significant ebbs in their popularity, only to bounce back later in the public's estimation. And so it was with Elizabeth II.

Five years after the death of Diana the nation came out in force to celebrate the queen's Golden Jubilee. It was an abrupt change in public mood as the people responded positively to Elizabeth II's half century on the throne. The queen had remained steady as ever through the sharp fluctuation in public sentiment, and in a speech before both Houses of Parliament that year, she thanked "people everywhere for the loyalty, support, and inspiration you have given me over these fifty, unforgettable years." Then Elizabeth did something entirely characteristic and promised "to serve the people of this great nation of ours to the best of my ability through the changing times ahead." And for that renewed commitment to her calling, the people had every cause to sing "God Save the Queen."

SELECT BIBLIOGRAPHY

Ashley, Maurice. *James II*. Minneapolis: University of Minnesota Press, 1977.

Bradford, Sarah. *The Reluctant King: The Life and Reign of George VI, 1895–1952*. New York: St. Martin's, 1989.

Carlton, Charles. *Charles I: The Personal Monarch*. New York and London: Routledge, 1995.

Clay, Catrine. *King, Kaiser, Tsar: Three Royal Cousins Who Led the World to War*. New York: Walker, 2006.

Erickson, Carolly. *Bloody Mary: The Remarkable Life of Mary Tudor*. Garden City, N.Y.: Doubleday, 1978.

———. *Bonnie Prince Charlie*. New York: William Morrow, 1989.

Fraser, Antonia. *King James I of England, VI of Scotland*. New York: Knopf, 1975.

———. *Royal Charles: Charles II and the Reconstruction*. New York: Knopf, 1979.

Gregg, Edward. *Queen Anne*. London, Boston, and Henley: Routledge & Kegan Paul, 1980.

Gristwood, Sarah. *Arbella: England's Lost Queen*. Boston and New York: Houghton Mifflin, 2003.

Hatton, Ragnhild. *George I: Elector and King*. Cambridge, Mass.: Harvard University Press, 1978.

Hibbert, Christopher. *George III*. New York: Basic Books, 1998.

———. *George IV: Prince of Wales*. London: Longman, 1972.

———. *George IV: Regent and King*, 1811–1830. New York, Harper & Row, 1973.

Holme, Thea. *Prinny's Daughter: A Life of Princess Charlotte of Wales*. London: Hamish Hamilton, 1976.

Larner, Christina. "James VI and I and Witchcraft." In *The Reign of James VI and I*, edited by Alan G. R. Smith. New York: St. Martin's, 1973.

Ollard, Richard. *The Escape of Charles II after the Battle of Worcester*. New York: Dorset, 1966.

Partridge, Robert B. *"O Horrable Murder": The Trial, Execution and Burial of King Charles I*. London: Rubicon, 1998.

Plowden, Alison. *Lady Jane Grey and the House of Suffolk*. New York: Franklin Watts, 1986.

Pollard, A. F. *England Under Protector Somerset: An Essay*. London: Kegan Paul, Trench, Trubner, 1900.

Roosevelt, Eleanor. *The Autobiography of Eleanor Roosevelt*. New York: Harper & Brothers, 1961.

Rose, Kenneth. *King George V*. New York: Knopf, 1984.

Ryan, William. *Queen Anne and Her Court*. New York: Dutton, 1909.

Skidmore, Chris. *Edward VI: The Lost King of England*. New York: St. Martin's, 2007.

Somerset, Anne. *Elizabeth I*. New York: St. Martin's, 1991.

Starkey, David. *Elizabeth: The Struggle for the Throne*. New York: HarperCollins, 2001.

St. Aubyn, Giles. *Edward VII: Prince and King*. New York: Atheneum, 1979.

———. *Queen Victoria: A Portrait*. New York: Atheneum, 1992.

Stewart, Alan. *The Cradle King: The Life of James VI & I, the First Monarch of a United Great Britain*. New York: St. Martin's, 2003.

Tillyard, Stella. *A Royal Affair: George III and His Scandalous Siblings*. New York: Random House, 2006.

Waller, Maureen: *Ungrateful Daughters: The Stuart Princesses Who Stole Their Father's Crown*. New York: St. Martin's, 2002.

Walters, John. *The Royal Griffin: Frederick Prince of Wales, 1707–51*. New York: Stein and Day, 1972.

Wardroper, John. *Wicked Ernest: The Truth About the Man Who Was Almost Britain's King*. London: Shelfmark Books, 2002.

Weintraub, Stanley. *Victoria: An Intimate Biography*. New York: Truman Talley Books/Dutton, 1987.

Wheeler-Bennett, Sir John. *King George VI: His Life and Reign*. New York: Macmillan, 1958.

Wilkins, W. H. *The Love of an Uncrowned Queen: Sophia Dorothea, Consort of George I, and Her Correspondence with Philip Christopher Count Königsmarck*. New York: Duffield, 1906.

Young, Michael B. *Charles I*. New York: St. Martin's, 1997.

———. *King James and the History of Homosexuality*. New York: New York University Press, 2000.

Zee, Henri van der, and Barbara van der Zee. *William and Mary*. New York: Knopf, 1973.

Ziegler, Philip. *King Edward VIII: A Biography*. New York: Knopf, 1991.

———. *King William IV*. London: Cassell, 1971.

ABOUT THE AUTHOR

MICHAEL FARQUHAR is the author of three bestsellers, *A Treasury of Royal Scandals, A Treasury of Great American Scandals,* and *A Treasury of Deception,* as well as his latest book, *A Treasury of Foolishly Forgotten Americans.* He is co-author of *The Century: History as It Happened on the Front Page of the Capital's Newspaper.* His work has been featured in a number of publications, including *The Washington Post,* where he was a writer and editor for ten years, specializing in history. He has appeared as a commentator on such programs as the History Channel's *Russia: Land of the Tsars* and *The French Revolution.* He lives in Washington, D.C.